Paperback Talk

This book is gratefully dedicated to my colleagues on the staff of The New York Times Book Review *over the past quarter of a century, for their aid, encouragement and sufferance.*

Paperback Talk

by

Ray Walters

Introduction by

Ian and Betty Ballantine

Author's Note

The author has made every effort to trace and obtain the permission of the copyright holders of the book covers and colophons reproduced in this book. These include Ace Books, Avon Books, Ballantine Books, Dell Publishing, Doubleday Anchor Books, New American Library, Penguin Books, Popular Library and Workman Publishing. He is grateful to Toni Mendez, agent of B. Kliban, for obtaining Mr. Kliban's permission to reproduce the illustrations on page 195. In the reproduction of the illustrations he received the aid of Steven Heller, art director of *The New York Times Book Review*. Most of the material in this volume originally appeared in *The New York Times Book Review* and is reproduced by permission of the New York Times Company. Copyright 1939, 1946, 1960, 1969, 1972, 1975, 1976, 1977, 1978, 1979, 1980, 1981, 1982, 1983, 1984 by the New York Times Company.

Published in 1985 by
Academy Chicago Publishers
425 N. Michigan Ave.
Chicago, IL 60611

Copyright © 1985 by Ray Walters

Introduction © 1985 by Betty and Ian Ballantine

Printed and bound in the USA

Library of Congress Cataloging in Publication Data

Walters, Ray, 1912—
    Paperback talk.

    Derived from the author's column, Paperback talk, and
articles contributed by him to the New York times book
review during the 23 years he was paperback editor of
that publication.
    1. Paperbacks—Publishing—United Sttaes.   2. Publishers
and publishing—United States.   3. Book industries and
trade—United States. I. Title.
Z479.W3   1984   070.5'73'0973   84-12456
ISBN 0-89733-108-7
ISBN 0-89733-109-5 (pbk.)

Contents

Preface

This volume is the fruit of a lifelong love affair I have had with the book world—a curious place inhabited by writers, agents, editors, publishers, critics, booksellers, librarians and, most important of all, readers. That world fascinates me because—as the editor Esther Margolis remarked to me recently—it resembles a diamond: small, multifaceted, precious.

My fascination began long ago, in the mid-1920's, when I was in high school. I happened to read Stanley Unwin's just-published and now classic *The Truth About Publishing*. I've never been the same since. It took another turn one summer in the early 1930's, when I was a college student vacationing in Europe and bought copies of the German Tauchnitz paperbound editions of fine works in English. Why, I wondered, weren't such wonderful things available in the United States?

Since World War II the nature of the book and the role that it plays in our society have changed more profoundly than during any period in the history of American book publishing. One of the key influences in these changes is the coming to America of the softcovered book—what has come to be called the Paperback Revolution. It was my good fortune to be able to observe that revolution as a close-up yet disinterested observer, first as the book review editor of the *Saturday Review of Literature*, then as an editor and columnist of the *New York Times Book Review*.

This volume is a selection of the pieces I contributed to the

New York Times Book Review, linked by afterthoughts and updates. Because it is literary journalism, it conveys, I believe, some of the immediacy and excitement of the moment at which it was written. Because much of it was printed in a weekly column called "Paperback Talk" during the 1970's and the early '80's, it is most relevant to those years. It will serve, I hope, as a modest contribution to the history of the publishing revolution of the mid-20th century that has yet to be written.

R.W.

Introduction

In reading through this collection of writings about the publishing industry over the past forty-five years, one is struck by the fact that Ray Walters appears to have been very consistently in the right place at the right time. This consistency is no accident. A columnist whose specific objective was to keep track of the paperbound publishing scene, he obviously recognized the need to know fully as much about the industry as a whole, and made it his business to do so.

Reading his columns now gives one a very good understanding of what the book trade was thinking and what it was doing at the time they were written: not only that, hindsight reveals that his reporting of book trade affairs was astute and concise. It quickly becomes clear that he recognized the relative importance of then current activities, sifting the merely sensational from the important, and giving proper dimension to both. The very fact that his work makes valuable and lively reading today speaks for its significance over the period of time when it first appeared.

Although the *New York Times* reviewed the lowly paperbound infrequently (if at all in the early years), Ray Walters' trade column had considerable impact on booksellers, who recognized a knowledgeable observer when they saw one. Hence, the column also had an effect on the consumer. It is not too much to say that Ray's writing helped the Paperback Revolution to develop and prosper.

As paperbounders, both reprint and original, my wife Betty and I have been working together and on the scene for a very long time—in fact, since its inception—in various incarnations: as Penguins, as Bantams, as Peacocks, and, for the longest period, under our own imprint. In the reprint business, we did not expect review attention. Even as publishers of originals (the war books and political specials of the Penguin years, and as Ballantine Books), we learned, along with later original paperbounders, to reach out for readers without the benefit of any budget for advertising, nor any hope of reviews. So recognition by Ray Walters of new paperbound trends, or of individual authors, was frequently the only recognition venturesome publishing might receive. His column, available by subscription, arrived in publishing offices early in the week preceding the Sunday when the *Book Review* section would appear. When his column concerned our own publishing we hurried to reproduce it and get it into the hands of booksellers all over the country. Ray's vitality was appreciated in cities not in the *New York Times* sphere of influence—in fact, his column was undoubtedly far more widely read than the august presence in which it officially appeared.

I remember talking to Ray about the emerging book chains— B. Dalton and Walden. Typically he wanted to visit their central buying offices. He always wanted to go to the heart of the matter, and having done so, always recognized what was important, and in this particular instance, secured the chains' cooperation in providing information for the *Times* best seller lists, thereby stabilizing the statistical base for that handy guide in the no-man's-land of conjecture about what was going to sell.

The arrangement of his columns in this book gives a fascinating you-were-there closeness to the rise and fall of trends in paperbound publishing. His writing has a sense of immediacy that loses none of its impact by reason of distance. On the contrary, the dual effect of being there at the same time that one is provided with an overall bird's-eye view achieves a clarity of understanding seldom enjoyed when one is enmeshed in the hurly-burly of competitive publishing. The connective tissue, the vignettes of powerful, trend-setting individuals, create a sense of unity, of growth and the passage of time.

His short author sketches take the mystery out of the paperbound "blockbuster". It is to be observed that consistently throughout the book Ray keeps quoting mass market rack size sales figures for best selling titles that far exceed the numbers being achieved today for the same level of "top" sellers. So that, in effect, one learns a great deal about today's marketplace by being able to make comparisons with its development.

Ray's perceptions cover the full range of the complex comings and goings among publishers and booksellers, authors and readers. He appreciates the showmanship of a Barbara Cartland while understanding the subtlety involved in introducing an author like Carlos Castaneda to the mass market. He consistently quotes hard publishing facts about numbers of copies printed, dollars paid, quantities sold. His canny observations on the birth, growth, development, trends and history of paperbound publishing, seen with the immediacy and reality of one who was on the spot when it happened, make him not only a participant in the Paperbound Revolution but a writer whose work is essential to anyone who wants to function in the highly competitive arena of American massmarket publishing— which necessarily includes hardcover since the two are now inextricably welded together. This book is a part of their working stock of basic information.

And, as any good book must, *Paperback Talk* provides, as we say in the trade, (accurately if ungrammatically) a very lively read.

Ian and Betty Ballantine
Bearsville, N.Y., 1985

The Paperback Revolution

The Beginning

Over a long weekend in May 1939, a time when the United States had barely freed itself from the throes of the Great Depression, some 500 bookpeople foregathered at New York's Hotel Pennsylvania, where the American Booksellers Association was holding its annual convention. Before and after panel dicussions of the problems of operating a store, booksellers from "as far away as Kansas City" broke bread and shared ideas during lunches and banquets and a day-long journey out to Flushing Meadows to see the fair that was celebrating "the World of Tomorrow." In the course of the socializing, publishers' representatives told the booksellers about—and took orders for—the most promising of the 10,000 titles being published that year.

New York was a natural place for the meeting. Except for several houses in Boston and Philadelphia and a sprinkling of university presses across the country, virtually all U.S. book publishing was concentrated in Manhattan and 40 percent of all the nation's sales were in the Northeast.

The cozy, rather provincial affair received scant attention in the press—even though the meeting included an address by Dr. Thomas Mann, in which the eminent Ger-

man emigré man of letters called books "mediators between the spirit and life," a timely topic in a spring when
Europe was edging toward war.

In another address, the best-selling novelist Edna
Ferber complained that $2 and $3 was too high a price for
a popular book — even as rumors circulated through the
corridors of the Hotel Pennsylvania that within a few
weeks a publisher would launch a series of paperbound
books costing only a quarter.

One Sunday morning in June 1939, a time when America's
best-selling books were *The Web and the Rock*, Thomas
Wolfe's third autobiographical novel ($3), and *The Grapes
of Wrath*, John Steinbeck's story of the westward trek of
Okies dispossessed by the Great Depression ($2.75), the
"Books and Authors" column of *The New York Times Book
Review* reported something up and coming.

June 18, 1939
A new experiment in providing good books at prices within the
reach of all is being launched by Robert F. de Graff, 386 Fourth
Avenue, New York City, who calls the series that he is publishing Pocket BOOKS. The first ten titles, to be published tomorrow, June 19, are:

Three novels that have served as the bases for popular
films: *Wuthering Heights* by Emily Brontë; *Lost Horizon* by
James Hilton, and *Topper* by Thorne Smith.

An inspirational self-help book, *Wake Up and Live!* by
Dorothea Brande.

A collection of light verse, *Enough Rope* by Dorothy
Parker.

A children's classic, *Bambi* by Felix Salten.

Two volumes of literary classics, *The Way of All Flesh* by
Samuel Butler, and *Shakespeare's Five Tragedies (Macbeth,
Julius Caesar, Hamlet, Romeo and Juliet* and *King Lear)* with in-
troductions by John Masefield.

A Pulitzer Prize-winning novel by Thornton Wilder, *The
Bridge of San Luis Rey.*

By eliminating excessive margins and by the use of special
lightweight but opaque paper Mr. de Graff has been able to
bring these books down to pocket size (4¼ inches by 6½ inches)

without sacrificing legibility. Each book is printed from type at least as large as that used in the original edition. The carrying weight has been further cut down by doing away with bulky cloth and board binding and substituting semi-stiff paper binding coated with Dura-gloss, which is moisture proof and does not easily become soiled. The books will sell at 25 cents per copy. Mr. de Graff is no newcomer to the business of publishing lower-priced books. Fourteen years ago he originated the Garden City Publishing Company's line of Star Dollar reprints. He left that organization to become president of Blue Ribbon Books, bringing out reprints of popular best-sellers at prices ranging down to 39 cents. A year ago he resigned to make an exhaustive investigation of what book readers want. The result of that investigation is his new series of Pocket BOOKS. New titles will be added from time to time to the ten excellent ones with which a beginning is being made.

The "Books and Authors" columnist failed to mention that Mr. de Graff had three more or less silent partners in his venture—Richard L. Simon, Max Schuster and Leon Shimkin, owners of Simon & Schuster, an aggressive 15-year-old trade publishing house, whose offices adjoined Pocket Books' quarters. The trio had put up about half of the $45,000 capital with which the venture was launched.

The idea of books in soft covers was by no means original. During the 19th century there had been several waves of paperback publishing in the United States, most of it popular and sometimes sensational fiction, commonly referred to as "penny dreadfuls" and "dime novels." During the 1920's and '30's, half a dozen book and magazine publishers, including Alfred A. Knopf and Lawrence E. Spivak, had attempted, unsuccessfully, to offer more serious works in the paper-cover style that had long been an integral part of publishing on the Continent and that had been brought to Great Britain in 1935 by Allen Lane's Penguin Books. Mr. de Graff had a formula that he believed would beat the jinx in this country. Pocket Books would be sold as if they were magazines—at newsstands, drugstores, cigar stores, as well as bookstores. By keeping production costs low and by selling hundreds of thousands of copies, their price could be kept at 25 cents, a bargain at a time when lending libraries were charging five cents a day.

By Labor Day, Mr. de Graff and his partners had reason to believe that their gamble was safe, as the "Books and Authors" columnist reported happily.

September 24, 1939

It begins to look as if the publishers of Pocket BOOKS have what the public has been looking for. Pocket BOOKS are now on sale in most large cities throughout the country (half a million copies of the ten titles have been sold) and distribution is about to begin in the smaller cities and towns. The best seller was Emily Brontë's *Wuthering Heights* and the one which attracted the fewest buyers was *Five Great Tragedies* of William Shakespeare. Four new titles have just been added: *The Good Earth* by Pearl Buck; *The Great Short Stories of Guy de Maupassant; Show Boat* by Edna Ferber, and *A Tale of Two Cities* by Charles Dickens. Additional titles will be issued regularly each month.

December 12, 1976

Ever since Gutenberg, publishers have been using colophons to identify their works—the sort of designs that advertising directors now call "logos." The logos readers remember most distinctly tend to be birds and beasts; viz., Knopf's borzoi, Bantam's rooster and Pocket Books' kangaroo, the last familiarly called "Gertrude."

Next month Gertrude will assume a new look, as a leaping marsupial designed by the leading graphic artist Milton Glazer. She's hopped a long way from the bespectacled, sedentary creature that adorned the first ten volumes with which Pocket introduced the modern paperbacks to the U.S. back in

1939   1943   1945   1962   1964   1977

1939. How did Gertrude get her name? Frank J. Lieberman, who designed her for a fee of $25, recollected the other day: "For some reason, I named her after my mother-in-law."

Pocket Books' spectacular success encouraged other publishers to launch similar lines. In August 1939, Allen Lane announced that he was bringing his line of Penguin Books to the United States. In November 1941, Joseph Meyers, a magazine publisher, announced a line of Avon Pocket-sized Books. But before either of these ventures could gain much momentum, the United States entered World War II and paper supplies were rigorously rationed.

Nonetheless, World War II did greatly widen the audience for the soft-covered book. During less than four years, the Army and the Navy, with the freely given cooperation of the hard-cover publishers, distributed to service personnel more than 100 million copies of reprints of more than a thousand worthy titles in the Armed Services Editions. Many soldiers and sailors, with lots of time on their hands, discovered that books provide pleasures and that a paperbound volume which could be slipped into the pockets of their fatigues was a handy form in which to read them.

Once the war was over and restrictions on paper were lifted, the Paperback Revolution accelerated. Within a few years two dozen publishers, with the help of a nationwide network of periodical distributors, were putting paperbacks into racks in stores in towns and neighborhoods where books had never been sold before.

The Industry Comes of Age

Twenty years after it began, the Paperback Revolution was providing something for everyone . . .

January 17, 1960

A traveling salesman grabs a copy of the latest John D. MacDonald mystery at the airport newsstand to kill time on a plane ride to St. Louis.

A mother of small children, faced by a domestic crisis, consults one of the two copies of Dr. Benjamin's Spock's *Baby and Child Care* — one for downstairs, one for upstairs — she bought at the checkout counter of the supermarket.

A high-school girl reads for junior English the copy of *Jane Eyre* sent by one of the three clubs that distribute paperback books through school and children's organizations.

A senior at Kent School in Connecticut buys Alfred Kazin's *On Native Grounds* from a rack in the school library because it promises to answer some of the questions about American literature his instructor recently raised in class.

A Dartmouth sophomore picks up at the college bookstore A. N. Whitehead's *Science and the Modern World,* required reading for a survey course he is taking.

An elderly resident of a Los Angeles suburb buys Ronald Knox's *The Belief of Catholics* from the rack in the lobby of her parish church.

An aspiring Beatnik visits San Francisco's City Lights Bookshop for John S. Wilson's *The Collector's Jazz: Modern.*

These and millions of other Americans — scholars and taxi drivers, teenagers and octogenarians — are visiting bookshops and newsstands, libraries and cigar stores to buy paperbound volumes on subjects as diverse as the Confucian odes and ways to improve one's poker game.

As the 1950's give way to the '60's, the paperback is "the latest" — as much a part of the times as hi-fi and stereo records, compact cars and ranch houses, bongo drums and five-children families, two-week jet vacations in Europe and electric can openers. Indeed, certain writers and their ideas — Jack Kerouac and his Beats, David Riesman and his lonely crowd, Jules Feiffer and his sick-sick-sickery, D. T. Suzuki and Zen Buddhism — have gained their wide reputations and currency largely through the soft covers.

Thanks in large part to paperbacks, the American book industry is enjoying a prosperity it has never before known. Last year, according to the best-educated guesses available, it sold a total of 300 million copies of the 7,000 paperback titles in print, accounting for close to one-half of all books sold and nearly one-fifth the industry's total dollar income, now at an all-time high. The sales not only kept the cash registers of booksellers ringing with unprecedented frequency, but proved a godsend to the men who tend newsstands in a period when magazine sales were sagging.

What is there about the softcover book that makes it one of this era's favored phenomena? It is inexpensive—although not as inexpensive as it once was. It is easy to carry—but no longer always easy to slip into a pocket. It is easy to buy—and becoming easier each month as the number of retail outlets increases. It is attractively packaged. Its contents are interesting—and increasingly so as the effects of American mass education spread.

Like most innovations, paperbacks at one time or another have stirred strong feelings. They have been condemned for having covers and contents unsuitable for children. "Trashy and lurid," "cheap pulp material," "profanity" were some of the objections to them recently expressed in a national survey of public and parochial school teachers. In a dozen cities—Chicago, San Francisco and Los Angeles among them—the police departments are vigilantly patrolling the newsstands, ready to seize any paperbacks deemed obscene or salacious.

Paperbacks have been resisted by some booksellers who complained that they took up too much space for the profit they brought; by librarians, who professed not to know how to catalogue and shelve them; by old-time publishers fearful they would upset the even keel of the industry.

And they have been lavishly praised—"the greatest thing since corn flakes," in the phrase of Bennett Cerf of Random House. "One of the greatest things that has ever happened to the book publishing business," says Harold E. Ingle, president of the American Association of University Presses. A. Whitney Griswold, president of Yale, believes "they assure that reading will continue to play its role in the educational process."

Why the sharp differences of opinion? Because its advocates and opponents have different images in mind when they praise and blame. In its short life the paperback has already assumed many facets.

During its first dozen years the softcover book remained, for the most part, a vehicle of entertainment and information for the masses. To keep prices low in the face of spiralling production costs, printing was done on high-speed rotary presses and cheaper methods of binding were introduced. In 1953, New

American Library, Pocket Books, Bantam, Fawcett, Popular Library, Avon and Dell, in about that order, accounted for approximately 85 percent of the sales.

A number of the recent comers to the industry were firms with backgrounds in magazine publishing. Two introduced practices that in time became general. Fawcett Publications, begetter of such periodicals as *True Confessions, Motion Picture* and *Woman's Day*, decided in 1950 to start a softcover line and distribute it through its own efficient sales organization. Because that organization was already handling New American Library's reprints of hardcover books, it tried something unique—a series of paperback originals. Its Gold Medal line gave writers like John D. MacDonald and Kurt Vonnegut their first chance to have their work published in book form.

At a time when many paperback firms were emphasizing smoking-gun thrillers intended for men, Fawcett and another magazine house, Dell Publishing Company, publisher of such magazines as *I Confess* and *Cupid's Diary*, introduced a romantic note into the paperback racks with reprints of novels by the likes of Victoria Holt. This development played a great part in getting women into the habit of reading paperbacks. As luck would have it, all this occurred at a time when multi-million-copy family magazines like the *Saturday Evening Post, Collier's* and *Liberty* were dying a slow death, thanks to the competition of television for the advertiser's dollars.

Nonetheless, the hard core of the mass market remained men who had formerly obtained their reading matter from lending libraries and in pulp magazines. This audience favored books of inspiration like Dale Carnegie's *How to Win Friends and Influence People* and stories of sex and violence like Mickey Spillane's *Kiss Me, Deadly*. Many publishers raised the false hopes of many males and raised the hackles of many Mrs. Grundys by bedecking their books in covers that made much of the fact that women are females, even if that fact was not pertinent to the book's contents.

Even as increasing numbers of paperbacks were being grabbed up by the masses, they were also becoming conveyors of high culture. During the 1950's the college population rocketed, thanks to the benefits offered by the Government under the G. I. Bill. Wouldn't these students prefer to buy their own copies of the fine books their professors assigned as supplementary reading rather than wait in line at the library?

The covers of many mass-market paperbacks in the late 1950's were designed to appeal to men and boys with time to kill and a desire to kill it through vicarious sex, murder and mayhem. These were designed by Harry Barton, Barrye Phillips, Tony Kokinos, Robert Stanley and Ray Johnson.

The first person to perceive and act on that opportunity was a young man fresh out of Columbia College named Jason Epstein. Mr. Epstein persuaded the business-like house of Doubleday to start, in April 1953, an imprint called Anchor Books, reprints of "serious" works that were out of print or too expensive for a "serious" reader's pocketbook. Its offerings included books like Edmund Wilson's *Literary Chronicles* and Sigmund Freud's *Origins of Psychoanalysis*.

Mr. Epstein's notion was not totally original, any more than Robert F. de Graff's had been. For many years Everyman's Library and the Modern Library had offered books of this sort in hard covers. Lately the inexpensive Penguin Books and New American Library's Mentor and Signet series, inspired by the British Penguin and the German Tauchnitz lines, had been offering works of comparable character. Their format and method of distribution, however, left something to be desired. Through the channels traditionally employed by Doubleday and other general trade publishers—bookstores, department stores and, most particularly, stores in college communities—the Anchor line found a warm welcome. Printing, paper and binding were of higher quality than those of the mass-market-distributed paperbacks. Cover designs were modernistic and often abstract.

Within a year several hardcover houses started similar lines of "quality" or "trade" paperbacks. In 1955, Cornell became the first university press to start a paperback line. By the end of the decade virtually every general trade publisher and university press had ventured into paperbacks, drawing on its own backlist and leasing rights to congenial titles from other houses.

Today, at the dawn of the '60's, the chief difference between "mass-market" and "trade" paperbacks are of price, format and size of printings. For mass-market paperbacks, prices now range from 35 cents (25 cents for mysteries and Westerns) to 95 cents. Printings range from 100,000 for a run-of-the-mill mystery to 8,500,000 copies for a novel like *God's Little Acre*. For the publications of the trade and university presses, the price range is commonly 85 cents to $2.95. Printings may be as low as 4,000 copies for a recondite treatise, and as high as 500,000 for *The Organization Man*.

What have been the effects of the Paperback Revolution on

Colophons used by publishers in the late 1950's.

These colophons, used by paperback houses between 1939 and 1959, demonstrate that while publishers' images of their houses have changed a bit over the years, the price tags on their books have changed a lot.

the book industry and the reading habits of Americans? It has not increased the number of bookstores: there are 1,450 of them by generous count, just about as many as a century ago. But, in many a city, bookstores that once stocked only the latest best sellers and the steadiest staples in hard covers now display in softcover form a rich cross-section of every field, old and new. The vast paperback department in one of Kroch's and Brentano's Chicago stores stocks 4,400 titles and numerous stores in other cities carry as many as 3,000.

The Paperback Revolution has put books on sale in some 85,000 other retail outlets. They have accustomed incalculable millions of Americans who never owned a book in their lives to acquire personal copies of what they read.

New areas in which they may sell their products are con-

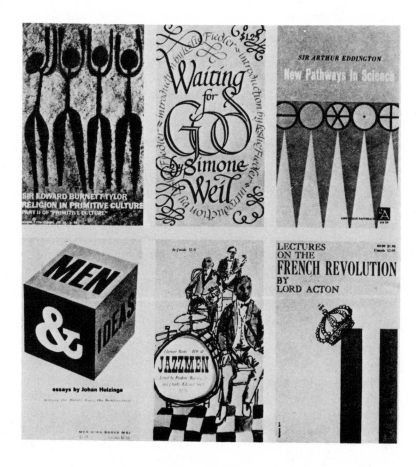

At the dawn of the 1960's, the trade paperback gave the graphics artist—
in the words of Ray Nash, professor of graphics arts at Dartmouth—"a
challenging and an expanding opportunity." These covers were designed by Alex Tsao, Irwin Primer, Ron Stachowiak, Elaine Lustig,
Jules Maidoff and Barbara Bert.

stantly being sought by the publishers, especially the large, aggressive mass-market firms. They are trying to increase their sales to the school and college population, which is growing each year as the birth rate rises. New American Library pioneered in paperbacks for classroom and collateral reading, but now virtually every one of the large houses has its own educational department.

As sales and markets expand, publishers are becoming nervously aware that the lode of literature suitable for reprinting is not inexhaustible. Last year alone about 600 titles were published in paperback for the first time. Competition for the reprint rights to books with a wide appeal has shot prices up to staggering heights. In the first years of the Revolution, authors and trade publishers were happy to receive a few thousand dollars for one of their books. Recently a half dozen best-selling novels have brought $100,000 or more. Rights to *Return to Peyton Place* went for $265,000.

Increasingly, both "mass-market" and "trade" paperback publishers are prospecting for original works of quality. NAL's Mentor volumes on ancient civilizations have won accolades within the industry. Ballantine has a notable series on engagements of World War II. Last year Lippincott inaugurated two series, one on music, another on medicine. Macmillan recently started a series of slender paperbound volumes of the new work of contemporary poets.

From time to time, some of the mass-market houses contract with an author to write a book for which they see a market and then arrange with a trade house to publish it in hardcovers before reprinting it themselves. Arthur Knight's history of the movies, *The Liveliest Art*, conceived by NAL's editors, was published by Macmillan a year and a half before it was printed in the Mentor series. On occasion the order is reversed. Dell published William Miller's *History of the United States* some time before Braziller brought it out in hardcover and the Book-of-the-Month Club distributed it to its membership.

The whole book world is watching these innovations closely. Indeed, no promising possibility is being overlooked in the booming paperback industry, 21 years old and beginning to feel and act like a grownup.

Definitions and Argot

By the late 1970's, the paperback industry had so expanded and had become so multifaceted that there was need
for definitions . . .

May 16, 1976

Like the truckers who swap information on their citizens-band
radios, paperbounders speak a jargon all their own. Herewith a
start at a compilation of the trade's ever-changing lexicon:

• *Racks.* The temporary resting place for newly-issued
mass-market paperbacks looking for buyers. These stands,
made of metal or wood, have pockets into which copies of
4¼-by-7 inch softcovered books may be slipped so that they
may attract the attention of browsers at newsstands, stationery stores and bookstores. As there are never enough
pockets to hold all of a month's releases, there is always a bitter competition for them among publishers. Books bearing an
especially alluring cover design or author's name will—as the
trade puts it—"jump out of the racks and race to the cash
register."

• *Dumps.* The happy temporary resting place for the
relatively few paperbacks that their publishers fervently feel
will become best sellers. Publishers supply these large, entic-
ingly decorated cardboard bins to retailers to display two
dozen or more copies in the middle of the busiest aisles of their
stores. The idea is that passing customers won't be able to
resist grabbing up a copy.

• *Shredders.* The ultimate unhappy end of nearly half of
all copies printed of mass-market paperbacks. Dealers return
unsold copies to their wholesaler, the wholesaler tears off the
front covers to be returned to the publisher for credit, then
stuffs the guts of the book into these destructive machines.

• *Shrinks.* To keep copies of their handsomely illustrated books pristinely suitable for gift-giving purposes, many
trade paperback publishers encase them in a tight cellophane
wrapping, attractive to the eye of potential buyers, safe from
the touch of smudgy fingers.

• *Simos.* More and more trade publishers are issuing
their new books simultaneously in hard and soft covers. The

high-priced hardcover editions garner the reviews, the more moderately priced softcover editions get the sales—proportionately one-to-eight or more in most cases.

March 27, 1977

The world of paperbacks is inhabited by two species of soft-covered creatures—mass-market and trade paperbacks. Exactly what, a friend asks, do those terms mean? To define them is about as easy as to explain the difference between Broadway, Off Broadway and Off Off Broadway to a theatergoer from out of town. But here's a try:

• *Publishers.* Mass-market books are the principal stock-in-trade of a dozen large New York-based firms, ranging alphabetically from Ace to Zebra. Trade paperbacks are issued by almost every book publisher in the land—including mass-market houses.

• *Format.* Mass-market paperbacks have a uniform page size, a pocketable 4¼ × 7 inches. Their type tends to be small and their paper soon yellows. The pages of trade paperbacks, on the other hand, vary from small to super-coffee-table size. Sometimes their form is peculiarly appropriate. A recently published book about Jimmy Carter's favorite crop is goober-shaped. Usually the trade paperback's paper is of superior quality, its type quite readable. Often the illustrations are numerous—sometimes they're the chief feature of the book.

• *Price.* From the time of its appearance on the American scene, one of the mass-market paperback's chief appeals has been its relative cheapness. But what started out at 25 cents a copy back in 1939 now costs $1.95 to $2.75.* There are not and never have been "usual prices" for trade paperbacks. These days some sell at $2.25 and even lower; some cost $7.95 and higher.

• *Subject matter.* When trade paperbacks made their debut a quarter of a century ago, they tended to be reprints of serious works of lasting significance. In recent years they have come to encompass the same wide range of enduring to trendy subjects as mass-market paperbacks. Indeed, a number of recent mass-market books are reprints of works originally published in trade format.

• *Distribution.* Trade paperbacks are normally on sale only in the bookstores that stock hardcover books. Mass-market paperbacks are available at all these stores—plus nearly 100,000 other retail outlets, including newsstands, variety stores and supermarkets. A trade paperback often remains part of a bookstore's staple stock for many years; it's a rare mass-market title that is accorded rack-space in a variety store or supermarket longer than 90 days after publication. A trade paperback is counted a "best seller" if it sells 50,000 copies or more; to earn the same accolade a mass-market book must have 750,000 copies or more in print.

With all this in mind, how can we define the paperback world's two species? The best we can do is this:

A *mass-market paperback* is a softcover book usually sold at newsstands, variety stores and supermarkets, as well as in bookstores.

A *trade paperback* is a softcover book usually sold in bookstores (and in some other special outlets) at an average price higher than mass-market paperbacks.

Can anyone here suggest anything better?**

*By early 1984, the price range of mass-market paperbacks had risen to $1.95–$4.95.
**No reader obliged.

Pioneering Paperbounders

• *Paperbounder.* A word popularized by Ian Ballantine to describe men and women who, like himself, live by the softcovered book. Herewith profiles of several who blazed trails during the Paperback Revolution.

Book Couple: Ian and Betty Ballantine

June 22, 1975
In a rambling old house high on a mountainside in the foothills of the Catskills, Ian and Betty Ballantine operate the Peacock Press of Bearsville, New York, an enterprise which produces series of war books and picture books for Bantam and hardcover books like *Gnomes* and *Faeries* for Harry N. Abrams. The building in which Peacock Press is quartered houses some of paperback publishing's most interesting mementos, for the

Ballantines have been in the business longer than any other Americans.

The couple's affair with the softcover book began back in 1938, when New York-born Ian Ballantine, as a Columbia College undergraduate, wrote a senior essay describing paperbound books as the great hope of publishing. A year later, while a student at the London School of Economics, he talked the late Allen Lane into appointing him American sales manager of his four-year-old enterprise, Penguin Books. Mr. Ballantine hurried back to the States with his British bride, Betty Jones, determined to make good. As a result of the newlywed's efforts, Penguin entered the American market in July 1939, only a few days after the debut of Pocket Books and the start of what has come to be called the Paperback Revolution.

In 1945, with a consortium of four major hardcover publishers and a magazine publisher, Mr. Ballantine founded Bantam Books; in 1952 he founded his own house, Ballantine Books. All along the way, Betty and Ian worked as close partners. Their joint career is a series of firsts: publishing original books about World War II . . . co-publishing original books with hardcover publishers . . . introducing the world of *Mad Magazine* to book covers . . . developing lines of science fiction and fantasy that helped make J. R. R. Tolkien's Middle Earth a campus favorite . . . popularizing the work of Paul Ehrlich and other environmentalists . . . sponsoring lines of books of regional interest . . . bringing the Sierra Club books and calendars to a national audience . . . issuing magnificent gift books and art albums at affordable prices.

Like the trail of most pioneers, the Ballantines' has not always been bathed in sunshine. Some of their innovations were ahead of their time. There were periods—if Ian Ballantine's critics are to be believed—when he spent too much time out in the grass roots gathering new seedlings and neglected to cultivate the garden at home.

After selling Ballantine Books, the Ballantines in 1974 started packaging books under the Peacock and other imprints. Ian continues to tour the country tirelessly, chatting with booksellers and authors to discover where the public's fancy may turn next, while Betty keeps store in Bearsville.

In 1985 the American Booksellers Association presented its Irita Van Doren Award to Mr. and Mrs. Ballantine for their "many contributions to the cause of the book as an instrument of culture in American life."

Doyenne: Helen Meyer

July 10, 1977

A long line of whiz kids have popped up and disappeared since the paperback changed the style of U.S. book publishing, but there are few persons—certainly only one woman—whose influence in the field has remained indisputably great through all its years. She's Helen Honig Meyer, who was president of Dell Publishing Company when it became the fourth firm to enter the field in 1944, and today is still the very active chairman of the board of what is now one of the three or four most active houses.

From her appearance you might guess that Mrs. Meyer is a grandmotherly suburban matron (which she is), from her tireless, energetic manner that she's in her early 50's (she's crowding 70). Talk with her a few minutes and you know for sure that she's a shrewd, strong-minded woman.

Recently, as Dell presented its archival collection of all the 9,000 paperback titles it's published to the Library of Congress (accompanied by an expression of hope that other publishers will follow suit), Mrs. Meyer had a moment for reminiscence. Some of her thoughts:

• Dell, like several other paperback pioneers, rose out of the pulp magazine business. George T. Delacorte was the publisher of *I Confess* and *Cupid's Diary* back in the 1920's when Miss Honig, a native of Brooklyn then in her teens, went to work for him as a clerk. The years passed, Miss Honig became Mrs. Meyer of South Orange, New Jersey, and the mother of two. Meanwhile, as the Delacorte pulp line proliferated, she tried her hand at everything in the business—even travelling as a sales representative. In time Mr. Delacorte rewarded her with the company presidency, making her the first woman to become chief executive of a major U.S. publishing house.

• When the German Tauchnitz-Albatross and the British Penguin softcover lines began to create a stir in the 1930's,

George Delacorte quickly sensed the possibilities of paperback publishing in the U.S. But his talks about forming a partnership with Richard L. Simon and Max Schuster fell through when the book publishers decided to set up their own Pocket Books in 1939. With paper hard to come by because of wartime rationing, Mr. Delacorte had to wait five years before launching Dell Books with a mystery called *Death in the Library*.

• At the start it wasn't easy to persuade newsdealers to handle anything so unusual as a book. Mrs. Meyer still smiles wryly when she recalls her troubles in lining up distributors in Chicago, storied scene of gangster-style circulation wars.

• With so many racks to fill each month, Dell had to look about for steady sources for reprints. Result: the founding of Delacorte, a hardcover house, and the acquisition of the long-established Dial Press during the early 1960's.

• Mrs. Meyer believes that a publisher's line should have a "good mix"—something for every type of reader. Thus, for the subway rider Dell has the Candlelight series, for the college student, Delta Books.

• She's particularly proud of her Laurel Leaf series, one of the best children's paperback lines. "I was always concerned that my children and grandchildren should read," she explains.

Mrs. Meyer doesn't have much time for reminiscence. Over the years George Delacorte left the running of his firm more and more to his sometime clerk. When he sold the company to Doubleday last year, it was understood that she would continue in charge for half a dozen years.

These days she's in her office every day, studying what the competition is up to, making plans and decisions for the future. In this business, she observes, no one knows what the situation will be even a year hence. "Who'd have thought that a John Jakes or a Rosemary Rogers would come along? . . . Now in October, we'll be printing one million copies of Thomas Thompson's *Blood and Money* . . ."

Following a practice common in the corporate world, Doubleday & Company, after acquiring the Delacorte publishing empire, in 1978 replaced Mrs. Meyer as chairman of Dell, but permitted her to continue as one of its "consultants" for several years. Mrs. Meyer later retired to Florida, from where she represented one of Dell's all-time best-selling authors, James Clavell, in foreign rights sales.

Dean: Oscar Dystel

December 31, 1978

Ever since May, when Helen Meyer retired as head of Dell Books, the paperback publishing corps has had a new dean. Characteristically, Oscar Dystel, who has presided over the affairs of Bantam Books for nearly a quarter of a century, hasn't rushed forward to accept the title. Bantam is generally acknowledged to be the leader in the field, accounting for nearly one-fifth of all mass-market sales. But Mr. Dystel, a short, slight man, is content with a low public profile.

Bantam Books, as it exists today, is Mr. Dystel's creation. When he became its president in 1954, the eight-year-old house—like the whole industry—was in a very bad way. Not long before, a sudden drop in the public's appetite for paperbacks had left publishers with 175 million unsold copies in their warehouses. Bantam's accountants were writing in deep red ink, its founding fathers were at loggerheads over policy, its presidency had been vacant for two years.

Mr. Dystel, a native New Yorker, brought Bantam qualifications that the industry has since come to consider most desirable for an executive—a Harvard M.B.A. and experience in magazine editorial and marketing work. He is a perennial enthusiast and a believer in team spirit. The highly capable staff with which he surrounded himself found itself regularly joining in all policy and planning discussions. Over the years there have been few personnel shakeups or even departures, a rare thing in book publishing. (Three Dystel-trained executives, however, have left to head other houses: Ron Busch to Pocket and Victor Temkin and Rena Wolner to Berkley.*

One of Mr. Dystel's first acts as Bantam's president was to visit distributors across the country to learn what they thought about its line and the way it should be promoted. He's made a point of keeping in close touch with them ever since, building a staff of 130 sales reps, the envy of the industry. This proved most effective as Bantam went into the school and college markets and, recently, into bookstores in a big way.

Over the years, Mr. Dystel has been alert to new trends but

---

*After a brief tenure at Berkley, Rena Wolner was named president of Avon, replacing Walter Meade who became an executive of the Hearst Group.

Ron Busch has left Pocket Books.—R.W. 6/85.

rarely goes overboard. He's pleased to see more originals being published and is as happy as anyone to have a blockbusting best seller, but he thinks that the backlist is equally important ("it pays the rent"). Nor, he insists, should the worthy book of middling prospects be overlooked. "We've distributed 1,772,000 copies of Robert M. Pirsig's *Zen and the Art of Motorcycle Maintenance*—who could have predicted that?"

Mr. Dystel got Bantam into the black within months after assuming its presidency and has kept it emphatically there ever since. In the last 25 years the house has had a variety of owners—an American publishing consortium, a West Coast entertainment conglomerate, an Ohio-based investment company, an Italian conglomerate; at present, it's controlled by Bertelsmann, a West German publishing conglomerate. All the absentee proprietors have refrained from interfering with a profitable operation.

Last month, at age 66, Mr. Dystel took a new title: chairman of the board. Does this mean he's looking forward to retirement? Not at all. "I look forward to working closely with the bright young people we've taken on in recent years," he says.

Not long after Bertelsmann obtained complete ownership of Bantam Books in 1980, it obliged Mr. Dystel to become a "consulting editor." Unhappy at this enforced inactivity, Mr. Dystel subsequently terminated his contract and opened an office as a publishers' consultant. In this role he arranged, in 1983, for a "leveraged buyout" of New American Library from its conglomerate owners by a cadre of its management.

Man on the Move: Peter Mayer

April 25, 1976

Season in, season out, there's one game always in progress along Publishers Row. Musical chairs. Only once in a blue moon—as back in 1958, when Robert Gottlieb led a guard of executives from Simon & Schuster to Knopf—do such switches have much significance except to residents of the Row. Another blue moon glowed a fortnight ago when Peter Mayer, lured by one of those Joe Namath-type contracts, moved from Avon Books to Pocket Books' top spot.

Avon was an also-ran paperback house when Mr. Mayer joined it as educational director 13 years ago, but as he rose to publisher he built it into one of the industry's leaders, with a well-balanced line that includes everything from reprints of prize-winning fiction to women's romances of the Rosemary Rogers school.

What's behind the move? Along the Row they're observing that Pocket pioneered U.S. paperback publishing in 1939, but through the years its primacy has eroded. Gulf & Western, the conglomerate that recently acquired the line through its purchase of Simon & Schuster, seems to be counting on Mr. Mayer to restore its ancient glory.

Two years later, Mr. Mayer found himself playing musical chairs again . . .

November 8, 1978

What is Peter Mayer going to do now? The question was one that publishing folk asked each other frequently last summer, after the head of Pocket Books suddenly parted ways with Richard E. Snyder, head of Simon & Schuster, Pocket's owner. The question is all the more tantalizing because Mr. Mayer is generally considered one of the most colorful, dynamic and innovative men in the business. In the past two years he has brought new vigor to the ailing veteran, Pocket Books. He accomplished this by paying attention to reprints and originals that sold millions of copies, as well as to imprints (Pocket's Archway and Quokka) of new and old classics selling only hundreds of thousands of copies.

The answer to the question is now out. Mr. Mayer is becoming chief executive of Penguin Books—which, like Mr. Mayer, was born in London 42 years ago. For him it seems a happy solution. His friends say he's been restive under the mass-market conditions that make it necessary "to publish a great deal of schlock in order to fill 30 rack pockets each month." At Penguin, which has a reputation throughout the English-speaking world for its high literary standards, the onetime holder of scholarships in politics, philosophy and literature at Columbia, Indiana University, Oxford and the Freie Universität in Berlin should find the going most congenial. His commitment, he says, is now to "ideas, reading,

English and the book," to "good books, exciting graphics and progressive marketing."

Mr. Mayer's old colleagues won't be seeing as much of him as before, because as operating head of Penguin International, based in London, he'll be overseeing Penguin's operations throughout the English-speaking world. But he hopes to be in New York frequently, watching over its American paperback line, as well as the operations of another of its subsidiaries, Viking Press.

April 18, 1982

Whatever became of Peter Mayer? Late in 1978, you'll recall, he moved to London to head Penguin Books, the oldest paperback house in the English-speaking world and the largest in Great Britain. Ever since, the publishing grapevine has buzzed with all sorts of rumors: that many old hands at Penguin considered him a brash American and were resisting his outlandish ideas. That he was in deep trouble with three unions. That he hadn't been able to halt Penguin's huge losses. Early in 1980, some gossips predicted that he wouldn't last out the year.

The other day Mr. Mayer, just off the plane from London, stopped by with lots of cheerful things to report. British book publishing is on the rise again, and Penguin is making good profits. While other houses have survived by cutting back, Penguin has grown.

When he took over, Mr. Mayer told us, Penguin was in a rut, depending on a large backlist and traditional merchandising methods. Now, to counterbalance the "high literary quality" titles favored in the past, its new editorial staff is adding works by popular authors and on new subjects, books like *The Far Pavilions, The White Hotel, The Soul of a New Machine* and *You Can Do the Cube.* There is no longer such a thing as "a typical Penguin cover"—the nature of each book is made clear by its cover design. So that its more varied offerings will reach a wider market, Penguin's beefed-up sales force works closely with news agents as well as booksellers. Some titles are advertised on television.

Mr. Mayer spends much of his time traveling, for he is responsible for Penguin's subsidiaries in Australia, New Zealand, South Africa, India, Canada and the United States. These are in no sense regional distributors, as they were in

Penguin's early days, but houses encouraged to develop and maintain their own traditions. Except for the Canadian house, all are in the black.

What of Viking Penguin, as the American subsidiary is called? The Viking hardcover line is profitable again, Mr. Mayer reported, the Penguin paperback line very much so. He is pleased that the Penguin American Library, a series of classics created by Kathryn Court, the editor-in-chief in New York, will also be published in Britain.

"Penguin," Mr. Mayer concluded, as he darted out to go to Colorado to visit some authors, "is a global federation held together by telex and computers." He might well have added, "And by Peter Mayer."

During 1983, Mr. Mayer spent an extended period in New York, reorganizing Viking Penguin to put its hardcover operations on a profitable basis. Then he returned to London and his global peregrinations.

The Product

- *Product.* A word used by many paperbounders on whose M.B.A. diplomas the ink is still wet, to describe the books published by their firm. The "product" falls into numerous categories and genres. The highest hopes and most intense promotional efforts are lavished on "the blockbuster."

- *Blockbuster.* (Sometimes called "the Super-Release" or "the Total Release.") A book with which many a paperback house heads its monthly list of publications. Many of these are the work of a "Big Brand Name Author" or are tie-ins to newly released movies and television specials.

The Big Brand Name Author

With paper-wrapped fiction vying with trade-marked cheesecake and aspirin for the favor of customers in supermarkets and drugstores, it's natural that the books that sell most briskly are by novelists whose previous work has pleased hundreds of thousands of readers. Every genre—mystery, saga, Western, science fiction, fantasy, horror, romance and the rest—has its own Brand Name Authors. So remarkable that they occupy a genre of their own are the Big Brand Name Authors. Writers who have delighted millions of readers with many riveting stories, usually about sex, power and money, frequently *romans à clef.* A Big Brand Name on the cover of a new release makes it — in the argot of paperbounders — "jump out of the racks."

Herewith brief reports on half a dozen typical Big Brand Name Authors:

Jacqueline Susann

May 8, 1977

Tomorrow night Irving Mansfield will be staying up late to be a guest on NBC's Tomorrow Show. He'll be doing a lot of that sort of thing during the next two months — appearing on television and radio talk shows, looking up old newspaper columnist friends from Boston to San Diego. Officially it's a tour to promote Bantam's just-published edition of Jacqueline Susann's posthumous novel *Dolores.* Privately it's a tour of duty by a quintessential showbizman in memory of his wife of 35 years. "I'm doing for it just what she'd be doing if she were here," he explained soberly the other day in his Central Park South apartment, close by his drawers of press clippings and an urn containing her ashes. He's determined that, like its three predecessors, it will make No. 1 on the best seller list.

Mr. Mansfield recalls that it wasn't until Jackie learned that she had cancer in the early 1960's that she abandoned a poor-to-middling career as a stage actress and television performer and determined to make it big as a writer. Her native storytelling talent enabled her to turn out novels capitalizing on what she knew best — "the dark underside of show biz," teeming with thinly veiled celebrities and sexy incidents. Jackie wrote them unaided; her husband collaborated with her in promoting them, pioneering in ways that have since become standard publishing practice. (The oldsters on Publishers Row are fond of recalling one gambit she used: breakfasting with distributors' deliverymen before they went out on their daily rounds and pleading with them to see that her books got into the best pockets in the racks.)

In 15 years the wife-and-husband team accomplished wonders: three novels and a nonfiction book about a pet dog, with worldwide sales of 50 million copies. Since its publication in 1960, her first novel *Valley of the Dolls,* chronicling the fortunes of a set of glamorous women who are addicted to pills, has sold nine million copies in the United States alone and still sells 4,000 copies a month.

Although *Dolores* was published in hardcover after Jackie's death in September 1974, Mr. Mansfield insists it's very much her own book. The idea of a novel about a President's widow had occurred to her long before John F. Kennedy's assassination. When Leonore Hershey, editor of *The Ladies Homes Journal*, suggested to Jackie S. that she write about Jackie O., Jackie S. agreed, but turned it into a *roman à clef.*

Before the year was out, *Dolores* had achieved Mr. Mansfield's ambition, attaining the No. 1 spot for two weeks on the paperback best seller list and selling some 2,530,000 copies. Ten years after Jacqueline Susann's death, all her books were in print and selling well.

Taylor Caldwell

May 22, 1977

Perhaps the most perdurable Big Brand Name author today is Janet Taylor Caldwell of Buffalo, New York, who at the moment has 35 novels in print from four paperback publishers. It's 43 years now since Miss Caldwell, a career woman by day, set up an office in her home and, with some help from her late husband, worked late into the night for four years to turn out *Dynasty of Death*, a saga about the intrigues of two munitions-making families. Her maiden effort was guided through the press by Scribner's legendary editor Maxwell Perkins, the mentor of Thomas Wolfe, F. Scott Fitzgerald and Ernest Hemingway. She's been spinning family sagas and making the best seller lists ever since.

This year, her 77th, is still very much Taylor Caldwell's prime time. Last fall her 1972 novel, *Captains and Kings*, about an Irish immigrant clan that made it big socially and politically in three generations, served as the basis of an NBC television miniseries and as a result enjoyed a 15-week run on the mass-market best seller list. This month Operation Prime Time, a challenge by 95 independent stations to the networks' monopoly of such entertainment, has been unreeling a six-hour miniseries based on her 1968 saga *Testimony of Two Men*—and Fawcett, which never let the book go out of print, rushed a new edition of 850,000 copies into the racks. Result: this week Miss Caldwell makes the list once more. And come October, Fawcett will be releasing her latest novel, *Ceremony of the Innocent,* about the involvement of one of Philadelphia's first families in an international conspiracy.

> Seven years later, Miss Caldwell had turned out yet another best-selling saga, *Answer As a Man* (1981) and had moved to Greenwich, Connecticut, where she was living with her fourth husband. Four paperback houses were keeping 33 of her books very much in print.

James A. Michener

July 30, 1978

In 1975, the paperback rights for E. L. Doctorow's novel *Ragtime* were sold for $1,850,000. In 1976, Colleen McCullough's *The Thorn Birds* went for $1,900,000. In 1978, Mario Puzo's *Fools Die,* along with renewed reprint rights to *The Godfather,* brought $2,550,000. Such events are blazoned in publications that usually pay little attention to the world of books.

A few weeks ago a contract that may involve more money than any of these was quietly signed by Fawcett Books and Random House. For "a very considerable sum" Fawcett acquired rights to James A. Michener's *Centennial,* and renewal rights to 14 of his older books.

Why was it done so quietly? At age 71, with a long string of successes behind him, Mr. Michener doesn't feel the need for the publicity hype that a paperback auction generates. Taxes being what they are, he doesn't think it worth his while to hold out for the topmost dollar—especially since he's had such a long and happy relationship with Fawcett. Back in 1965, the late Bennett Cerf of Random House sold the rights to *The Source* for the largest sum Fawcett had paid up to that time— $700,000.

Mr. Michener, it goes without saying, is one of the Internal Revenue Service's favorite writers. In a "particularly conservative estimate," *Fortune* magazine placed his income from his 1974 novel *Centennial* at $2,100,000.

Over the years Mr. Michener, a onetime Pennsylvania schoolteacher and Manhattan textbook editor, has won his huge following by his ability to chronicle, in an engrossing fictional style, the history of a nation or region. *The Source* told the story of what is now Israel, *Hawaii* of the 50th state, *Centennial* of Colorado, *Chesapeake* of Maryland's eastern shore.

In another way, Mr. Michener is now demonstrating that he isn't the hype type. Instead of hustling to every television talk show to promote his latest book, he's now in South Africa, doing research on his next one. If you should want to see what he's like away from his typewriter, you'll have to attend one of the meetings of the many public causes that occupy his spare time.

The book about South Africa turned out to be another history in the form of fiction. *Covenant* (1981) sold 2,325,000 softcover copies. Since then, Mr. Michener has published *Space*, a fictional account of the U.S. space program, and *Poland*, a fictional history of that nation, with paperback sales in each case approaching 2,500,000 copies. Thereupon he took up residence in Austin, capital of Texas, and set to work to give his magic touch to the history of the Lone Star State. Meanwhile, he laid plans for paying his respects to the largest state of them all, Alaska.

If Mr. Michener's income makes him the I.R.S.'s favorite novelist, the length of his books should make him the favorite of truckers and manufacturers of paper and ink. Consider the case of one of his earlier novels . . .

November 30, 1975

With its 1,088 type-packed pages, James A. Michener's *Centennial* may well be the longest mass-market paperback published to date. A lady at Fawcett Books, with an office intercom in front of her, a pocket calculator in one hand and a copy of the book in the other, has come up with some reckonings:

• More than 10,000 miles of paper 7-by-14½ inches wide were required to print the 2,800,000 copies now on the market. That's 3,300,000 pounds from 3,800 rolls.

• If the printed pages were placed end to end, the total would stretch around the globe 15 times.

• Fifty thousand pounds of ink were required to print the edition.

• Seventeen thousand man-hours were required to print and bind the copies.

• Sixty-seven trucks carrying approximately 42,000 copies each were required to deliver the copies across the country.

We'll take the lady's word for it. Stupefying.

Some Big Brand Name Authors found their huge and loyal followings through the mass-market paperback. One of the first was . . .

Sidney Sheldon

August 24, 1975

A while back, when he had six Broadway plays, 25 motion pictures, more than 200 television scripts, an Academy Award, two Screen Writers Guild Awards and a Tony to his credit, Sidney Sheldon found himself passing the time of day with the editor of *Variety*, the weekly bible of show biz. "What kind of writing do you do?" the editor asked curiously.

Now, with his novel *The Other Side of Midnight* 1975's No. 2 paperback best seller (after *Jaws*), Mr. Sheldon is a garlanded unknown no longer. He's being deluged with fan letters, requests for autographs and personal appearances.

Fame has sneaked up as quietly on the book as it has on the 59-year-old native of Chicago. Published in hardcover last year, *The Other Side of Midnight* won respectable reviews and creditable sales (almost 60,000 copies). But it didn't start making history until last February when Dell brought it out in soft covers. During its first month in the racks it sold one million copies. Now there are 2,800,000 copies in print and reorders at the rate of 100,000 copies a week.

In the trade it is agreed that the book's success is due to word-of-mouth among satisfied readers. That pleases Mr. Sheldon. "My ambition is to be a storyteller," he says, "to keep the story moving and readers turning pages."

He wrote the novel over several years, in time stolen from television script writing and producing. When he began it, he had only a general situtation in mind—a man falls in love with a woman whose husband will not give her up—and let the plot develop as he went along.

Now that Mr. Sheldon is a brand-new Brand Name in the paperback racks, Dell has reissued *The Naked Face*, his only previous book. A thriller about a psychoanalyst who discovers that someone is trying to kill him, it was highly praised and had modest sales when it was first published in 1970. Meanwhile, in his antique-filled mansion in Bel Air, California, Mr. Sheldon's at work on a more ambitious novel, the story of a lovable comic who destroys those he passes on his way to fame.

Sidney Sheldon's claim to Big Brand status now seems secure. The reprint of *The Naked Face* sold more than two million copies; *The Stranger in the Window*, about a lovable comic, was a big best seller in both hardcover and paperback. Similar success awaited Mr. Sheldon's three succeeding novels.

Another writer who rode the paperback trail to become a Big Brand Name was . . .

John Jakes

October 7, 1979

In the history of U.S. book publishing, there's never been a success story quite like that of John Jakes and his Kent family. It began quite modestly, at a table in a midtown Manhattan restaurant back in March 1973. Over lunch, two executives of Pyramid Books, one of the smaller mass-market paperback houses, told Lyle Kenyon Engel, a veteran book packager, about the types of books they were looking for: Westerns, spy stories and—oh, something to tie in with the upcoming American Bicentennial celebration.

Never at a loss for ideas, within a few weeks Mr. Engel submitted a detailed outline for a series that would carry one family through the dramatic events of the nation's history. He even had an author lined up. Unhappily the first one he'd turned to was "too busy." More happily, the second was ready, willing and able, a man who "at heart was a history teacher with brio": John Jakes, a 47-year-old advertising man who had already turned out some 50 books, including science fiction, children's stories and historical novels. A tireless fellow, he does all his own research, writing and typing in the basement of his Dayton, Ohio, home.

The compound of appealing characters, derring-do, sex

play and vivid descriptions of our national past that Mr. Jakes fabricated under Mr. Engel's supervision turned out to be just what millions of Americans, the majority of them male, were looking for. The first volume, *The Bastard*, told of Philip Kent, byblow of British nobility, arriving in Boston in time for the Tea Party; it was published rather quietly (600,000 copies) in October 1974. Readers' word-of-mouth enthusiasm did the rest. By the time the fourth volume, *The Furies*, in which four of Kent's grandchildren scramble for gold in the West and try to cope with the rising abolition movement during the 1830's and 1840's, was published in January 1976, the initial print order was 1,500,000 copies. Next February, when the eighth volume, *The Americans*, carrying the Kents through the period of San Francisco's Barbary Coast, Newport's "marble cottages" and the Johnstown flood, is published, the starting print order will be three million copies. Already a total of 25 million copies of paperbacks about the Kents have been carried to the checkout counters.

> Thus far Mr. Jakes has resisted the urging of his paperback publisher that he bring the Kent Chronicles up to the present. He's moved to Hilton Head, South Carolina, and written two historical novels about the friendship of two families, one in Pennsylvania, the other in Carolina, and how it was strained by the Civil War. That a Big Brand Name established through the paperback racks could exert equal magic at the bookstore counters where hardcover fiction is displayed was demonstrated by the sales of *North and South* (1982) and *Love and War* (1984): for the former, 262,000 hardcover copies, 2,100,000 in paperback reprint; for the latter, a first printing of 270,000 hardcover copies.

Danielle Steel

March 19, 1978

When the paperbounders of Publishers Row get together these late winter days, their talk often drifts to the subject of Brand Names—those well-established writers whose mere name on a book's cover will turn it into a best seller. Somebody has estimated that the average age of the Brand Names is now a bit beyond 60. Where will the next generation of Brand Names come from? What can a publisher do to help his authors qualify for the golden circle?

Once upon a time, the Jacqueline Susanns, the Taylor Caldwells, the James Micheners established their ability to write best sellers through sales in hardcover. In recent years, that's been changing. A tattler of the high-flying set like Sidney Sheldon, a chronicler of horror like Stephen King, a science fictioneer like Frank Herbert, a fantasist like J. R. R. Tolkien might first be published in hardback, but it wasn't until their work began leaping from the mass-market racks that the book world took them seriously. Historical romancers like John Jakes, Rosemary Rogers and Kathleen Woodiwiss became Brand Names without ever publishing a book in hardcover.

To meet the challenges of changing times, Dell Books is developing a new strategy. According to its editor, Bill Grose, from now on that house will take pains to turn their most promising authors of originals into names that every bookbuyer will recognize. Next month, for example, it will send out 1,200,000 copies of *The Promise*, a contemporary love story, the work of Danielle Steel. Dell will spend $300,000 on every promotional gimmick known to the book trade, from television, radio and newspaper advertising to shopping bags and spectacular bookstore displays.

January 6, 1980

At age 32, Mrs. William Toth has lived the sort of life that millions of women love to read about. Her father was the scion of a Munich beer dynasty, her mother the daughter of a Portuguese diplomat. After studying to be a fashion designer in New York, she worked for a show-biz publicity firm and married a French banker who maintained homes on both sides of the Atlantic. Today she lives with her second husband, a social services counselor, and her two children on San Francisco's Russian Hill.

During the past three years, under the name of Danielle Steel, Mrs. Toth has published six paperback originals about the glamorous life she lived and observed on her way to Russian Hill. Her dream, conceived when she was a girl, is to inherit the literary mantle of Jacqueline Susann.

There's more than a touch of Susann in her just-published

To Love Again (Dell), a "contemporary romance" crowded with incidents borrowed from newspaper headlines. It tells of a woman, distraught when her Italian couturier husband is kidnapped and murdered, who finds love again in the arms of an American fashion magnate. Miss Steel's growing legion of fans has encouraged Dell to give it a 1,100,000-copy first printing. In her own words "a shy type," she has up to now avoided author tours, but she's going on the road in behalf of her new book this week.

Miss Steel has some reservations about having her novels published as original paperbacks. That was the only form in which Dell was willing to publish her first, *Passion's Promise*, four years ago. She's happy with the editorial help the Dell staff gave it and its successors. But she's delighted that Dell's sister house, Delacorte Press, has agreed to bring out a novel she's just finished in harcover next year. "There's more prestige in hardcover," she says.

Thereafter Delacorte published some of Miss Steel's romances in hardcover, Dell some as paperback originals. A dozen years after her debut, she had published 18 best sellers that had racked up sales of some 50 million copies. A number achieved the No. 1 spot on the hardcover best seller list, certainly entitling her to the mantle once worn by Jacqueline Susann.

Women's Romances

March 25, 1979

Never underestimate the influence of a woman. It's an adage that paperback publishers never forget. After all, 60 percent of the 430 million softcover books sold each year are bought by women, most of them between the ages of 21 and 49, to be read—as the market analysts put it—"for pleasure."

Many of the books these women read for pleasure are, of course, the current best sellers—gossipy *romans à clef* like Sidney Sheldon's *Bloodline*, suspensers with a literary touch like Graham Greene's *The Human Factor*. But the women who regularly buy the greatest number of books seek most of their reading pleasure on the shelves marked "Romance," "Historicals" or "Gothics."

"In spite of the feminist movement," observes Leona Nevler, editor-in-chief of Fawcett Books, "women are as hungry as
ever for romantic fiction." Every major publisher issues a half-
dozen or more such books each month. They break down into a
number of sub-genres. Their covers make clear what lies
within. Some are placarded as "in the tradition of Georgette
Heyer"—or Victoria Holt or Phyllis Whitney. The "glitter and
elegance of Regency England" is recalled by the cover design of
the Historicals, the brooding romance of *Wuthering Heights* is
suggested by the covers of the Gothics.

By the bye, Gothics, with their covers showing a manor
house on a moor from which a single lighted window looks out
on the night are relatively rare these days. "That sub-genre died
in the late '60's," according to Miss Nevler, "after the market
became flooded with too many poor imitations of the Brontës."

Chaste Damsels

September 12, 1976

The setting is exotic—a South African ostrich farm, a planta-
tion on the edge of the Sahara, a boutique in a French village.

The plot line is simple: girl meets boy and is interested.
Many complications set in. Sixty thousand words later, the ob-
stacles duly overcome, the heroine yields on the last page to
her suitor's kiss on the mouth and the pair walk off hand in
hand.

These are the stock-in-trade of Harlequin Enterprises Ltd.
of Toronto, owned by Torstar, a Canadian-based conglomerate
whose properties also include *The Toronto Star.* Harlequin
started out in Winnipeg back in 1949 as a softcover reprinter of
hardcover books. Many of these came from Mills & Boon, a
long-established London publisher of romantic novels by
writers in all parts of the British Commonwealth. In time the
Canadian firm staked out a worldwide market for its paperbacks, then bought out Mills & Boon.

Nowadays Harlequin issues a dozen such romances a
month, distinguished from another by little except their
locales and the names of some 120 little-known authors. Most
of the writers are British or Australian; a few—like Janet
Dailey and Roberta Lee—are Americans. The 350,000 copies of
each title destined for the U.S. market are printed in Buffalo.

Harlequins are so rigidly edited that—as the firm's

marketing director puts it—"a buyer knows exactly what she's getting, just as if it were Ivory Soap or Coca-Cola." Many a reader is proud of owning a thousand or more of the 2,000 titles published so far, and some aspire to become "completers."

Comparable vigilance is expended on their distribution. More than 70 percent of the copies must be sold in the first ten days, more than 80 percent in 90 days, by far the highest rate in the business. Then the novels are sent to a "pool" of back titles, from which they may be reissued sometime in the future.

Queen of Romance: Barbara Cartland

April 13, 1975

The name of Barbara Cartland isn't apt to light up the eyes of readers of literary reviews, but its appearance on a paperback cover is enough to make several hundred thousand romance-hungry women plunk down $1.25 for a copy at the nearest checkout counter. This month Pyramid Books publishes *The Complacent Wife* and *The Irresistible Buck* and Bantam *The Impetuous Duchess*—bringing Miss Cartland's record to over 16 million copies of 91 titles printed in the United States since 1968.

A Cartland fan knows what to expect. The setting is Britain in Regency, Victorian or Georgian times. The leading lady typically is a nice young thing who must hurdle all manner of complications until she ends up in the arms of the true love (a young man with a title or position) whom fate has in store for her. The prose is rich in adjectives, sped along by chunks of crisp dialogue. To Miss Cartland, love-making is word-play, not a body-contact sport; her heroines remain pristine to the final pages. ("Randal's lips held Sorela's and in that first kiss he knew an ecstasy that had in it something of the Divine. Man and woman made one.")

The creatrix of all this bliss is the quintessence of the legendary English eccentric. The daughter of an Army major, Barbara Cartland was one of London's "bright young people" in the 1920's, a leader in war volunteer work in the '40's, a crusader against fluoridation in the '60's. In the last 15 years she has published well over 150 books—uncounted romances, four autobiographies, half a dozen biographies, numerous volumes on

nutrition and other causes dear to her heart. Three of her plays
have had London productions.

What explains her current success with the sighs and strat-
egems of yesteryear? Miss Cartland recently told a man from
The New Yorker: "It's the pornography and lack of romance in
modern life that people wish to escape."

November 6, 1977
If you're an American in London and Barbara Cartland invites
you to tea, you're due for a very royal, very English reception.
The Great Lady of Romance Fiction will send her white Rolls-
Royce around to your Mayfair hotel to drive you the 20 miles
out to Hertfordshire, where she'll be waiting to welcome you to
Camfield Place, the stately country mansion where she's been
living—and working—for the past 25 years.

Some people describe Miss Cartland as looking like a cross
between Mae West and Liberace. Everyone would have to
agree that, though now a widow and in her 78th year, she has
enough ideas and energy for both combined. Over tea and
sweet cakes, she talks a royal blue streak.

Earlier this afternoon, between 1 and 3:30, she dictated to
two secretaries nearly 7,000 words of her 225th book. It's called
Chieftain With a Heart and will be published in the United
States sometime in 1978. Her contract with Bantam requires
her to produce two 60,000-word novels about the romances of
passionate virgins each month. She spends some time reading
works of history every day so that at night her subconscious
will help her plot her next book. Over the years she's travelled
widely in search of fresh backgrounds for her stories. This
winter she hopes to take a look at Haiti and the Caribbean.

Writing comes easily for Miss Cartland because she's been
doing it, day in, day out, since the 1920's, when, as one of London's bright young people, she wrote a gossip column for *The
Daily Express.* She believes dictation produces the most readable style of writing, for then even exposition sounds like conversation and reads fast. Most readers, she declares, skip long
paragraphs.

The popularity of her novels has zoomed during the 1970's
and they're now best sellers in almost every country except the
Soviet Union and China. Total worldwide sales to date: 80
million. She believes this is because pornography is on its way

out and we're entering a new romantic age. What does she think of the best-selling Harlequin Romances? "Nice stories. But you get the feeling that their authors never experienced really passionate love. As I have."

After tea, Miss Cartland takes you on a quick tour of the house, proudly pointing out its superlative view of two small lakes and a forest beyond, identifying the busts of some of her forebears in the hallway. As you're about to start out on your ride back to London, she presents you with a jar of one of her favorite foods—honey—and explains that, as this is Friday, she expects her two sons to arrive shortly for their regular weekend visits. Glen McCorquodale helps her with the literary side of her activities, Ian McCorquodale with the business. "Together," she says with a laugh, "we've been called the operators of the Barbara Cartland factory."

Bodice Rippers

August 7, 1977

"What does a woman want?" Sigmund Freud once demanded, not without some exasperation. He might have found an answer in the literary sub-genre practiced by such best-selling writers as Kathleen E. Woodiwiss and Rosemary Rogers, most of which are set in the past, particularly the 18th and early 19th centuries, published by Avon Books.

The discoverer of this literary lode is Nancy Coffey, one-time Manhattan fourth-grade teacher, one-time children's book editor, who struck it rich under the sort of circumstances that make publishing such a fascinatingly chancy business.

Back in 1971, Avon, bothered by the rocketing prices being demanded for reprint rights, spread word through the writers magazines that it was in the market for originals. Among the deluge of manuscripts that immediately poured in was a bulky romance, *The Flame and the Flower*, by Kathleen Woodiwiss, a small-town Minnesota housewife. Miss Coffey carried it away with her over a weekend and in turn was carried away. ("The most important thing about any story is its ability to grab your interest on the first page and keep you reading to the last.") It was published, with slight editing, in 1972. Copies to date: 2,580,000.

Miss Coffey's success with Kathleen Woodiwiss attracted

other authors who write in much the same style. Some male chauvinists call them "rape sagas" and "bodice rippers" because of the many pages they devote to erotic encounters and because words like "passion" and "fury" appear on their covers.

Miss Coffey protests such references to her romances. She acknowledges that they're definitely not descendants of *Jane Eyre*, as the Gothics are. Nor are they first-kiss-on-the-last-page stories like the Harlequins, formula stories that differ only in exotic setting. Nor are they bare outlines for stories, which Miss Coffey believes Barbara Cartland's are. They are the fantasies of typical modern women — like their authors — acted out in glamorous periods of the past, with just the amount of sexual detail contemporary women crave.

November 4, 1979

That current rage, the rape saga or bodice ripper, has an unlikely creatrix: Kathleen E. Woodiwiss, born in Louisiana 40 years ago, a tall, dark-haired, soft-spoken former fashion model, who now lives with her husband, a retired Air Force major, and three young sons in rural Minnesota. She is, in her own words, "just an ordinary housewife."

The circumstances under which Mrs. Woodiwiss begat the literary sub-genre are equally curious. About ten years ago her husband gave her a typewriter for Christmas, and just for fun she began pecking out a novel about the time of the American Revolution. Her inspiration for the plot and incidents came to her during naps and moments of reverie, not from real life or actual historical incidents. Her heroine was the object of rape and violence who ended up marrying the man who had assaulted her.

At the urging of her husband and friends, Mrs. Woodiwiss submitted the bulky manuscript to ten hardcover publishers, who rejected it, some on the grounds that it was too long to be commercially practicable. Finally it ended up in the slush pile of Avon Books' Nancy Coffey, who promptly accepted it. The rest, as they say, is paperback history.

Since then, during the school year ("I save the summers for my boys"), Mrs. Woodiwiss has written three more ravishing sagas: *Ashes in the Wind*, *The Wolf and the Dove*, and *Shana*. Total sales for the four: ten million copies.

October 24, 1976

With ten million copies of her four novels in print, with three million of her latest—*Wicked Loving Lies*—in circulation only two weeks after publication, Rosemary Rogers is surely one of the contemporary queens of Historical Romance.

Miss Rogers has come a long and unlikely way in her 40-some years. In her native Sri Lanka she shocked her traditional family by insisting on quitting her servant-staffed home to take a job with a newspaper, where she confounded her boss by refusing to be restricted to the women's pages. Four children and two divorces later, she was living in California, working as a secretary by day and trying her hand at novel-writing by night. When one of her daughters remarked that the kind of book she was writing resembled Kathleen Woodiwiss's *The Flame and the Flower*, she sent her manuscript off to its publisher. Avon Books editor Nancy Coffey fished it out of her slush pile, published it as *Sweet Savage Love* late in 1973. This and two others—*The Wildest Heart* (1974) and *Dark Fires* (1975)—evoked so much fan mail that Avon had to set up a club to handle it.

Naturally Miss Rogers is not working as a secretary any more. When she's finished her current cross-country publicity tour she'll go back to her house on the beach in romantic Carmel, California, spend her days sleeping, her nights turning out more tales about young women who use their natural endowments to getting around and ahead in history's most fabulous circles.

September 19, 1976

What are the fabricators of Gothic novels doing now that there's no great demand for accounts of romantic encounters on the moors?

Well, for one, down in Fort Worth, Texas, there's Tom E. Huff, who was a teacher at Paschal High School and in his spare time wrote some 20 Gothics under such pseudonyms as Edwina Marlow and Beatrice Parker. When the rage for the Kathleen Woodiwiss-Rosemary Rogers kind of historical romance set in, he tried his hand at that. His *Love's Tender Fury*, written under the name Jennifer Wilde and published by Warner

Books, has just finished a four-month run on the mass-market paperback best seller list.

These days Mr. Huff, a tall, quiet, mid-30ish bachelor, lives inconspicuously (sorry, no interviews!), devotes his full time to more Jennifer Wilde tales and a serious biography of Tallulah Bankhead. The thousands of Fort Worth women who grabbed up their share of *Love's Tender Fury's* 2,313,625 copies had no idea they were patronizing a local boy who's made good.

A P.S. from Nancy Coffey: She turned down Jennifer Wilde's *LTF* when it was submitted to her in manuscript, detecting its masculine authorship through its "plethora of violent sex."

The Right Words: A Lexicon for Writers

December 3, 1978

In the Chicago offices of *The Critic*, a magazine published by the not-for-profit Thomas More Association, the staff recently stole time from its appointed duties—assessing books of religious and social significance—to create a kit that would help its readers win fame and fortune by writing a best-selling "romantic novel." The kit consists of the following "choicest words":

For titles: Island, Passion, Desert, Desire, Mistress, Blaze, Gypsy, Storm, Fire, Frenzy.

Key words for the text: ravish, bodice, vengeful, lusty, pierce, azure, blush, groan, plea, rip, flail, secret, thunder, tender, tremble, lurk, glow, feeble, fondle, filmy, flush, deserted, steely, tight, dank, coarse, flood, rough, thunder, flicker, divine, curving, ample, flame, harsh, frigid, cruel, moan, satin-like, sigh, clutch, sunder, flashing, devour, heat, urgent, thrust, tear, torrent, fragile, massive, impetuous, pulse, tense, rounded, tickle, scalding, candle, crash, burst, desolate, probing, race, farewell, maleness, bosom.

Names for heroes and heroines: Daphne, Rupert, Miriam, Roger, Lance, Desiree, Linda, Isobel, Storm, Rolfe. (Lance is the only acceptable male name not beginning with "R.")

Now all you have to do to become a best-selling romantic novelist is arrange them in the proper order.

A Critic's Riposte

October 12, 1980

The Harlequin phenomenon has always received far more attention from business news publications than from the literary press. When critics mention the books at all, it is to call them insipid tales of virginal innocence. Ann Douglas, who teaches English literature at Columbia University, begs to differ. In a recent issue of *The New Republic*, she brands them "soft-core pornography," stories that "crudely elaborate the physiological and psychological conditions of girls in love." She quoted what she said is a "typical passage" that describes the hero's "razor-like features" as he "presses" the heroine to his "contours," which are "bruisingly sharp."

War of Romance: Harlequin vs. Silhouette

October 12, 1980

"*Time* and *Newsweek*, Crest and Colgate, Coca-Cola and Pepsi-Cola flourish side by side. In the American marketplace, there's place for both of us." So we were assured last February by an executive of Silhouette Books, as he announced plans for a series of "contemporary women's romances" to contest the near-monopoly of that genre by Harlequin Books.

It hasn't worked out quite that cozily. The two houses are now engaged in a bitter publishing war.

The Harlequin series is a phenomenon without precedent. In 1979 nearly $70 million worth of its titles were sold, giving the Toronto publisher ten percent of the U.S. mass paperback market. At a time when sales of paperbacks have been "flat" and their price tags have rocketed (as high as $3.95), Harlequin's sales have steadily increased, while their price tags remained constant ($1.25 and $1.50).

If Harlequin's near-monopoly of the romance market was to be contested, the owners of Silhouette would seem to be the logical challengers. They are Simon & Schuster and Pocket Books, which distributed the Harlequin line until late in 1979, when the Canadian company set up a U.S. subsidiary to assume that function.

In establishing its line, Silhouette proceeded very much as if it were producing a bar of soap to compete with Ivory. It hired a number of Harlequin veterans, both authors and merchandisers. It conducted research that convinced it that the potential market for such romances in this country was not merely the 12 million women that Harlequin was aiming for, but 20 million. It began plugging its series vigorously on popular radio and television shows. It made arrangements for a pantyhose manufacturer to offer Silhouettes as premiums. It now reports that its sales since May, when it began releasing six titles a month, have been "better than our expectations." And it has announced its determination to become "the leading romance publisher not only in the United States, but throughout the world."

Harlequin hasn't taken this competition complacently. It's taken Silhouette into the law courts, charging it with "unfair competition" on some 30 points—to which Silhouette has filed countersuits. Thus far, Harlequin has won just one round—a "preliminary injunction" barring Silhouette from packaging its romances in covers said to be deceptively similar to its own. The courtroom battles may drag on for many months.

Meanwhile, Harlequin too is wooing American romance lovers in the practiced ways of product merchandisers. This month, for example, it's conducting sweepstake drawings for free vacations in the sort of glamorous lands that its devotees enjoy reading about. Last Thursday it threw a "thank-you party" for some of its most faithful fans who live in the Philadelphia area, the ninth such bash it's staged. As usually happens, a number of the guests present proudly reported that they bought every Harlequin title as soon as it went on sale and carefully stored their collections in boxes at home.

Romance in the 80's

July 19, 1981

"There's no place closer to the American heartland than Kansas City—which is why market researchers so often use it to gauge changing fashions in popular taste." Vivien Lee Jennings, who told us this, has reason to feel that way—she is president of Rainy Day Books, a five-store chain based in Fairway, Kansas, a suburb of Kansas City.

Partly for business, partly for pleasure, Mrs. Jennings reads 50 books a week, most of them "romances," novels centered on the relationship of a man and a woman told from the woman's point of view, and discusses them with customers in her stores. She attends many of the conventions of romance fans and writers that are springing up across the land. She reports her findings in a monthly newsletter called *Boy Meets Girl.*

Here's a rundown on some of the things Mrs. Jennings told us recently:

• There are now eight sub-genres, ranging in sophistication from "soft romances" for teen-age girls to "sensual romances" for their mothers and grandmothers.

• Bodice-rippers, those stories featuring rape and violence that crowded the best seller list not long ago, are definitely "out." However, the products of an exceptional writer like Kathleen Woodiwiss continue to have a loyal audience. Gothics are still in eclipse.

• Certain historical periods—especially the British Regency—still enchant readers, but contemporary settings and situations are increasingly favored.

• The roles played by men and women are being more and more equalized. Today's heroes are less "macho," more sensitive. They are not always handsome or physically perfect. In one recent book, the hero has lost a hand through service in Vietnam. Heroines no longer have to be "gorgeous," merely "cute." Even "an ugly stepsister" has a chance.

• When the principal characters are truly in love, they remain faithful to each other. This, Mrs. Jennings suggests, may be a reflection of the current "new morality."

• A light touch, a bit of humor now and then, is very much appreciated by readers.

May 9, 1982

The Borough President of Brooklyn came over the Bridge to Manhattan to welcome the guests at the opening ceremonies. Rosemary Rogers and Jennifer Wilde, a.k.a. Tom E. Huff, told how devoted they were to each other and to each other's novels. One delighted woman won the drawing that entitled her to dinner at a posh French restaurant with an Indian prince, Khedker of Khed Anjanvel, as her escort. Fifty authors autographed books for their fans. At a score of seminars, writers, editors and art directors described how they work. All the while, reporters and television cameramen roved about, looking for good angles for their stories.

Such was the spirit of the two-day Romantic Book Lovers Conference, attended by 350 writers and readers from all parts of the country, held last month at New York's storied St. Regis Hotel under the auspices of Long Island's Institute for Continuing Education and a fan magazine named *Romantic Times.*

Next month, June 4–6, the Romance Writers of America will hold their second annual conference aboard the Queen Mary, now docked in Long Beach, California. The RWA has survived an internecine war and now has six regional organizations and a number of local chapters across the country.

These social events are the most visible manifestation of a revolution in popular reading taste that is currently engaging some 20 million American women. Their purchases of what the book trade calls "brand-name romances" now bring the mass-market paperback houses more than $200 million a year, approximately one-quarter of their total income. At a time when their business is touch-and-go, the publishers regard the brand-name romance as something to be cherished and nurtured.

The bitter "love war" between Harlequin and Pocket Books' Silhouette line since 1980—the competition for rack space, authors and the favor of readers—has been having far-reaching consequences:

• In the past two years, the number of romantic titles published and their dollar sales have increased nearly ten-fold. Bookstores have joined variety stores and supermarkets in stocking them.

• Virtually every mass-market paperback house now has a brand-name romance line or plans to start one. Notably successful are Dell's Candlelight Ecstasy series and Jove's Second Chance at Love line. It's still too early to tell how Bantam's new, prodigiously market-researched Circle of Love will do. Coming in the near future: Ballantine's Love and Life, New American Library's Adventures in Love and Late Love and Avon's Looking for Mr. Right.

• As the titles for these new series suggest, the appeal of brand-name romances has greatly widened. Now there's something for every kind of reader, from the teen-ager to the woman who uses a walker, from the high-school dropout to the Ph.D. Both Harlequin and Silhouette are starting lines to provide longer reads and more sophisticated treatment of sexual encounters.

• Many of the more veteran writers of brand-name romances have become brand names in their own right. Janet Dailey, whom Silhouette lured away from Harlequin, is by far the best known, but 64 others have large enough personal followings to be profiled in Kathleen Falk's *Love's Leading Ladies* (Pinnacle).

• A number of editors with a special feel for what readers will like—Harlequin's Vivian Stephens, Silhouette's Karen Solem and Bantam's Carolyn Nichols among them—are scouring the country for promising new talent. Thanks to their efforts, scores of young writers are getting their work published for the first time.

• Because marketing specialists play a key role in the brand-name romance business, television and other forms of promotions are used more extensively than for other types of books. Currently, Harlequin is putting free samples of its romances in packages of Hefty garbage bags.

The number of American women aged 26 to 45—the most avid group of romance readers—will grow by 3.7 million by 1986, according to one marketing survey. "At the moment, it's an almost limitless market," says Bantam's publisher Jack Romanos. Vivien Lee Jennings, editor of the newsletter *Boy Meets Girl*, takes a less sanguine view: "Stores have only so much space to display paperbacks. If the flood of new lines keeps increasing, only the very fittest will be able to survive."

Mrs. Jennings's observations were on target—as became quite evident in June 1984, when the Romance Writers of America held its annual conference in Detroit. By that time, 140 romance novels were being published every month, contributing 40 percent of all the mass-market paperback industry's annual sales.

But this prosperity was illusory. Although Harlequin and Silhouette had formally withdrawn their legal suits and countersuits in late 1981, they continued to wage their war of romance vigorously in the marketplace. The cost of the conflict was high. In the spring of 1984, Harlequin's owners revealed that its North American sales had fallen from $22 million in 1982 to $10 million in 1983 and its share of the romance market, once 90 percent, was now down to 44 percent. Returns of unsold copies, once

20 percent, were now 45 percent. Quite probably Silhouette was having a comparable experience, although it divulged no facts or figures, in keeping with the policy of Gulf & Western, the conglomerate that owns Simon and Schuster, Pocket Books and Silhouette.

The war of romance ended abruptly on the eve of the RWA conference, when the two giants announced that Harlequin would buy the Silhouette line for "more than $10 million" and Simon and Schuster would resume its role of U.S. distributor of Harlequin Books.

A reporter attending the conference found most of the publishers present pleased by the prospect of a less glutted market. Editors and writers told him that there was a slight increase in the popularity of the Regency romance genre and a growing demand for stories about women active in contemporary business life. Interludes of sex were enjoyed by readers in the mid-'80's, they added, but far more important were depictions of abiding, romantic love.

Men's Action Stories

September 20, 1981

If you drop into one of those open-at-all-hours convenience stores whose clientele is largely men and boys, you're certain to see a rack filled with paperbacks that have a very virile look. At the center of their covers handsome, dynamic men brandish guns menacingly. In montages behind them there are often buildings aflame or evil men lurking or shapely women posed seductively. Large legends—usually larger than the books' titles or the names of their authors—indicate they're part of a continuing series: *The Destroyer #44* or *The Hook #2*. The price of these 200 pages of fast-moving prose is a uniformly modest $1.95.

In the trade, these are called "men's-action stories." In one form or another, they've been around since the Civil War. American men and boys, Walter Mittys at heart, dream of being supermen, vigilantes who singlehandedly give the bad guys what's coming to them when the forces of law and order are remiss. In the dime novels of the late 19th century and the pulp magazines of the early 20th, they read about the exploits of Nick Carter and Doc Savage. In the 1950's the Paperback Revolution brought them stories with "macho" titles, like Mickey Spillane's *My Gun Is Quick*, *The Big Kill* and *Kiss Me, Deadly*. John F. Kennedy, through his professed fondness for Ian Fleming's superspy James Bond, made the genre respectable—indeed, chic—in the '60's.

In 1974, a critic for *The New York Times Book Review* gave good marks to a half a dozen of 25 series with titles like The Executioner, The Inquisitor and The Revenger then being issued on a regular basis. Most of them disappeared not long after, a consequence of the market being inundated with volumes lacking originality or any sort of wit.

Two series that the critic rated highly are still alive and doing well—but only after some corporate conflicts. In 1978 Harlequin Enterprises Ltd., the Canadian company that has set sales records with its series of women's romances, proposed a purchase of American-owned Pinnacle Books. Pinnacle, the book trade learned to its surprise, was still publishing men's-action stories most profitably—14 series of them! The most successful was The Executioner, written by Don Pendleton, a veteran of the U-boat service who lived in suburban Los Angeles. Three dozen Executioner titles had sold 25 million copies in ten years. A close runner-up was The Destroyer, the work of a team of writers, with sales of 20 million copies of two score titles in ten years. It looked like a perfect marriage. But the Federal Trade Commission vetoed Harlequin's proposal.

Harlequin countered by setting up a Gold Eagle Books imprint of its own in Los Angeles and hired Andrew Ettinger, the editor who had helped Mr. Pendleton develop the Executioner series to run it. Mr. Ettinger arranged with Mr. Pendleton to follow him. Pinnacle sued to prevent the move. After many a legal skirmish, it was agreed that, although Mr. Pendleton could move, Pinnacle could reissue the old Executioner titles to take advantage of the campaign Harlequin would stage in behalf of its new line.

Under the Gold Eagle emblem, the Destroyer, a.k.a. Mark Boylan, now has a new enemy. Instead of fighting the Mafia as in past stories, he's taking on international terrorists. In *The Executioner #39: The New War*, for example, his mission is to "rescue or terminate an agent caught in the jungles of Central America."

Meanwhile, Pinnacle's Destroyer goes on its heroic way. In *The Destroyer #45: The Spoils of War,* the heroes Remo and Chiun take care of a crisis in a banana republic. The series is now being written by Walter Murphy, a onetime New Jersey newspaperman who, critics say, makes the series stand out from the crowd because he applies touches of humor.

Now that they realize that the men's-action story is enjoying renewed life, other paperback houses are getting into the game or stepping up their participation. For example:

• New American Library is offering The Mercenary series about Marc Dean—"danger was his business . . . and his pleasure."

• Warner Books has Dirty Harry, "who makes killers wish they'd never been born" and The Hook, "gentleman private eye . . . violence is his middle name, sex his signature."

• Jove Books has The Hawk, whose "latest mission is to tear apart an underground sex-crime ring."

The profits that series like these can make are not huge, but they're tidy. If they develop a faithful following, they're sure to sell at least 60,000 copies of each title. One of the problems publishers face in increasing their market is to get them displayed in places besides convenience stores. Supermarkets and variety stores, two great mass-market outlets, refuse to stock them because, their managers say, the shoot-'em-up covers will offend women customers.

Westerns

October 9, 1977

Along Publishers Row, Bantam Books' Marc Jaffe is known as one of the most astute of paperback editors. Mention "Westerns" to Mr. Jaffe, as we recently did, and you hear the voice of a man talking about a first and still cherished love.

When he got his first job in publishing back in 1948, Mr. Jaffe recalls, it was as a Western editor for New American Library. In those days most softcover buyers were males, their favorite reading stories about a cowboy and his horse. Dwight D. Eisenhower, who was on his way to the White House, acknowledged that he greatly enjoyed "oaters." The Big Names of the genre included Zane Grey, Ernest Haycox, Wayne D. Overholzer, Nelson Nye, Max Brand and Louis L'Amour. Their books sold hundreds of thousands of copies, and all publishers vied for their work.

All this began to change during the 1960's, by which time Mr. Jaffe had become Bantam's editorial eminence. The Big Names slowed down or died. No new writers appeared to claim their places. A flood of inferior television shows about barroom shoot-outs surfeited the public's appetite. "I don't see many Western manuscripts these days," Mr. Jaffe says sadly. The relatively few Westerns in the racks at present are mostly reissues of works by the departed.

Small wonder, then, that of Bantam's current authors Mr. Jaffe's particular favorite is Louis L'Amour. He recalls fondly how he first met him in an Elko, Nevada, saloon during a convention of the Western Writers of America back in 1960. A native of North Dakota who now lives in suburban comfort within a coyote howl of the Beverly Hills Hotel, Mr. L'Amour has been turning out novels about the Old West at the rate of three a year for the past quarter of a century. His copies-in-print total 71 million, far exceeding Zane Grey's.

Wide-open Spaceman: Louis L'Amour

June 15, 1980

Today, Father's Day, the man whose books are reckoned to have sold more copies during the past year than those of any other writer is taking it easy with his family at his home in the hills of southern California. The rest is well deserved. Last week he weathered a grating tour of eight Midwestern cities—Chicago, Moline, East Moline and Rock Island in Illinois, Davenport and Des Moines in Iowa, Omaha in Nebraska, Kansas City in Missouri—talking with press and television interviewers, autographing copies of his books for admirers, accepting keys to the cities of Davenport, Des Moines, Omaha and Kansas City.

In a few days he will be on the road once more, again traveling in a superluxury bus of the style favored by Dolly Parton and Loretta Lynn, as he visits Nashville and Knoxville in Tennessee, Little Rock in Arkansas, Tulsa and Oklahoma City in Oklahoma. In Knoxville he will be made an honorary citizen of the city, in Oklahoma City an honorary citizen of the state. In Nashville, next Friday night, he will be saluted in music and words by the Charlie Davis Band on the stage of the Grand Old Opry.

All this hoopla may be a bit perplexing to the habitues of such literary haunts in the effete East as Manhattan's Elaine's or Washington's National Press Club, but in the heartland country he's touring, when it comes to writers, Louis L'Amour is the real stuff.

Mr. L'Amour, a strapping, courtly man now in his 70's, quit school when he was 15, roamed the West as a miner, rancher and lumberjack, visited the Far East as a seaman, served a tour of duty as a tank officer during World War II. His hankering to become a writer was encouraged by several university professors he became acquainted with while living in Norman, Oklahoma, ultimately leading to the publication of his first novel, *Hondo*, by Fawcett in 1953.

Mr. L'Amour has so immersed himself in the records and relics of the frontier that his stories are considered not "horse operas" or "oaters," but valid historical novels of the American West. Their pictures of spunky men and women struggling to survive against the forces of evil and nature have so delighted readers in all parts of the world that his 75 books now have 100 million copies in print. Sixty-two of his titles, published by Bantam and Fawcett, have sold one million copies each. With Mr. L'Amour's books, unlike most paperbacks, a very high percentage of copies printed are actually sold.

Right now, Mr. L'Amour has two new titles in the racks, both published by Bantam. *Yondering* is a collection of stories inspired by men and women he encountered during the youthful years he spent "yondering" around the country. *The Warrior's Path* is the 15th in his saga about the Sackett family, who moved ever westward as the frontier opened.

In the spring of 1984, as his 88th work of fiction was about to be published, Louis L'Amour was awarded a special Congressional Gold Medal for lifetime literary achievement, the first novelist in American history to be so honored.

The Adulters

October 9, 1977

There's a new breed of tale about the Old American West in the paperback racks—"the adult Western." In 1975 Playboy Press began publishing a series of novels, bearing the byline of one Jake Logan, that recount the escapades of strong men whose romantic interests are by no means confined to their horses. It appears that's just what hundreds of thousands of men and boys were looking for. During the next five years, 23 Jake Logan stories sold close to four million copies.

Who is Jake Logan? Let's put it this way: Jake Logan is the inspiration of Bob Gleason, an editor at Playboy Press. Mr. Gleason has been a Western fan since he was a boy and helped Clair Huffaker write some of his novels. It seemed to Mr. Gleason that many a first-rate young writer would like to do an occasional Western, but unlike members of Louis L'Amour's generation, is turned off by the thought of punching them out year after year. But fans prefer books with tried-and-true names on the title pages . . .

Mr. Gleason's solution has been to commission books from writers who've made reputations and even won prizes in television and other media and are willing to help save an endangered literary species. They not only must conceive a historically plausible plot—one revolving around a hero with all the traditional skills who also "cuts a fine figure in the bedroom" but also do their own very careful research. Mr. Gleason edits the finished manuscript to conform to the other volumes in the series. For a month or two of work the writers are compensated generously under a royalty arrangement, but the name of the author is always Jake Logan.

June 15, 1980

Jake Logan's success has attracted a number of rivals. Under the pseudonym Tabor Evans, a posse of writers is turning out a series of macho adventures in the West of the 1880's, featuring a marshal called "Longarm" for Jove Books. Under the name J. D. Hardin, a veteran writer of Westerns who lives in Greenwich, Connecticut, is writing a second series of adulters for Playboy. Pocket Books has introduced an "adult" writer called Zeke Masters, and New American Library is starting a series called The Trailsmen. Whimsically, NAL labels the latter "X Brand Westerns."

Writers' Roundup

July 4, 1982

If you happened by the Inn at Loretto—a resort hotel at "the end of the Santa Fe Trail"—in Santa Fe, New Mexico, this past week, you found it thronged with folks sporting Western gear and talking about the books they're writing. Nothing too special about that, pardner. They were members of the Western Writers of America, a professional association that was holding its 29th annual roundup—five days of confabs and trade talk, climaxed by a banquet at which a half dozen Golden Spur Awards were conferred on the authors of new books about the Old West.

Most of the WWA's 400 members live in Texas and California, which accounts for the tradition that the annual gatherings are held west of the Mississippi. The attendance last week was only about 200, including a small posse of paperback editors from New York. This number reflects the general state of the economy and the fact that the popularity of the Western—which, like most fictional genres, follows a cyclical pattern—is currently on the downside. Louis L'Amour is the only writer of Westerns to make the best seller lists in recent years. Most practitioners currently regard their writing as a part-time activity. Advances for a novel run in the $750 to $1,500 range. Many members are trying their hand at non-fiction about Indians and the West; in some cases, it pays far better.

In the brotherhood, the new "adult Western"—stories in which the hero has objects of affection other than his horse—are often castigated. As one WWA member puts it, "They saddle upon a respectable pioneer West the loose code of morals of today, while things simply were *not* that way." Nonetheless, with advances of $2,000 and up being offered by publishers of adult Westerns, some old hands are writing them—under pseudonyms, of course.

Mysteries

The Legacy of Sherlock Holmes

May 4, 1975

For some years now, the word along Publishers Row has been that Americans have little interest in stories of crime perpe-

trated in the classical British style. Now, rather suddenly, the sales of Doubleday's hardcover edition of *The Complete Sherlock Holmes* are leaping and bounding. Little wonder that four paperback houses are hurrying to reprint volumes of old Holmes tales, an opportunistic move made possible by the fact that the works are now out of copyright.

October 26, 1975

Mention Sherlock Holmes and the picture that leaps to mind is one created by an artist named Sidney Paget to illustrate the first collections of stories published between 1892 and 1905. Most of the stage and film actors who have assumed his role since have tried to bring that image to life. Now you won't have to possess copies of the rare original editions to savor Paget's sketches as you read Conan Doyle's Victorian melodramatics. Softcovered editions of the first four volumes have been released: *The Adventures of Sherlock Holmes* and *The Memoirs of Sherlock Holmes* (A & W Visual Library) and *The Hound of the Baskervilles* and *The Return of Sherlock Holmes* (Schocken).

The Spirit of Agatha Christie

October 2, 1977

Every writer of melodrama knows that a last act should teem with surprises and happy endings, but it's a rare one who's able to arrange his own life story that way. Agatha Christie, that rarest of the rare, was able to create excitement even after the curtain fell on her own life.

When Miss Christie died in January 1976, at the age of 85, her 86th mystery novel, *Curtain,* was at the top of the hardcover best seller lists. Now, nearly two years after her death, she's still taking curtain calls:

• Pocket Books has distributed 2,500,000 paperback copies of *Curtain,* in which Miss Christie's famous sleuth Hercule Poirot returns to the scene of his first murder case, an English country boarding house, and figures out which one of its residents is going to be murdered and why. Pocket paid $925,000 for the reprint rights, many times as much as it paid to include Miss Christie's classic *The Murder of Roger Ackroyd* on its first list back in 1939.

• Bantam Books has disposed of 1,250,000 copies of a posthumous Christie whodunit, *Sleeping Murder,* within the past three weeks. It paid $1 million for the privilege of paperbacking this account of how the spinster sleuth Miss Jane Marple uncovers the deadly truth about a young woman's dreams of her childhood.

• Three of Miss Christie's four U.S. paperback publishers will be issuing new editions of her books during the coming month. In all, she now has 79 softcover titles in print in this country. It's estimated that nearly 95 million copies of her works have been sold in the United States, 400 million throughout the world.

• Next month, St. Martin's Theatre in London will be celebrating the 25th anniversary of the premiere of *The Mousetrap,* the longest running play in history. Three of her plays are currently on the London stage.

Crime Comes Back

October 26, 1980

When Agatha Christie died back in 1976, many literary seers declared that an age was ending. The kind of crime story of which she was the premier fabricator, an ingeniously plotted puzzle, urbanely acted out by upper-middle-class English people, already seemed terribly old-fashioned. No one, they predicted, would want to read that kind of thing anymore.

It seems that the seers' crystal balls were a bit clouded. Consider:

• For the past four years, Penguin Books has been publishing the Penguin Crime Monthly, reprints of such practitioners of the classic British whodunit as Julian Symons, Michael Innes and Peter Lovesey. Printings are modest (25,000 copies or so) and so are the cover prices, but the sales are constant.

- For the past three and a half years, Harper's Perennial Library, another bookstore-oriented line, has been releasing one oldtime mystery a month by the likes of Nicholas Blake, Cyril Hare, Michael Gilbert and Andrew Garve. They're doing quite well.
- For the past year and a half, Bantam has been releasing two stories a month by such classic British ladies of crime as Patricia Wentworth, Catherine Aird and June Thomson.
- This month, Dell Books is inaugurating two series, each offering two classic-style whodunits a month, Murder Ink and Scene of the Crime.

What's behind this current crime renaissance? Insiders cite a number of influences:

- Back in 1977, Workman Publishing Company issued a 500-page, large-format paperback, *Murder Ink*, the work of Dilys Winn, founder of a Manhattan bookstore called Murder Ink. It's a prodigious smorgasbord of writing and pictures about the crime story past and present—its authors, sleuths, perpetrators and their motives, victims, supporting characters, scenes and accessories of crime, mystery films and shows. It sold more than 85,000 copies within a year.

Miss Winn's book helped attract a younger generation of readers to the genre and re-whetted the appetites of old addicts. According to a Gallup poll taken about the time, 53 percent of all college graduates relish crime stories. According to an independent survey made not long after, the average fan consumes three books a week.

- Some 300 colleges now offer courses in the genre, emphasizing the works' literary style and the challenges they offer to deductive minds. As a result, once-faded writers who have achieved "academic respectability" are in demand in large-city and college-town bookstores.
- Miss Winn's bookstore is by no means unique. Stores specializing in mysteries have sprung up in half a dozen cities across the country and serve as watering places for the devoted.

Some crime fanciers think that, the way things are going, there will soon be a resurgence of popular interest in the hard-boiled whodunit, of which Dashiell Hammett and Raymond Chandler were masters. Others have their doubts. "The British-style crime story is great escape reading," is the way Bantam's editor Linda Price puts it. "It's nice nowadays to get into a world where there's no blood and gore, where everything is genteel and the bad guy gets what's coming to him in the end."

Meanwhile a number of new American writers of talent have appeared on the scene. For example:

Profile of a Newcomer: Gregory Mcdonald

April 10, 1977

You'll find his kind in every newspaper city room—the reporter who dreams of putting on his hat and coat some fine day and striding forth to win fame and fortune writing books, doing his own stories in his own way. Every year a few make it all come true, usually as writers of nonfiction. Among the very, very few who have made it of late as fiction writers is Gregory Mcdonald.

For seven years Mr. Mcdonald, a Boston boy, son of a CBS newsman, author of one failed novel, wrote feature stories and did an interview column for the *Boston Globe.* When he walked out of the newsroom to live at home with his typewriter in 1970, he did what came naturally—wrote about a newspaperman named Irwin Maurice Fletcher, who, in the course of covering the California drug scene, finds himself part of the action and has to maneuver his way to safety. He wrote in a way that came naturally, in the lean, economical style, relying largely on dialogue and action, that he'd acquired while the *Globe's* graphics director was enlarging the paper's type face and reducing the wordage of his column.

When *Fletch* won the Edgar Allen Poe Award for Best Mystery of 1975, Mr. Mcdonald, who'd never been much of a mystery-story reader, found himself being toasted by the greats of the genre.

Fletch had fair sales in hardcover. But when Avon Books sent him out on a promotion tour on behalf of its paperback reprint last year ("What an experience! Being interviewed, instead of doing the interviewing!") Mcdonald became convinced that the softcover book is his natural medium ("People who read for entertainment naturally turn to paperbacks"). So when his second book, *Confess, Fletch,* a thriller about dirty doings in the Boston art world was ready, he had Avon bring it out as a paperback original ("A winner!" wrote the *New York Times* reviewer Newgate Callender.)

Nowadays everything's going all right for Mcdonald. Avon has just reissued *Running Scared!* the novel about a tragic love affair in Cambridge he wrote when he was 23 and just out of college. He's hard at work on another novel about which he remains tight-lipped. His brightest moment occurred several months ago when he made a "personal appearance" at the *Boston Globe* Book Fair and found his old police reporter friends waiting to give him a rousing reception.

Fifteen years after striding out of the city room of the *Boston Globe*, Gregory Mcdonald had made his mark in the annals of crime. He'd turned out nearly a dozen novels about Fletch and a Boston police commissioner named Flynn. Two of his books had won Edgar Allen Poe awards. He'd served a term as president of the Mystery Writers of America. In 1985 Warner Books published a collection of the interviews he wrote for the *Globe* as a trade paperback.

All the while, the fraternity of mystery story fans remained faithful to its old idols . . .

The Wolfe Pack

December 21, 1980

Every January, for nearly half a century, members of a strictly all-male organization called The Baker Street Irregulars, have forgathered in a New York hotel to celebrate the birthday of Sherlock Holmes. Every December, for the past three years, feminine as well as masculine admirers of a writer who many mystery story buffs insist is the only American worthy of mention in the same breath with Conan Doyle, have been staging a get-together to honor him and the sleuth he created. The writer: Rex Stout (1896–1973), onetime yeoman on Teddy Roosevelt's yacht, onetime hotel manager, one of the founding fathers of Vanguard Press, author of nearly 70 novels in a variety of styles. The sleuth: Nero Wolfe, the gargantuan, gourmandizing recluse in a brownstone on New York's West 35th Street who, with the help of a highly mobile aide named Archie, solved some 70 cases. The 25 volumes about Nero Wolfe that Bantam and Jove currently have in print are reported to be among the briskest sellers in the whodunit genre, and reissues of others are planned for the near future.

Just a fortnight ago, The Wolfe Pack, which has 700 members, aged 15 to 80-odd, in nine states, held its annual "black orchid party" at the Hotel Biltmore. The celebration followed the Stout canon to the letter. A jolly Santa Claus was slipped a lethal brew, just as in one of the Nero Wolfe stories, and those present were challenged to discover whodunit. Erudite speeches were delivered about Stout's craftsmanship, and games were played that assumed a familiarity with the Wolfe lore. The exotic dishes served were straight out of *The Nero Wolfe Cookbook*, a collection of recipes Stout published in his food-loving sleuth's name back in 1973.

Science Fiction/Fantasy

From "Trash" to Mainstream Literature

February 5, 1984

In their leisure reading, Americans are increasingly looking at faraway places. A planet where human beings are struggling with environmental problems. Outer space, where a Boss exploits an army created by genetic engineering. A distant land called The Land, to which a young man who had been shunned by his neighbors on Earth is miraculously transported and where he leads a war against the forces of evil. Such are the locales and subjects of three recent best sellers, respectively *God Emperor of Dune* by Frank Herbert, *Friday* by Robert A. Heinlein and *The One Tree* by Stephen R. Donaldson.

During 1983, these and two dozen other books belonging to the literary genre known as science fiction/fantasy have made the best seller lists. Recent arrivals to the list include *The Robots of Dawn*, Isaac Asimov's story of a human detective from Earth who goes to the planet Aurora to investigate the murder of a robot, and *Moreta: Dragonlady of Pern*, Anne McCaffrey's account of a battle against ecological disaster in a far-off world. High on the lists is the cautionary tale George Orwell wrote 36 years ago; his *Nineteen Eighty-Four* sold more than one million paperback copies in the last weeks of 1983.

The present rage for stories about remote times and places is evident too at the many conventions where fans gather to toast popular authors, share the enthusiasm they feel for the books they've recently read and buy trinkets, art works and mementos. One or more such affairs are held somewhere in this country just about every week. All records were shattered in September 1983, when 6,500 persons from every part of the United States and from Canada, Western Europe, Australia and Japan showed up in Baltimore for the five-day 41st Annual Science Fiction Convention. This get-together, known to its devotees as the Worldcon, is one of the few literary functions of any kind where fans and professionals—authors, artists, editors—meet on an equal footing.

A feeling of community, indeed of family, has characterized the genre's readers and writers for decades. It manifested itself at the first Worldcon, held during the summer of 1939, when New York City was staging a world's fair to celebrate "the World of Tomorrow." In that spirit, 200 men and a score of women, most of them in their teens and early 20's, convened for two days at a hall on East 59th Street, retiring periodically to a nearby cafeteria for food and further talk. The novelist-editor Frederik Pohl, who was there, has described them as "toadish" and "loners." Another observer put it more generously—the gathering was made up of youths who for one reason or another were not athletic, had high I.Q.'s and got their fun by exercising their imaginations. They all shared a passion for stories that offered answers to the question "What if . . .?" in the tradition of H. G. Wells and Edgar Rice Burroughs. This was a form of literature popularized during the '20's and '30's in magazines like Hugo Gernsback's *Amazing Stories* and John W. Campbell Jr.'s *Astounding Stories*.

Like all good families, the sf/fantasy community cherishes its traditions and patriarchs. Gernsback and Campbell are commemorated by the Hugos and the Campbells, annual awards for outstanding new work. Many of today's most popular writers—Arthur C. Clarke, Ray Bradbury and Messrs. Herbert, Heinlein and Asimov, to name a few—have been practicing their craft steadily and prolifically for decades. There is a constant demand in the marketplace for the early works of these and lesser known writers in the genre. Donald A. Wolheim, who was around at the first Worldcon, like Mr. Asimov, and who is now one of the leading publishers in the field, has observed, "Good science fiction doesn't date, and its readers are loyal."

How the community grew over the past four decades is

vividly shown in the attendance record of the Worldcons. Four hundred devotees showed up for the meeting in Portland, Oregon, in 1950, 568 in Pittsburgh in 1960, 620 in Heidelberg, West Germany, in 1970, 3,114 in Brighton, England, in 1979, 4,275 in Chicago in 1982. As the affair has moved about, fans have shown up from all parts of the globe, although the great majority are Americans. Recently, nearly as many women have attended as men. All generations are represented, but the majority of the conventioneers continue to be young.

Over the years, the sf/fantasy community has found new members through a variety of print and electronic media. During the 1940's, millions of boys flexed their imaginations as they pored over comic books that graphically depicted the fantastic adventures of supermen. During the late '50's and '60's, when many of the magazines that published fiction began to die off as a result of television's competition for advertisers' dollars, another generation of youths found similar stimulation in reprints of the better short stories and novels of the past offered by Ace, Ballantine and other paperback houses.

It was television that won science fiction a sizable feminine following for the first time. In the late '60's, *Star Trek*, a series about the voyages through space of a ship called the *Enterprise*, manned by a crew of human beings and an inscrutable pointy-eared creature named Mr. Spock, attracted a cult of "trekkers." "The *Enterprise* crew captured the hearts of millions of girls and young women," recalls Vonda M. McIntyre, who was one of them and years later became a writer of prizewinning science fiction herself. Several paperback houses issued series of original stories featuring the same characters in new adventures, and the trekkers grabbed them up.

Motion pictures too helped enlarge the science-fiction family. As a self-described "Terry the Toad" in a small California town, George Lucas was greatly impressed by the fantastic visions presented in comic books and paperbacks. After he grew up and became a Hollywood director, he made several outer-space films, one of which, *Star Wars*, in 1977 broke all box-office records. Mr. Lucas's own novelization of that film became one of the year's paperback best sellers.

What of the current rage for fiction in which the emphasis is on fantasy rather than fiction? The inspiration for it came from the other side of the Atlantic. An Oxford don, J. R. R.

Tolkien, envisioned Middle-earth, a place whose civilization is superior to ours, in *The Lord of the Rings*. When the trilogy was reprinted in paperback late in the late '60's, it enraptured a whole generation of idealistic college students. Among them was Stephen R. Donaldson, who has since created The Land.

As the sf/fantasy community proliferated, many old-timers expressed fears that the newcomers would be only transient admirers. To their pleasant surprise, the loyalty of many trekkers, star warriors and Middle-earth fans appears to be abiding. The teen-agers of yesteryear are being joined by their juniors. New *Star Trek* novels are being published regularly, and a host of books tied to *Star Wars* have sold well—particularly Joan D. Vinge's *Return of the Jedi*. Mr. Donaldson is only the most successful of a new generation of fantasists. More significantly, many of the new recruits have taken to reading the classic works of the genre.

Even as it achieved widespread popularity, sf/fantasy rose in critical favor. It had a long way to rise. Paul A. Carter, a history professor at the University of Arizona, writing of the "golden age" of Hugo Gernsback and John W. Campbell Jr. in his book *The Creation of Tomorrow*, recalls that at the time their magazines were scornfully referred to as "pulps" and the stories they published as "trash."

A number of events and trends enabled sf/fantasy—in the words of Fred Lerner, a fan who works for a New Hampshire engineering firm—"to escape from the cultural ghetto, to become part of the mainstream, to achieve respectability." Mr. Lerner enumerated some of them in a talk at last fall's World-con—the arrival of the atomic bomb and nuclear power, the sputnik launching and the moon landing, the concern about environment inaugurated by Rachel Carson's *Silent Spring*, the energy problems posed by OPEC, the dawning of the electronic age, the feminist movement.

These developments won the genre entree into the halls of academe. During the '50's and '60's, it became an arm of "futurological research" and the study of "possible alternatives." In the '70's, as growing numbers of students elected the sciences and other "practical subjects" for their majors, the endangered literature departments of many colleges and universities began offering courses in the genre. There are now several learned societies and an academic journal devoted to its study.

The coming of feminism inspired writers with new perceptions. Alice Mary Norton was a singular pioneer when she entered the field in the late '40's under the name Andre Norton. During the '60's, she was joined by such gifted writers as Marion Zimmer Bradley, Kate Wilhelm, Ursula LeGuin and Anne McCaffrey; during the '70's, by C. J. Cherryh, Vonda T. McIntyre and Joan D. Vinge. Mrs. LeGuin made history when one of her novels was awarded both the Hugo and the Nebula, two of the genre's most coveted prizes. Unlike most of sf/fantasy's patriarchs, whose training was in science and technology, many of these female newcomers had backgrounds in the humanities and the social sciences. "Women," the writer Jacqueline Lichtenberg says, "brought to the genre an interest in people as people."

Telling evidence that sf/fantasy has entered the cultural mainstream is its frequent appearance on the best seller lists. Now that the earlier devotees of the '60's and '70's have more money to spend, they buy the latest books by their favorites. In the golden age of science fiction, it was difficult for even the most esteemed authors to make a living from their writing. Now some writers are receiving advances that would have seemed incredible then—Messrs. Clarke, Herbert and Heinlein in the neighborhood of $1 million. The scientist Carl Sagan is getting a $2 million advance for his first novel.

Any lingering doubts fans may have had about the respectability of their favorite reading was wiped away by the recent award of the Nobel Prize in Literature to the British writer William Golding. Two of his novels, *Lord of the Flies* (1955) and *The Inheritors* (1962), and a collection of novellas, *The Scorpion God* (1972), are counted in the genre. "On the evidence of these two novels alone," the British critic Colin Middleton Murry observes in *Twentieth Century Science-Fiction Writers*, "Golding is arguably the finest writer to have worked within the classic tradition of Wellsian scientific romance."

With sf/fantasy now enjoying unprecedented popularity and respectability, its writers are naturally ebullient. A number have expressed their feelings in addresses and interviews. Ursula LeGuin says, "We are in an extraordinary, enviable position as inheritors of the least rigid, freest, youngest of all literary traditions."

This freedom and lack of rigidity, Susan Schwartz remarks, allow writers to churn out "sword and sorcery" fantasies for adolescent males in which "lightly clad women shriek and are abducted by heroes heavy of testosterone and light on brains" or romantic tales for women about places where "ladies embroider, cast spells and wear medieval garb, while their lords battle dragons, orcs and archaic diction." Other writers, according to Jacqueline Lichtenberg, see that "by depicting people as elves and magicians or robots in imaginary worlds, it is possible to comment on problems and suggest things they can do about themselves and their future."

It is in this optimistic spirit that sf/fantasy basically differs from much "mainstream literature" of the recent past and from such a currently popular genre as horror/occult. Our world seems bent on self-destruction, William Golding observed when accepting his Nobel Prize. "Either we blow ourselves off the face of the earth or we degrade the fertility of the earth bit by bit." But, he added hopefully, "Words can change the course of history."

"Think how far we have come just in this century!" C. J. Cherryh exclaims. "From Kitty Hawk to the moon! In the next century, we'll probe the stars!" Frederik Pohl too is looking forward hopefully—"Science fiction can serve mankind with tales that are cautionary as well as predictive. Orwell's *Nineteen Eighty-Four* probably helped save us from a terrible fate this year. Disaster may come in the years ahead—but there's hope after that. Science fiction can tell us how to get to Utopia."

A Flourishing Genre

February 5, 1984

In all, 1,047 volumes of science fiction and fantasy were issued in 1982—more than 12 percent of all the fiction published in the United States. There were twice as many titles in science fiction as fantasy. Three-quarters of both groups appeared in paperback. Nearly half of the books were new editions.

At last count, more than 125 book publishers were playing the sf/fantasy game, ranging from such giants as Doubleday, Berkley and Bantam to midgets like Phantasia Press of Huntington Woods, Michigan. Editorial direction is usually in the hands of men and women who have devoted their lives to the field. Del Rey, the most spectacularly successful house, is headed by Judy-Lynn del Rey, who began as a gofer on a magazine, and her husband, Lester, a pioneering sf editor-writer. DAW books, another prolific house, is run by Donald A. Wolheim.

Almost all sf editors give every manuscript submitted a look; the old-timers are inclined to boast a bit about the present-day name writers they discovered in their slush piles.

Sire of Sword and Sorcery: Robert E. Howard

April 30, 1978

On June 11, 1936, Robert E. Howard, 30, the loner son of a Cross Plains, Texas, physician, heard that his mother had lapsed into a terminal coma. Distraught, he shot himself with a revolver he always carried with him to take care of unseen "enemies." Little notice was paid to the tragedy outside of his central Texas hometown, although Howard had been able to eke out a living—$12,000 over 12 years—writing fantasies, Westerns, pirate stories, detective and adventure yarns for the pulp magazines.

Now, nearly half a century later, Howard is one of the hottest properties along Publishers Row. Twenty-seven books flaunting his byline, issued by six houses—and countless volumes by other writers that are unabashed imitations—are keeping bookstore cash registers ringing.

What explains Robert E. Howard's great life after death? All of his tales that are alive today are fantasies: sword-and-sorcery stories. Their heroes are indomitable males—King Kull, Solomon Kane, Bram Mak Morn and, greatest of all, Conan—swaggering through fabulous adventures in faraway places and fantastic times. Although they vary greatly in quality, all are written with compulsive, raw energy in a style that's a cross between Hemingway and the King James Bible.

The rise of Howard's popularity coincided with the fortunes of the fantasy genre—small but steady during the 1950's and '60's, rocketing through the '70's. But fame might have come more easily if he hadn't left his affairs in such a mess. Very few of the more than a million words he wrote were in the form of finished books, making it necessary for publishers to find collaborators and editors to tie the short stories together, complete manuscripts, flesh out plot ideas. The confused condition of his estate encouraged some opportunistic publishers to freeboot his work, and frightened away some of the more responsible houses. But that's all been straightened out during the last year. Robert E. Howard's literary legacy is now administered by Conan Properties Inc. of Pasadena, Texas, headed by four men who have been Howard devotees for years. From now on, they promise, collaborations and pastiches will be the work of writers who have already achieved reputations as fantasists.

By the mid-'80's there were 34 volumes by Howard in print from nine publishers. Four were edited by or collaborations with the well-known sf/fantasy writer L. Sprague de Camp. Fourteen were issued by Donald M. Grant, a small publisher who periodically issues profusely illustrated, numbered editions of Howard's work. Ace has 11 volumes of Conan tales in paperback. Several movies about Conan and other swaggering swordsmen have helped keep Howard's memory green.

Ecological Prophet: Frank Herbert

March 17, 1977

A planet that's a complete desert, where in order to survive human beings must conserve and make the best possible use of every molecule of water.

That's the notion that Frank Herbert, a West Coast newspaperman and prolific science fiction writer, had in mind a half dozen years ago when he sat down to write what turned out to be a long epic novel about the people of a planet called Dune. The project proved to be the knottiest, most time-consuming he'd ever undertaken, so he wrote it in installments, with long intervals in between to support himself by teaching and quickie writing jobs.

Unwittingly Mr. Herbert hit pay dirt, for as he wrote ecology took root and blossomed into a worldwide movement. The manuscript of *Dune,* the first volume, was turned down by a score of publishers until it finally found a home at an unlikely house, Chilton, a publisher specializing in technical books. The first printing was 2,200 hardcover copies. *Dune* (1965) sold pretty well; *Dune Messiah* (1970) better; *Children of Dune* (1975), in which, ironically, grass grows throughout the planet and intrigue flourishes within the rulers' palace, became a best seller. To date, nearly two million copies of the trilogy have been sold; now Berkley has one million paperback copies of *Children of Dune* in print.

These days Mr. Herbert, 56 and a grandfather, lives on a six-acre farm in northwestern Washington, close by British Columbia, where he experiments with ecological-age agricultural methods. He doesn't like to be told that he's now the father of a cult. "When a writer begins to think of himself as a guru," he says, "he's finished."

At the urging of his present publishers, Putnam and its paperback sibling Berkley, and to the delight of his cult, Mr. Herbert has continued chronicling the story of Dune. In 1981, he published *God Emperor of Dune*, an account of the arid planet 3,500 years after the events of the original trilogy; it sold 165,793 copies in hardcover and had a one million-copy printing in paperback. In 1984, *Heretics of Dune* was on the hardcover best seller list for 20 weeks. But Mr. Herbert's greatest hour of glory came at Christmastime in 1984. The release of a multi-million dollar film production of *Dune*, on which he had collaborated, occasioned the publication of a 1,400,000-copy paperback tie-in edition of the book that had had a 2,200-copy first printing 20 years before.

Lord of The Land: Stephen R. Donaldson

February 18, 1979

What should you do after you've sent the manuscript you've been working on full time for nearly five years to every publisher listed in *Literary Market Place*—and it's been returned every time without a word of encouragement?

Such was the quandary Stephen R. Donaldson faced just three years ago. The son of a medical missionary in India, a graduate-school dropout, Mr. Donaldson was living near Glassboro, New Jersey, supported by his wife, a professional social worker. As an admirer of C. S. Lewis's Narnia, Frank Herbert's Dune and—most important of all—J. R. R. Tolkien's Middle-earth, he had dreamed up a world of his own and had chronicled one man's adventures in it through three long volumes. He was about to start submitting his novel to British publishers when it occurred to him that Ballantine Books must be "getting rich" from the rage for *The Lord of the Rings*. He decided to resubmit the manuscript to Ballantine, a house that had rejected sample chapters a year or two before.

Then, as befits a fantasy, a miracle occurred. There had

been a recent change in management at Ballantine. Lester del Rey, the veteran science fiction/fantasy editor-writer, was now in charge of its fantasy line. Mr. del Rey not only enthusiastically accepted Mr. Donaldson's trilogy for paperback publication, but arranged with Holt to bring it out first in hardcover.

The Chronicles of Thomas Covenant, the Unbeliever is the story of a leper, shunned by his neighbors, who is miraculously transported to The Land, a mysterious, beautiful country where he is hailed as a savior in a struggle against the forces of evil. It's jam-packed with swords and sorcery, perils and heroism. The science fiction/fantasy press hailed it ("a highly imaginative epic to be savored through successive readings"), the Science Fiction Book Club distributed it, Holt sold 12,000 sets at $30 in the past year.

Ballantine and Mr. del Rey are now working hard to spread the word about The Land across the country. They've published the trilogy serially in softcover—first *Lord Foul's Bane*, then *The Illearth*, this week, *The Power That Preserves*. The public's response has necessitated printings of 250,000 copies.

Last week Mr. Donaldson received good news from England, where he'd already been hailed as "Tolkien's successor." His trilogy has been awarded the British Fantasy Society's first prize for 1977–78. At 31, he's trying to take it all in stride. He now lives in Albuquerque, New Mexico, where he's plotting new chronicles for Thomas Covenant.

In the wake of the acclaim from the British, life continues fantastically for both Thomas Covenant and his creator. Mr. Donaldson continues to live in Albuquerque with a second wife, whom he met while he was a panelist at a fantasy convention, and has completed a second trilogy about The Land, all of which achieved bestsellerdom when published in both hardcover and paperback under the Del Rey/Ballantine imprint.

Horror

June 27, 1982

"Bridgewater was such a lovely place to live, a quiet place where nothing ever happened . . . Until little Emma Winthrop invented a playmate named Abigail . . . Until Abigail taught Emma how to make strange things happen with her mind . . . Until Emma learned how to move objects, arrest heartbeats and create grisly fires . . . Until blood flowed like water and people began to die . . . A masterpiece of modern horror in the tradition of Stephen King's *Carrie.*"

Thus Pinnacle Books advertises Yvonne McManus's *The Piercing,* a novel it is stuffing into the mass-market racks this week. Similar descriptions are being offered by a dozen other publishers for three dozen books they're releasing this summer, paperbacks bearing such titles as *Hobgoblin, Nightmare Country, Don't Talk to Strangers* and *Creepshow.* If their covers don't say it's Stephen King whose tradition is being followed, they're apt to call up the names of such other contemporary "masters of horror" as V. C. Andrews and John Saul.

Next to women's romances and science fiction/fantasy, the tale of horror and the occult is now the most widely read genre of fiction. "As horror becomes commonplace in the real world," observes Berkley Books' editor Roger Cooper, "the public increasingly feels a need for make-believe macabre to serve as a catharsis. Hence its current popularity in books, as well as in movies."

Tales of terror have been part of our literary tradition at least since 1818, when Mary Wollstonecraft Shelley published *Frankenstein,* but it's only in the last 15 years, as popular movies and popular fiction have kept close company, that they have assumed their present-day characteristics. The trend began with Ira Levin's *Rosemary's Baby* in 1967 and accelerated with William P. Blatty's *The Exorcist* in 1971 and Peter Bench-ley's *Jaws* in 1974.

During three recent summers, horror stories have headed the best seller lists. In 1979 there was V. C. Andrews's *Flowers in the Attic,* Stephen King's *'Salem's Lot* and John Saul's *Cry for the Strangers;* in 1980 Peter Straub's *Ghost Story* and Miss Andrews' *Petals in the Wind;* in 1981 Mr. Straub's *Shadowland* and Miss Andrews' *If There Be Thorns.*

With the hunger for horror growing so rapidly, it's perilous to predict where the genre is headed. It seems likely, however, that for the next several years three writers will be casting long shadows: Stephen King, John Saul and V. C. Andrews.

Guru of Ghoul: Stephen King

September 19, 1976

He discovered his calling in a box in an attic over his aunt's and uncle's garage in a small town in Maine—piles of paperbacks his father had left behind when he deserted the family years before. Novels and collections of short stories by such masters of horror as H. P. Lovecraft, Ray Bradbury and A. Merritt.

The revelation befell Stephen King when he was only 12 or 13 and it has guided him ever since. In high school and college he lapped up frightening tales in books and magazines, on the radio, at the movies. When he became a private-school English teacher he had to live in a trailer and round out his $6,400 yearly salary by doing odd jobs in a laundry and at a gas station to support his growing family—but somehow he managed to find time to concoct terrifying tales of his own.

Dawn began breaking for Mr. King in his 28th year. In 1974 Doubleday paid him a $2,500 advance for one of his manuscripts. *Carrie*, the story of a woman possessed, created a small stir among horror aficionados when it was published in hardcover, but New American Library's paperback reprint sold a breathtaking 1,500,000 copies. A question his wife asked him while he was teaching the Dracula legend to his class—what would it be like if a vampire descended on present-day Maine?— sowed the seeds for his second novel. *'Salem's Lot* sold rather well in hardcover (60,000 copies), fantastically well (two million copies) in paperback.

Mr. King's head may teem with dark, ghastly visions, but it has plenty of room for practical thoughts that turn to gold. A contract he negotiated with Viking Press and New American Library in 1977 assured him $2,500,000 for three more novels. That trio and half a dozen other books he's published since have enjoyed runs on both the hardcover and paperback best seller lists. For example, *Christine* (1983), the story of a car that kills at large among the high-school set of a small town, sold 303,589 copies in hardcover, 3,125,000 in paperback. *The Talisman* (1984), a chiller about a young boy who can travel between two parallel worlds, on which Mr. King collaborated with Peter Straub, broke all records for hardcover sales in a single week at both the Waldenbooks and B. Dalton chains. *Danse Macabre* (1981), his idiosyncratic history and critique of the horror story, was not only a best seller, but established him as the genre's leading guru.

All the while, the indefatigable Mr. King was churning out other eerie stories under a pseudonym. When New American Library put *Rage* (1977), *The Long Walker* (1979) and *The Running Man* (1982) in the mass-market paperback racks, his fans failed to detect that the "Richard Bachman" whose name was on their title page was really Mr. King. They were soon allowed to go out of print. But when NAL issued a fourth Bachman opus in hardcover late in 1984, shortly after the publication of *The Talisman* and revealed Mr. Bachman's true identity, *Thinner*, the story of the weird consequences of a car crash, soon gave Mr. King the rare distinction of having two hardcover books on the best seller list at the same time.

Mr. King still lives in Maine but, needless to say, he no longer teaches school and his home is not a trailer but a 24-room Victorian mansion.

Mistress of the Macabre: V. C. Andrews

January 27, 1980

"After we escaped Foxworth Hall, we managed, somehow, to keep striving toward our goals. . . . But how we managed to survive—that's another story." Concluding sentences like that kept our great-great-grandmothers waiting on tenterhooks for the next installment of the multi-volume novels so popular during the Victorian age.

Actually, they're the last words of *Flowers in the Attic* by V. C. Andrews, which Pocket Books published as an original paperback late in 1979. Copies kept jumping out of the racks so fast and furiously that in three months a total of 1,648,000 copies had to be printed to keep up with the demand. Quite a record for a first novel that, booksellers tell us, has sold largely through word-of-mouth recommendations of readers.

Indeed, so many readers have been inundating the publisher's New York offices with queries about when the promised sequel will be available that Pocket Books has had to change its plans. *Petals in the Wind*, originally scheduled for November, has been pushed up to June.

What's all the excitement about? *Flowers* is an old-fashioned horror-chiller about four children, members of a family named Dollanganger, whose mother keeps them locked up in the attic of their grandfather's mansion. Greed, cruelty, incest and psychological child abuse are its outstanding ingredients. Apparently just what millions of Americans—especially 12-to-14-year-old girls—want to read about.

And who is V. C. Andrews? She's Cleo Virginia Andrews, a 55-year-old former fashion illustrator and commercial artist who lives with her mother in Portsmouth, Virginia. A victim of progressive arthritis, she's confined to a wheelchair. Several years ago she abandoned her sketchbook, curled up with a typewriter and let her macabre imagination run free. Her work brought her a seemingly endless stream of rejection slips until she found the literary agent who showed *Flowers* to Pocket Books' originals editor. The rest, as they say, is paperback history in the making.

> In the five years following the Dollangangers' debut, Miss Andrews published three more books about the family, all composed of the same ingredients, each selling more furiously than its predecessors. In all, a total of more than 14 million copies. Many writers who find a following through the mass-market racks later achieve best seller status in hardcover as well. For some reason, that magic has not worked for Miss Andrews. Each of her Dollanganger stories was subsequently published in hardcover as well, but only about 5,000 copies of each were bought, most of them by libraries.

A Comer: John Saul

July 1, 1979

The movie screens are shaking up large audiences with scary films this summer, but one man who won't be going to any of them is John Saul, author of the season's most successful occult novel, *Cry for the Strangers* (Dell). "When I'm at home alone, sitting at my typewriter turning out one of these stories," he confesses, "I just about scare myself out of my wits. A movie would just be too much."

Mr. Saul, who is 37 and lives in quiet, sylvan Bellevue, Washington, across the lake from Seattle, has joined that growing band of writers whose books regularly become paperback best sellers without first appearing in hardcover. His record: *Suffer the Children* (1977), 1,350,000 copies. *Punish the Sinners* (1978), 1,036,000 copies. *Cry for the Strangers,* out just a month, has 1,300,000 copies in the racks and is No. 8 on this week's mass-market paperback best seller list.

Mr. Saul found his eerie calling in a calculated, quite rational way. Ever since majoring in drama at San Francisco State College, he's dreamed of becoming a playwright, but has been put off by comments that his scripts read better than they act. For many years he supported himself as an "office temp" and as an aide to a drug abuse therapeutic organization. In 1976, while he was visiting New York, a literary agent suggested that he study what was selling well in the bookstores. That was the year of *The Omen, Where Are the Children, 'Salem's Lot, Audrey Rose* and *Carrie.* He set his frightening imagination to work and in 28 days turned out *Suffer the Children.*

Mr. Saul has already completed his dreadful tale for the summer of 1980. This should give him time to pursue an old love—he'll be collaborating on a musical.

> John Saul's writing for the stage has yet to make theatrical history, but his tales of horror continue to play a significant role in book publishing, with paperbacks selling well over one million copies: *Cry for the Strangers* (1979), *Comes the Blind Fury* (1980), *When the Wind Blows* (1982) and *The God Project* (1983).

The Show-Biz Connection

> *Tie-in.* A book, either an original or a reprint, released in time and promoted in such a manner as to benefit from and contribute to the popularity of a movie or television feature.

February 25, 1979
"The future of the paperback lies in show-biz. In fact, some people are saying that the softcover book is becoming more closely tied to the entertainment world than to hardcover publishing."

That outburst from an officer of a major paperback house sent us hurrying to discover whether the industry is about to go Hollywood. Here's what we found:

• In the early 1970's, screen versions of *The Exorcist* and *Jaws* helped sell 4,500,000 copies of each of the William Peter Blatty and Peter Benchley novels on which they were based.

• In 1975, Ken Kesey's *One Flew Over the Cuckoo's Nest* had already sold 3,129,000 copies in paperback when a film derived from it was released; the Academy Award-winner enabled it to sell 2,200,000 more copies in the following year.

• In the winter of 1975–76, a seven-part dramatization of Irwin Shaw's 1970 novel *Rich Man, Poor Man,* was shown on television in prime time. The book had already sold 1,475,000 copies; sales of 3,325,000 more copies soon followed.

• During 1977, an ABC television miniseries called *Roots* attracted a record-breaking number of viewers. Within 12 months 1,174,000 hardcover copies of the nonfiction book by Alex Haley on which it was based had been sold. A paperback reprint then sold 3,677,000 copies more.

• In 1978, similar television specials occasioned extremely large softcover printings of five books: James A. Michener's novel *Centennial,* 2,500,000 copies; Gerald Green's novelization of his own script for *Holocaust,* 1,700,000 copies; a novelization of *Battlestar Galactica,* 1,565,000 copies; John Jakes' *The Bastard,* 1,200,000 copies; Howard Fast's novel *The Immigrants,* nearly one million copies.

• Buoyed by such sales records, some paperback houses are now releasing at least one tie-in a month.

"Every New York editor-in-chief spends as much time reading the show-biz papers as he does the book-trade journals," we're told. "He's on the phone every morning, discussing what's new with his house's West Coast representative. Whenever he discusses a prospective title with his staff, the sales people are sure to ask, "Does it have any tie-in possibilities?"

Western Rep: Charles B. Bloch

July 23, 1978

He looks something like a veteran U.S. senator, Southern-style. The name of his firm, Charles B. Bloch & Associates, suggests that he's in public relations. His modest offices, above a real estate office on a commercial-residential street, would befit an accountant. But in the dream-factory town of Los Angeles, things are not always what they seem. Charles Bloch is the Western representative of Bantam Books, and he is one of the reasons that house looms so large in the paperback industry.

Other softcover publishers maintain Hollywood bases. Avon, Dell, Warner have full-time editors. New American Library has the part-time services of a film-company executive. Pinnacle is now based in Century City. None enjoys the combination of experience and resourcefulness Mr. Bloch brings to his job.

Mr. Bloch, a native New Yorker, has been highly visible in Hollywood since 1946, when he moved there to represent a news photography service. In 1958 chance carried him into the paperback world. Victor Weybright, NAL's co-founder and publisher, tired of being considered a "reprinter . . . a second-class citizen" in the publishing world, hired Mr. Bloch to help him develop some literary properties of his own. One of Mr. Bloch's first coups in behalf of NAL was a multi-book deal with Irving Wallace, then a little-known but promising writer. The advance Mr. Bloch got him from NAL enabled Mr. Wallace to quit film scripting and concentrate on novel writing. NAL let Simon & Schuster bring out the Wallace books first in hardcover, then issued them in paper, to the considerable profit of everyone concerned. Mr. Bloch has been doing that sort of thing ever since—for NAL, for Dell, for the last 14 years for Bantam.

To succeed as a West Coast literary rep as Mr. Bloch has, a man's work becomes pretty much his life. Between 8:30 and 9:30 most mornings, he's on the phone in his Spanish-style North Hollywood home, talking with Marc Jaffe and other Bantam editors in New York about projects afoot and possibilities being pondered. The rest of the day he's at his office, a three-minute walk away, going over manuscripts and projects with his three associates.

Until recently, much of Mr. Bloch's time was devoted to movie novelizations. "The studios would let you have rights for virtually nothing, figuring that a paperback could only help them promote their film. Now that they see there's a lot of money to be made from them, they're commissioning the novelizations themselves and auctioning off the rights."

He hasn't given up novelizations entirely—almost every

month Bantam publishes one of his tie-ins. But now Mr. Bloch spends much time searching Bantam's rich backlist for titles that would make movies or television shows. When he finds a promising one, he looks around for the right people to get the project moving. But, he insists, "my primary function is to develop writers. I suspect that I work with more unpublished writers than most editors."

How does Charles Bloch find writers to develop? "There aren't any real watering holes for writers out here, the way there are in New York." So he works hard to maintain a high profile, lecturing regularly at the University of Southern California, appearing frequently at writers' workshops. Next month he'll be a star performer at a conference on the University of California's San Diego campus.

Mr. Bloch suspects that in years to come what he's doing for Bantam will be followed and expanded upon by the rest of the industry. There's an enormous amount of undeveloped talent in the West, he says, and if the paperback houses know what's good for them, they'll take pains to develop it.

Novelizer: Alan Dean Foster

July 13, 1980

Their covers are adorned with "scenes from the film" and with banners flaunting the names of the stars, the producers, the director. Only at the bottom, in relatively small type, is there mention of the person who wrote the story within. There are a score of such books in the mass-market racks these days, novels tied to recently released, very popular movies.

Many of these are "novelizations," readable narratives transformed from the film's shooting script. The novelization is a bit of literary legerdemain nearly as old as Hollywood. A friend of ours, cleaning out his attic recently, came across a crumbling copy of *Manhandled*, the novelization of a 1924 Gloria Swanson movie.

How does a novelizer feel about playing a supporting role in one of the latest multi-million-dollar Hollywood productions? We asked the question of Alan Dean Foster, novelizer of the current best seller, *The Black Hole* (Del Rey/Ballantine), based on the new Walt Disney space-opera film. Mr. Foster assured us that he's quite content with his role.

Mr. Foster, who was born on the Bronx's Grand Concourse 33 years ago, attributes his present success to two long-held interests. As a boy, he got hooked on the science fiction magazines his father and uncle brought home. After his family moved to California, he fell under Hollywood's spell, studying and teaching film-making at the University of California at Los Angeles and the University of Southern California.

Mr. Foster has been publishing stories and novels for eight years and now has two dozen books bearing his byline in print. Ten of these are novelizations of the popular *Star Trek* television shows. Last year, his novelizations of two outer space movies, *Alien* and *The Black Hole*, each occasioned printings of nearly 1,500,000 copies.

Novelizing, Mr. Foster finds, is a demanding but satisfying craft. As a rule, he is allowed only four weeks to turn out a 65,000-word manuscript. To write it, he is given a copy of the screenplay and a collection of still photographs from the show. Sometimes he is permitted to look at models of the sets used during the filming. He cannot see the movie itself, for almost always the cutting is still unfinished.

His most important resource, Mr. Foster says, is his own imagination. As an old student of film-making, he understands that, because the running time of a movie must be kept short, scriptwriters and actors have to leave gaps in the narrative and character development. "I add details that will make the story more credible and try to make the characters full-bodied human beings. My aim is to write a real novel, something a reader will enjoy even if he hasn't seen the movie and perhaps never will."

Film Director as Novelist: George Lucas

July 3, 1977

This summer we're seeing something rare, perhaps completely new in the way of novelizations—a best-selling book that derives from the longtime, driving vision of the man whose name is on the title page.

When George Lucas was growing up in Modesto, California, he was an avid reader of fantasy. As a film major at the University of Southern California he produced a 30-minute fantasy, *Electronic Labyrinth*. In 1967, just out of college, he talked

Warners into backing his production of a full-length fantasy, *THX 1138*. Three years ago he persuaded 20th Century-Fox to underwrite yet another fantasy—*Star Wars*, a story of a long-ago time in a galaxy far, far away that some critics are already hailing as this year's best picture and the wise men in the trade are predicting will set new box office records.

Logically, perhaps inevitably, once he had started production of *Star Wars*, Mr. Lucas sent his lawyer with a draft of a book version to the New York firm his friends assured him was the current leader in fantasy publishing. Judy-Lynn del Ray, who runs Ballantine Books' science fiction-fantasy division, knew a good thing when she saw it. She bought the book and rights to several tie-in properties.

The *Star Wars* novelization is essentially Mr. Lucas's work. In its preparation he received some help from two old friends from his USC days who are partners in the production—producer Gary Kurtz and advertising-promotion chief Charles Lippincott—and from Carole Wikarska, Mr. Lippincott's assistant.

The 150,000-copy first printing, released last November, sold briskly for a paperback original; but when still photographs from the film were added in later editions and the movie was released nationally, sales began rocketing off into outer space.

Within a year, the *Star Wars* novelization had four million copies in print.

And what of the attractions offered on the little home screen?

The Television Miniseries

September 14, 1980

In 1976, ABC televised a miniseries called *Rich Man, Poor Man* and Dell Books quickly disposed of 3,325,000 copies of the Irwin Shaw novel on which it was based. The next year, ABC showed a miniseries called *Roots* and Dell distributed 3,677,000 copies of the Alex Haley book that served as its inspiration.

Are television and Dell going to enjoy similar good fortunes this week? Beginning tomorrow night and continuing through Friday evening—12 hours in all—NBC will televise a miniseries called *Shogun*, the story of an Englishman's experiences in

17th-century Japan. Will millions of Americans watch it from beginning to end, then hurry out to buy copies of Dell's edition of the book from which it is derived—a novel written by James Clavell, the executive producer of the series? Despite a lukewarm preview notice or two, the author-producer of *Shogun* and his publisher feel certain they will. They have some good reasons for their confidence. Long before the television people began hyping it, Mr. Clavell's massive (535,000-word) novel was one of the biggest-selling and most avidly read works of fiction in recent times. Published by Atheneum to glowing reviews in 1975, it had a 32-week run on the hardcover best seller list and continues to sell 10,000 hardcover copies (at $19.95) a year. Published in paperback by Dell in June 1976, it sold 3,500,000 copies during the next four years.

During the past summer, Dell has been making extraordinary preparations to make the most of the excitement that they believe the miniseries will create. There are 3,100,000 copies of a television tie-in edition either already in the racks or on their way there. Supermarket chains such as Safeway, which normally relegate paperbacks to a quiet corner, have been persuaded to display dumps-full of them in every section of their stores. The campaigns they've been staging in bookstores have led officials of the Dalton and Waldenbooks chains to predict that they'll sell more copies of *Shogun* than any other book in 1980.

Shogun lived up to the high hopes of its sponsors on both Broadcasters Row and Publishers Row. After the five-night miniseries was over, NBC found that it had won a 51 percent share of the television-viewing audience, second only to *Roots* in 1977; Dell discovered that it had disposed of 3,500,000 copies of its tie-in edition, exceeded only by *The Complete Scarsdale Medical Diet* in paperback sales during 1980.

The Television Miniseries, PBS-style

February 26, 1978
What would happen if noncommercial television adopted some of the commercial networks' ways, collaborating with a publisher in promoting one of its miniseries and the novel from

which it is derived? Last fall, Masterpiece Theatre, producer of some of the little tube's best programs, joined forces with a publisher to find out.

During the 13 weeks Masterpiece's *I, Claudius* was showing on the Public Broadcasting System's 271 stations, advertisements run by the sponsor, Mobil Oil, contained references to Vintage Books' paperback editions of Robert Graves' historical novels on which the series was based. In turn, the covers of the books and display material sent to bookstores were tied to the show. When the series ended recently, Vintage found that it had sold 91,000 copies of *I, Claudius,* 85,000 copies of *Claudius the God.* Far short of the multi-million copy sales racked up by such commercial novel-commercial television tie-ins as Irwin Shaw's *Rich Man, Poor Man,* but gratifying nonetheless.

The PBS-style of television tie-in enjoyed another good year in 1982, when Penguin sold 66,000 copies of its edition of Charles Dickens' *The Life and Times of Nicholas Nickleby* and Vintage disposed of 63,364 copies of Nancy Mitford's *Love in a Cold Climate.*

TV Tie-Ins: A Chancy Game

June 1, 1980

"A game without rules." That's the way many paperbounders describe the television tie-in game, a sport that can bring rich rewards or considerable losses. Nearly everyone who's played it has a horror tale or two to tell about networks changing air dates at the last minute, too late to get copies of their books into the stores in time. Moreover, the percentage of winners is low. Of some 20 titles published in the first four months in 1980, only two sold well enough to make the best seller lists.

Despite its chanciness, we found several publishers willing to hazard a few generalizations about the television tie-in:

• A "one-shot show," even a very good one, is not likely to make many watchers rush out to buy the book on which it is based. Viewers must spend several nights with a subject to feel an urge to read about it.

• A miniseries that dramatizes a novel in several installments frequently, but not always, creates a demand for the tie-in book. Back in the season of 1976–77, the miniseries *Rich Man, Poor Man* sold four million copies. But a 1980 series called *Moviola* made it possible for Pocket Books to place only 850,000 copies.

• Programs aired serially over the Public Broadcasting System network occupy a special place in the hearts of book-buyers who favor trade paperback editions. In some cases the sales are large—over 500,000 copies in the case of Julia Childs' cookbooks. More often the sales run in the 30,000-to-50,000 copy range, as in the case of most of Penguin's paperbacks tied to Masterpiece Theatre. Mystery Theatre, which recently featured stories by the veteran British writer Dick Francis, is credited with making *Whip Hand*, his 20th novel, his first American best seller.

• Books by and about television performers who have won a loyal following over the years have a special appeal to book-buyers. Fans of the Mr. Bill Show have bought 340,000 copies of the book about him. Fans of Phil Donahue, the morning talk show host, have bought 300,000 hardcover copies of his autobiography.

Writers in Tinseltown

August 17, 1980

What was the writer's lot in Hollywood in the good old days? Some of the "insults, insights and famous lines" Gary Herman serves up in his new compendium, *The Book of Hollywood Quotes* (Quick Fox), make it painfully clear:

• "The writer is a necessary evil."—Irving Thalberg, studio chieftain from 1919 to 1933.

• "Writers clutter up a story conference."—Eddie Mannix, M-G-M executive during the 1930's.

• "Since arriving here, I have written four versions of *Abraham Lincoln*, including a good one, playable in the required time. That, of course, is out. Seven people, including myself, are now working in conference on the fifth one, which promises to be the worst yet. If I don't get out of here soon, I am going crazy. Perhaps I am crazy now."—Stephen Vincent Benet, poet.

• "Let me tell you about writing for films. You finish your book. Now, you know where the California state line is? Well, drive to it, take your manuscript and pitch it back. No, on second thought, don't pitch it back. First, let them toss the money over. *Then* you throw it over, pick up the money and get the hell out of there."—Ernest Hemingway, novelist.

The writer's lot is quite different, now that Tinseltown is a place of free-wheeling entrepreneurs. Herewith notes on four remarkable cases:

• Harold Robbins published his first novel in 1948, not long after leaving a job in the shipping room of Universal Pictures. He's been writing ever since, 16 books that have sold more than 50 million copies. Pocket Books will have copies of his latest, *Memories of Another Day*, in the racks next week. So that he might control the way in which his books are turned into films, Mr. Robbins set up his own production company. It released *The Betsy* in 1977, now has *Lonely Lady* in the works.

• During 14 years as a sergeant in the Los Angeles Police Department, Joseph Wambaugh published three critically acclaimed books based on his experiences. Unhappy about the way the large studios went about filming them, he raised $3 million — $850,000 of his own money — to form his own production company. Its version of *The Onion Field* was well reviewed last year, and one of *The Black Marble* is now in production. Meanwhile, William Morrow, the publisher, is becoming Mr. Wambaugh's close associate. It has invested in his company and plans to publish his next novel under its new Perigord Press imprint.

• Three years ago, Steve Shagan, with half a dozen film scripts to his credit, felt that it was time to escape "the straitjacket that restricts the screenwriter." He was already the author of two quietly published novels; he decided to try again with *The Formula*, a suspenser about a long-lost Nazi secret. When word of what he was up to began to circulate through Beverly Hills, publishers and movie producers began propositioning him. For Mr. Shagan, it's turning out most happily. As producer, he was in charge of the making of the soon-to-be-released M-G-M film version. The book, a best seller in hardcover, was just published in paperback by Bantam.

• As a young man, James Clavell, Australian-born son of a British naval officer, visited a movie studio and was tremendously impressed by the power enjoyed by the men who sat in the producers' and directors' chairs. During the past 25 years he's been achieving some of that power himself by writing, directing and producing films in Hollywood, the best known of which is the 1966 picture *To Sir, With Love*, in which Sidney Poitier starred as a black teacher in an English school.

But as far as the public at large is concerned, Mr. Clavell is known for three best-selling novels, inspired by his experiences in Asia. Back in 1960, a screenwriters' strike left him with time on his hands. To keep busy, he wrote *King Rat*, a novel based on his ordeal as a Japanese prisoner of war. He says that he wrote his second, *Tai-Pan*, about the birth of Hong Kong, to convince "friends" that the success of his first hadn't been just luck. His third, *Shogun*, recounts an Englishman's adventures as a samurai in 17th-century Japan. Published in paperback by Dell in June 1976, it sold 3,500,000 copies during the next four years.

The Show-Biz Connection: Pros and Cons

December 7, 1980

"The future of the paperback lies in show-biz. In fact, some people are saying that the softcover book is becoming more closely tied to the entertainment world than to hardcover publishing."

When we printed that outburst from an officer of a major paperback house a few years ago, none of his neighbors on Publishers Row seemed inclined to dispute it.

And how is the tie-in business at the dawn of the 1980's? "Disastrous!" That's the word of Chuck Thegze, who ran Avon Books' now-closed Hollywood office. The only representative of the East Coast houses still operating on the West Coast is Bantam Books' Charles B. Bloch. New York editors continue to watch Hollywood's offerings, but with a more discriminating eye. The $450,000 that Dell paid for rights to *F.I.S.T.*, which bombed at both box offices and checkout counters, is now a legendary disaster. One hundred thousand dollars is considered a "high sum" for tie-in rights. Ironically, Warner Books, a sibling of a major screen company, has declared that in the future any "movie book" it publishes must be good enough to achieve a satisfactory sale well in advance of the film's release. In general, first printings are modest, in the 100,000-to-200,000 copy range.

February 22, 1981

Just four years ago, when Jimmy Carter was getting settled in the White House and the future of book publishing looked certain and bright, Pinnacle Books, a middle-sized paperback house owned by a Dallas-based conglomerate, made a surprising announcement. Since it could not afford to compete with the large houses in the auctions of reprint rights to blockbuster titles, it had long specialized in women's romances and men's action stories. To gain easy access to southern California's pool of creative talent and to Hollywood's many film tie-in projects, however, it announced it was going to move its headquarters from Manhattan to Los Angeles' Century Park, an office complex on the old 20th Century-Fox lot.

This weekend, as Ronald Reagan is getting settled in the White House and the future of book publishing is quite cloudy, Pinnacle is sending its staff and office furniture back East, to quarters in the garment district of Broadway. Why? Stanley Reisner, who became head of the house last year, says it's a matter of logistics. "Our printers and other suppliers, our distributors are in the East. It was cumbersome trying to operate a continent away from them."

Whatever became of those high hopes held for being close to Hollywood? During the past year or so, most film tie-ins have turned out disastrously. Pinnacle stayed clear of them. And what of southern California's talent pool? "There isn't a book community there as there is in New York," Patrick J. O'Connor, Pinnacle's editorial director, told us. "The area is full of young writers whose driving ambition is to be involved in film-making. They regard any association with a book as merely a step toward that goal. Dozens of them have brought me one of their scripts and asked me to find someone capable of turning it into a best-selling novel so that a film will be made. I always tell them, 'Write it yourself.'"

Even so, Mr. O'Connor, who before joining Pinnacle was Popular Library's editorial director, is returning to Manhattan with mixed feelings. He says that he has signed up a number of highly promising writers for Pinnacle and has placed some of their manuscripts with East Coast hardcover houses. He plans to go West frequently to see his new-found friends. And Pinnacle will maintain a small editorial office there to keep the two coasts in touch.

Despite this cooling of affections between Publishers Row and Hollywood, three major paperback houses—Pocket Books, Berkley Books and Warner Books—as properties of conglomerates, remain siblings of movie firms.

Children's Books

November 13, 1977

There was a time, not so long ago, when the offices that housed children's book departments were the most relaxed sanctums on Publishers Row. In some 50 houses knowing editors quietly went about their business of acquiring and developing worthy manuscripts—2,000 picture-and-storybooks for the young and "young adult" novels for teen-agers a year—confident that they would duly reach all the youngsters for whom they were intended. In this they were helped by a well-organized community of librarians and schoolteachers who bought 85 percent of all the children's books sold. The remaining 15 percent found their way into the relatively few bookstores that had children's departments to be bought by grandmothers and fond aunts for Christmas and birthday presents. Usually the grandmothers and aunts chose books they themselves had enjoyed when they were young.

In those days a children's book publisher hoped to recover the cost of launching a new title within several years. If it attracted a following, he expected it to become a staple on his backlist and sell steadily for decades, perhaps making a small fortune for him and its author.

The coming of the Paperback Revolution after World War II had little effect on the situation. Most publishers did not want to spoil the good thing they had going by offering "cheap editions." Most librarians were reluctant to buy books that would "soon wear out."

Suddenly, in the late 1970's, the children's book world realized that its lot had greatly changed and it was in the midst of a crisis. Federal appropriations for libraries had been abruptly terminated. In the wake of galloping inflation, many states and communities had slashed their budgets. Librarians, no longer able to buy books so openhandedly, began buying some of the paperbacks that a score of firms were reprinting of works that had sold well over the years. Meanwhile accountants, who were now casting long shadows over every section of the book business, invaded the children's departments and demanded that henceforth the editors issue only books whose costs might be retrieved within six months or a year.

All this was happening at a time when tests and studies

made by educators showed that the average schoolchild was not reading as much or as well as the child who occupied his desk back in the '40's and '50's. For this television, poor teaching, the stresses of social change were all blamed — the cause was moot.

The urgency of the crisis was not lost on the publishers, especially those who issued paperbacks. "Getting the kids interested in books as a form of entertainment as well as a means of learning is our most challenging problem," declared Lou Wolfe, chairman of Bantam Books. "If we get them into the book habit early, we have them for life."

"If we're going to stay in business," said Walter Meade, Avon Books' publisher, "we'll have to re-gear our editorial procedures and promote and merchandise our young people's lines in the same way we do adult books." The refrain was taken up at other houses which had established children's book lines in the '60's. Scholastic, which for years had been selling paperbacks to students through their classroom teachers, took steps to sell its publications through book and variety stores.

One of the first effects of the editorial re-gearing was a marked increase in the sums some authors were given for reprint rights. Bantam, for example, paid Roald Dahl $1 million for seven of his books that had won a following over the years. Most of the mass-market houses started series of originals to supplement their reprint lines. These were designed to appeal to children and their parents, rather than to teachers, librarians and grandmothers. For the very young there were new and expanded series of picture books; for their older brothers and sisters, how-to books, biographies and novels illuminating a world their grandmothers never knew.

It was not always easy to get booksellers to take children's books seriously. Some of the old-timers were apprehensive whenever two or three teen-agers came in to browse. The publishers made use of the same sales and promotional devices that had proved successful with adult books. Bookstores, supermarkets and variety store chains were provided with racks to display the titles invitingly, encouraged to set up or expand "family reading centers."

Especially cooperative were "the large bookstore chains with a supermarket air," according to George Nicholson, children's editor at Dell. "They set up separate sections where young people feel free to roam. They invite school groups to pay them a visit and stage personal appearances of popular authors. This is helping us enormously."

There are a dozen writers—like Judy Blume—whose names have become household words among today's young set. But what about the hundreds of fine authors, many of them winners of Newbery and other awards, whose names are not? "In selling books directly to children and their parents," according to Bantam editor Ron Buehl, "it's expedient to present them as part of a series. If young people like a book that has an easily remembered series name or design on its cover, they're apt to buy another book bearing it." Which explains why New American Library has a new series for teen-agers branded Signet Vista, Avon one named Flare and Fawcett one called Juniper.

Nowadays the paperback is considered an integral part of the children's book world. With only rare exceptions, every new volume that finds a discernible public in hardcover is paperbacked either by its original publisher or by a mass-market house.

Blooming Pioneer: Judy Blume

February 5, 1978

The campaign the paperback houses are waging to get parents into the habit of buying books for their children takes a giant step forward next Wednesday. On that morning NBC's Today Show, a national television program counted most effective in promoting books and authors, will offer a rare feature—an interview with a writer of children's books named Judy Blume.

Pioneering in her field is an old story for Mrs. Blume. Ten years ago she began writing stories dealing with hitherto unmentionable matters that trouble youth—menstruation *(Are You There, God? It's Me, Margaret)*, wet dreams *(Then Again, Maybe I Won't)*, parents' divorce and remarriage *(It's Not the End of the World)*. Her ten books, told in the language and from the point of view of a young person, have made her not only one of the most controversial children's writers, but one of the best selling.

Judy Blume, who started out as Judy Sussman 40 years ago in Elizabeth, New Jersey, now lives in New Mexico with her two teenage children and her second husband, a Los Alamos physicist. The publicists at Dell Books, her paperback publisher, are confident that she'll capture the hearts of the Today Show's viewers. "She's petite, peppy and charismatic," they say. "We had her as a guest at our recent sales conference. You should have seen how she made those hard-boiled sales reps choke up as she read some of the letters she's received from her readers."

Mrs. Blume's charisma and understanding of her young readers' world have served her well. Often when she made a personal appearance at a bookstore, hundreds of young placard-bearing "Bloomies" showed up to get a glimpse of her and have her autograph a copy of her latest book. Six weeks after the publication of her *Superfudge* in 1981, Dell reported that it had sold more than one million copies.

Realism for the 80's: Young Adult Fiction
July 20, 1980

YA. You've probably seen those two letters inconspicuously printed on the inside jacket flap of many hardcover books, but unless you're in the book trade, it's unlikely you understand their significance. Even *Webster's Unabridged* fails to explain that "YA" means that the book is intended for reading by "young adults." Professional librarians adopted that term for teenagers back in the 1940's. Paperback publishers do not use it on their books, but it crops up frequently in their conversations. "It's an amorphous concept, but we don't seem able to get along without it," one of them told us the other day.

Young adults are becoming an increasingly important force in the world of paperback publishing. More than 35 percent of softcover books are now sold in bookstores which teenagers increasingly visit, spending money in hand. They particularly like the supermarket atmosphere of the large chain stores, the Daltons and Waldens. The more personal air of "carriage trade" and "mom-and-pop" bookstores turns them off.

What kind of books do they buy? Surveys show that they frequently buy the same paperbacks as their elders—Harlequin-type romances and science fiction. They're apt to grab up the same best-selling novels—books thick with violence, eeriness or sex. But they're also avid customers for stories about boys and girls of their own age confused with "real-life" situations that they've come to know about through experience or from watching television.

These realistic novels, the work of such writers as Norma Klein, M. E. Kerr, Paul Zindel and Robert Cormier, and some of the works of Judy Blume, now constitute the main thrust of the young adult book trade. In paper covers they sell in great numbers—many titles more than 500,000 copies—to schools and public libraries as well as to individuals through bookstores. Their prices are lower than most adult paperbacks—currently $1.95 and $2.25—but unlike most adult paperbacks, very few— nine percent—are returned unsold.

Scarcely a decade ago, a young woman living with her husband and two small children on Manhattan's Upper West Side, who had already published a score of short stories in the popular magazines, decided it was time to try something different. The realism of D. H. Lawrence and James Joyce had long been a part of the mainstream of the modern novel. Why not bring it to a story for young people?

Norma Klein's *Mom, the Wolf Man and Me* created a bit of a sensation when it was published in 1972. And no wonder. For it told the story of how a young girl felt when a strange man moved in with her mother, a liberated woman who'd never been married. The book won prizes and sold well.

It turned out that this was one of the first of a stream of novels written in the same spirit. The same year, a woman from upstate New York named M. E. Kerr told, in *Dinky Hocker Shoots Smack!* of a young girl's campaign to get some attention from a mother absorbed in doing good public works. In 1975 a young woman from New Jersey named Judy Blume published *Forever,* an account of a girl's first love affair written in the frank idiom that every mid-70's teen-ager knew by heart.

In the years since, these and other young adult writers have touched virtually every social problem an adolescent is likely to encounter or hear about. Wet dreams, menstruation, masturbation, life in a divorce-split home, homosexuality, incest, drugs, racism, teen-age violence—they've all been treated in realistic novels for young adults. Some have stirred up local censorship, leading to their removal from library shelves and increased sales at local bookstores.

The men in the young-adult book trade have especially kind words for the work of Paul Zindel and Robert Cormier. Mr. Zindel, a Staten Island high-school chemistry teacher, was already at work on *The Effect of Gamma Rays on Man-in-the Moon Marigolds,* the play that was to win him the 1971 Pulitzer Prize, when he published *The Pigman,* a harrowing story about two teen-agers who abuse an elderly man who had befriended them. His later *Pardon Me, You're Stepping on My Eyeball!* is another account of tension between the generations.

The young-adult writer currently in highest critical favor is Robert Cormier, a longtime newspaperman who lives in Leominster, Massachusetts. In the past five years Mr. Cormier has published three novels—*I Am the Cheese, The Chocolate War* and *After the First Death*—all of which are seen through the eyes of young people and have unhappy endings. "The beautiful thing about Cormier's books," an editor who is not his publisher told us, "is that they're so well-written that they can be enjoyed by readers of any age. That's why the young adult book is such an amorphous thing."

Teen-age Tattler: S. E. Hinton

April 18, 1984

"By almost any standard, Miss Hinton's performance is impressive. At an age when most youngsters are still writing 300-word compositions, she has produced a book alive with the fresh dialogue of her contemporaries, and wound around it a story that captures, in vivid patches at least, a rather convincing slice of teen-age America."

When he wrote those words back in 1967, the novelist-historian Thomas Fleming, like other reviewers of a young-adult novel called *The Outsiders,* only partially recognized the significance of the phenomenon he was heralding. The book's author, Susan Eloise Hinton of Tulsa, Oklahoma, had written it during her 16th summer, had sent it to a literary agent recommended by a friend's mother and had sold it to a New York publisher when she was 17.

The Outsiders, like three more novels she's written since—
That Was Then, This Is Now (1971), *Rumble Fish* (1975) and *Tex*
(1979) are about what Miss Hinton knows well—teenagers con-
tending with the bewilderments of adolescence, with bouts of
alcohol, sex, gambling, gang fighting and heists in her native
Oklahoma. Although she's now a graduate of the University of
Tulsa and married, she hasn't lost her sharp ear and eye for life
as it really is for the late 20th-century American teen-ager.

Miss Hinton has become a phenomenon of our time, too,
because her books have been published at a time when the
paperback houses were making strenuous efforts to find a new
market for their young people's books. All four were first published in hardcover and accepted—with some reservations—by
the children's librarian establishment. But as Dell reprinted
them in soft covers, it sent her—even though she confesses to
being a shy type—on personal appearance tours of bookstores,
contributing to the enthusiastic acceptance of her work by the
teen-agers themselves. To date, they've shelled out their own
spending money for eleven million copies of her books. Scarcely
a week passes when all of them aren't among the best-selling
young people's books at the major bookstore chains.

Although girls play significant roles in Susan Eloise Hinton's tales, they're all told from the point of view of a teen-age
boy. And the S. E. Hinton byline suggests that their author is
male. "That way I reach a much wider audience," explains Miss
Hinton, whose friends call her Susie. "Girls read boys' books,
but boys don't read girls' books."

Romantic Realism

February 1, 1981
Today's teen-age girls are tough-minded kids. The books they
buy with their spending money are novels that depict the ugly
side of society they know through experience or from watching
television, a society fraught with unwed pregnancy, broken
homes, homosexuality and incest.

Until recently, that was the accepted word along Publishers Row. But during the past few months the word has been
modified. The major bookstore chains and many independent
stores report that among their top current best sellers are
eight novels of a quite different sort, part of a new line called
Wildfire, published by Scholastic Book Services.

Bearing such titles as *Dreams Can Come True, Just Sixteen, That's My Girl* and *Love Comes to Anne*, wrapped in glossy photographic covers and bearing $1.50 price tags, the Wildfires follow a certain formula. The heroines are 16-year-old girls who live in a typical American town or small city with a pair of strong parents whom they respect and secretly admire. They dress in jeans and plaids and speak the vernacular of the '80's, but are faced with youth's eternal problems: how to interest a boy who interests them, how to be sure they're really in love, what to do if they really are. The story always ends happily, with no closer physical contact than an old-fashioned kiss.

The Wildfires originated in the grass roots. Back in 1979, a number of booksellers told representatives of Scholastic, a New York-based firm that has been publishing magazines and books for classroom use for 60 years, how uneasy they were about the hyper-realistic stories they had to sell teenagers. One of Scholastic's enterprises, the Teen Age Book Club, distributed novels—many of them original—that offer the combination of romance and realism the booksellers sought. Why didn't Scholastic publish such stories for bookstore sale?

Scholastic gave Ann Reit, senior editor of the Teen Age Book Club, the happy task of developing such a line. Miss Reit recruited a corps of 24 veteran writers she knew could turn out 40,000- to 50,000-word novels according to the prescription. The first titles appeared in the bookstore racks just a year ago. For six months they languished in the racks and then suddenly started selling like—well, wildfire. To date there are ten titles in print, with sales totaling 1,500,000 copies. More are scheduled for later this year, as well as another series, Wishing Star, that will depict girls coping satisfactorily with such contemporary situations as dividing one's time between divorced parents.

The extraordinary popularity of the Wildfire stories prompted several mass-market publishers to launch competitive series, in the course of which elements of soap-opera melodrama were introduced. By far the most successful of these was the Sweet Valley High series, bearing the byline of Francine Pascal and produced by Cloverdale Press, a Manhattan packager, for distribution to the trade by Bantam Books. During a single week in the spring of

1985, 16 of the top-selling young adult books were about what went on at Sweet Valley High.

Special Books for "Special" Children

January 25, 1981

As part of their all-out effort to meet the crisis in children's book-buying and reading, the paperback houses have launched innovative series to meet the needs of children with special tastes and problems. For example:

• For 6-to-12-year-olds who need an excuse to develop their latent skills in reading, writing, using numbers, reasoning and imaging, Dell has revitalized its Home Activity Series. These present challenging puzzles, funny stories and whimsical games under such titles as *Be A Detective* and *Make A Book.*

• For the millions of subteen-agers who watch Bill Cosby's Saturday morning television show Fat Albert and the Cosby Kids, Dell has a series derived from it. These employ folksy language to tell stories with a bit of a moral—for example, about the "little dude" who borrows things with no intention of returning them. Every page has an illustration in color.

• For the eight million children—15 percent of the school population—who are unable to read at the level considered normal for their age, Bantam has a series called Hi/Lo. These fiction and nonfiction books deal with subjects of interest to teen-agers in pictures and words that subteen-agers can understand. *Cutting A Record in Nashville,* for example, treats a subject of interest to 14- and 15-year-olds in a style suitable for nine-year-old readers.

• For kids who like to let their imaginations roam as they read, there are three challenging series: Bantam's Encyclopedia Brown and Choose Your Own Adventure, Pocket's Which Way Books. In Choose Your Own Adventure, the reader becomes the book's protagonist and, through his choice of alternatives, determines the course that the story takes. In *Deadwood City,* a typical volume, the reader rides into a town in the Old West, only to find a gang of desperadoes on his trail. What should he do? He makes a choice—or choices—from 37 possible endings, all of them surprising and all of them festooned with black-and-white sketches.

How did American children and their parents respond to the efforts of the publishers to re-gear the editing and marketing of their young people's lines? Most enthusiastically. For 1980, reported sales approached $57 million, nearly 70 percent higher than the year before. For 1983, sales approached $66 million. All this at a time when sales of most other types of books, paperback and hardcover, were either "flat" or down a bit.

The Library Connection

July 25, 1982

The nation's school and public libraries may not have the prodigious sums to spend for books that they had back in the 1960's and early '70's, but they are still highly cherished on Publishers Row. Particularly by houses that issued paperbacks.

The disdain most librarians once showed for softcovered books vanished in the past several years, as their budgets were slashed and the prices of books rose. Libraries have increasingly adopted the practice of buying a few hardcover copies of books to keep on their shelves and many relatively inexpensive copies of the same titles in paperback for their patrons to take out and read at home. According to one survey, in 1981 the public libraries spent $13.2 million—ten percent of their budgets—to buy paperbacks, one-quarter of all the books they purchased. One large mass-market paperback publisher declares that one-fifth of its total business is now done with school and public libraries.

The particularly close relationship that exists between paperback publishers and children's librarians was evident at the recent annual conference of the American Library Association in Philadelphia. In the vast exhibition hall nearly 40 firms competed for the librarians' attention. Because of the considerable sums these librarians still have to spend, they continue to play a pivotal role in that field of publishing. Most of them took courses in children's literature in library school and are anxious that the standards they learned to respect be maintained.

At the conference every year, the Association for Library Service to Children, an affiliate of the A.L.A., presents awards to two new books for young people—the Caldecott Medal for a picture book, the Newbery Medal for a work of literature. A book that wins one of these prizes, we're told, automatically sells 50,000 copies to libraries across the country. No other prize—not even a Pulitzer or a National Book Award—has any such discernible effect on book sales.

The Classroom Connection

May 11, 1980

If you were in high school nowadays, what books would your English teacher be escorting you through because they are "literary classics"? One way to find out quickly is to chat with representatives of the paperback firms that maintain "educational sales" departments. Their duties include attending some 75 regional and national meetings where teachers foregather in the course of a year. There they undertake to persuade the "influentials" to adopt their publications, even as they keep their ears open to discover what's "in" and what's "out" in the world of pedagogy.

The reps have been doing this sort of thing a long time: New American Library's Signet and Mentor lines and Pocket Books' Washington Square Press led the way in the 1950's and were subsequently joined by Dell, Bantam and Avon. The literally thousands of titles they keep in print for the school trade are among publishing's hardiest staples, selling steadily year after year.

Fashions change but slowly in the English classroom. Not surprisingly, Shakespeare is easily today's No. 1 author, with *Hamlet, Macbeth, Othello* and *Romeo and Juliet* high on the best seller list. Runners-up include *Huckleberry Finn, Wuthering Heights, Pride and Prejudice, Jane Eyre, Moby Dick* and *Walden*. Of late, there's renewed interest in Upton Sinclair's *The Jungle,* Jack London's *The Call of the Wild* and Owen Wister's *The Virginian*.

As these works are all out of copyright, many houses attempt to make their editions something special through an attractive format or with a preface by a well-known contemporary writer or critic (as NAL does with Stephen King's introduction to Robert Louis Stevenson's *Dr. Jekyll and Mr. Hyde,* Irving Howe's foreword to George Eliot's *Daniel Deronda).*

Some houses do exceedingly well with recent books that are still in copyright, as is the case with Bantam's *The Catcher in the Rye,* NAL's *Animal Farm* and Penguin's *The Grapes of Wrath.*

Censorship

July 25, 1981

"So far as writers are concerned, there is no longer a law of obscenity." So wrote Charles Rembar in *The End of Obscenity,* a book widely reviewed when it was published 13 years ago. As an attorney, Mr. Rembar had played a central role in the legal battles that lifted the bans on *Lady Chatterley's Lover, Tropic of Cancer* and *Fanny Hill.*

Mr. Rembar was unduly optimistic. One of the reasons for the grave mood pervading the recent convention of the American Booksellers Association in Atlanta was the passage by the Georgia Assembly of a law that declares it to be a misdemeanor of the highest degree to display publicly in a place frequented by minors "any book, pocketbook or magazine" containing material that may "provoke or arouse lust or passion." According to Maxwell Lillienstein, the A.B.A. counsel, this is the first time in his recollection that something less than obscene has been banned in this country. Laws of a similar sort, but not as far reaching, are on the books in Pennsylvania and in several municipalities in Los Angeles County, California.

Similar apprehension was in the air this past week as censorship and its implications were discussed at a series of meetings during the American Library Association convention in San Francisco. Judith Krug, director of the A.L.A.'s Office for Intellectual Freedom, reports that protests by local groups against the circulation of certain books by school and public libraries have tripled during the past year, with 34 states heard from. Such favorite targets of the past as J. D. Salinger's *The Catcher in the Rye,* Kurt Vonnegut's *Slaughterhouse Five* and dictionaries that define "bed" as a verb have been joined by the Boston Women's Health Collective's *Our Bodies, Ourselves,* Judy Blume's stories for young people and Don Brede's novel of adolescence, *Hard Feelings.*

The retreat from the victories celebrated by Mr. Rembar began in 1973, when the United States Supreme Court ruled, in the case of Miller v. California, that criteria for obscenity must be set by "local community standards." It has been accelerated in the past year or two by the nationwide swing to conservatism and the proliferation of groups campaigning for their conception of morality.

The situation has been complicated by the fact that in many communities, books, particularly paperbacks, are sold in the same stores as "sophisticates"—as the trade calls such magazines as *Playboy* and *Penthouse*. In at least one instance a prosecutor, anxious to please a local group, suggested to dealers that they refrain from selling certain books and magazines until a court had ruled as to whether they were obscene. Few retailers have the time or competence to judge each of the hundreds of new titles they offer for sale each month.

To meet the rising tide of vigilantism, businessmen and professional people concerned about the fate of the book maintain a New York-based organization to exchange information and take legal action when that seems advisable. Media Coalition, Inc., is an alliance of the American Booksellers Association, the Association of American Publishers, the Council of Periodical Distributors, the International Periodical Distributors Association and the National Association of College Bookstores. The American Library Association cooperates through its Office for Intellectual Freedom. At the moment, Media Coalition has suits in the courts contesting the constitutionality of both the Pennsylvania and Georgia laws.

How does an author whose works are a particular target of protestors feel about it? The question was asked Judy Blume at a press conference during the A.B.A. convention. "The parental groups responsible just don't want to deal with reality," she replied. She called the trend "saddest for the kids—it stops real communication between them and their parents."

The Campus Connection

Bad Times for Good Books

July 1, 1979

"The best books of the past?" the manager of a large Fifth Avenue bookstore asked rhetorically. "Whenever anyone asks about them, I say go down to the basement and look at our paperback section. The best books are alive and well in soft covers."

That was back in the late 1950's and much has changed since then. Most booksellers have gotten over their notion that paperbacks are second-class citizens and now integrate them with hardcover books according to their subject throughout the store. But, unhappily, at the same time the "best books of the past"—classics of literature and the social sciences, important works of scholarship—have become increasingly hard to come by in any edition. Attribute this to the recent twists in our national social values and the turns of American education.

During the '50's and '60's, college enrollments in the liberal arts reached unprecedented heights. Instructors, shunning textbooks, prescribed long reading lists of important works for their courses. Almost every book publisher hastened to help meet the demand. The shelves of every bookstore—certainly every one near a campus—were crowded with the paper-covered riches of the past. It looked as if the textbook would soon be a dodo.

Then, with the coming of the '70's, the rocketing production costs of books—mostly for paper—turned the tide. Many budget-bound students complained they couldn't afford the high price tags paperbacks now carried and instructors returned to the use of textbooks. The sales of many academically-oriented paperbacks fell below the total (7,000 copies a year) their publishers considered necessary to keep them in print. Most houses reduced their lists drastically; some dropped them completely.

The situation was further aggravated by the appearance of a new breed of student—career-oriented, "practical"—who concentrated on courses leading to an M.B.A. or other professional degree. Enrollments in the humanities fell precipitously. At the same time, many literature departments remained reluctant to "teach" authors of works published after 1950, nipping a potential market for serious contemporary fiction.

The state of good books in this last year of the '70's would be grimmer still if it weren't for the university presses, those not-for-profit, campus-based houses dedicated to the spread of knowledge. Their way has been led by the University of Chicago Press's director Morris Philipson, who years ago helped create Random House's Vintage line. Chicago now has 800 paperback titles in print and each year is adding 25 more that it calculates can sell 4,000 copies within four years. Yale, Harvard and a number of other university presses are planning similar programs.

Nor have the leading New York-based academic publishers—Harper, Norton, Oxford, Penguin and Vintage—abandoned the cause. Their editorial directors tell us that the decline in their paperback sales bottomed out two years ago, that business is now looking up a bit.

Unrequired Reading

April 24, 1977

Back in the 1960's, the *New York Times Book Review* periodically published accounts of what students on representative campuses across the country were choosing to read for their own pleasure. By this time, according to these reports, every young man and young woman who had not already enjoyed J. D. Salinger's *The Catcher in the Rye*, William Golding's *Lord of the Flies* and John Knowles' *A Separate Peace* was hastening to do so—in paperback, of course, for this was the first "paperback generation." They were, a critic noted at the time, "members of a distinctive youth culture that sought writers who spoke for themselves alone."

Before the decade was half over and demonstrations protesting the Vietnam War were making front-page headlines, a number of distinctive new trends began to appear:

• Science fiction/fantasy claimed a center spotlight on many campuses—first at Harvard, then across the country—as an Oxford don named J. R. R. Tolkien pied-pipered a growing band of youths to his Middle-earth. Similar cults appeared devoted to the works of writers like Frank Herbert, Arthur C. Clarke and Robert Heinlein. "The kids don't like what they see of the real world," a paperback distributor whose business was oriented to the college bookstores of the Northeast told us at the time. "They're trying to find a better world in such books."

• Contemporary values were questioned through the novels of Kurt Vonnegut, Richard Brautigan and Ken Kesey, through the Doonesbury cartoon books of G. B. Trudeau, through works that defy categorization like Carlos Castaneda's Don Juan quartet and Robert Pirsig's *Zen and the Art of Motorcycle Maintenance*.

• In their concern for environmental matters, students

avidly read Rachel Carson's *Silent Spring,* Paul H. Ehrlich's *The Population Bomb* and D. L. and D. H. Meadows' *Limits of Growth.*

• The feminist movement, incited by Betty Friedan's *The Feminine Mystique,* created a new public for historical and hortatory volumes like Susan Brownmiller's *Against Our Will,* novels like Erica Jong's *Fear of Flying* and Judith Rossner's *Looking for Mr. Goodbar.* The same cause was served by Tom Robbins' satiric novel *Even Cowgirls Get the Blues.*

• The undergraduates' relentless search for psychological self-help was served by Eric Berne's *Games People Play,* Thomas A. Harris's *I'm OK, You're OK,* Ken Olsen's *The Art of Hanging Loose in An Uptight World* and in numerous books about such movements as transcendental meditation (TM) and est.

Then came the 1980's and a career-oriented college generation . . .

The Taste of the '80's

April 4, 1982

Last year, feeling that campus bookstores should be helped in their efforts to encourage students in the habit of buying books not prescribed for courses, the Association of American Publishers joined the Association of College Bookstores in sponsoring a monthly list of "Campus Best Sellers." Somewhat to its dismay, the lists so far have been dominated by books about cats, cubes and preppies—the same titles as on the national best seller lists. A far cry from a decade or two ago, when undergraduates had their own set of literary idols.

Alive in Academe

February 15, 1981

"Many college and university literature departments are reluctant to 'teach' fiction published more recently than 1950," we reported a while back. This statement evoked questions from a number of readers. When colleges do venture to teach the works of living writers nowadays, whose do they choose? What books are going to represent contemporary literature in the minds of members of the '80's generation?

We passed the questions along to a number of publishing folk whose job it is to watch developments in academe—education sales directors of the large paperback houses and the editors of the Frederick Ungar Company's Modern Literature Series, books designed to help students with their courses. In addition, Prof. David H. Richter of Queens College checked with some of his colleagues. Herewith some generalizations based on their impressions:

• So-called "elite" colleges and those in the Northeast tend to be traditional in setting up their courses. Institutions in the South and particularly in the burgeoning Sun Belt are more innovative, emphasizing authors from their regions. Veteran writers like Eudora Welty, Robert Penn Warren and Walker Percy are being rediscovered or accorded greater attention. Stories about Indians and Chicanos are finding appreciative readers in the classrooms. A recently published overview of the Sun Belt that is proving quite popular is Max Apple's new anthology, *Southwest Fiction* (Bantam).

• The short story is enjoying a classroom popularity that it has not known for many years. One reason, teachers acknowledge, is that a long, intricate novel "overtaxes the reading-attention span of many of today's undergraduates." Another is the high quality of writing to be found in much new short fiction. Teachers are said to be enthusiastic about two new anthologies—Bill Henderson's *Pushcart Prize V* (Avon) and William Abrahams' *Prize Short Stories of the Seventies* (Washington Square Press).

• The proliferation of women's studies courses is leading many young people to read the fiction of Joan Didion, Margaret Drabble, Mary Gordon, Doris Lessing, Toni Morrison, Tillie Olsen and Eudora Welty.

• Little that is being written in Europe these days is causing any excitement on the campuses. However, the belated discovery, in the '70's, of Gabriel Garcia Marquez's *One Hundred Years of Solitude* has incited interest in the works of Luis Borges, Jorge Amado and other Latin American authors.

• The withering of the black studies programs that blossomed during the '60's has left James Baldwin, Ralph Ellison and Toni Morrison the only black writers currently receiving much academic attention.

• The fascination that science fiction/fantasy continues to

hold for many young people is reflected in courses that feature the work of such writers as Ray Bradbury, Frank Herbert and, especially, Ursula LeGuin.

• Many writers who were toasts of the campuses during the '60's and '70's continue to find readers there. A number of these are remembered for single novels—J. D. Salinger *(The Catcher in the Rye)*, Ken Kesey *(One Flew Over the Cuckoo's Nest)*, John Knowles *(A Separate Peace)*, Alan Sillitoe *(The Loneliness of the Long-Distance Runner)*. Of late there has been renewed interest in John Fowles *(The Collector, The French Lieutenant's Woman)*. The works of Thomas Pynchon, Richard Brautigan and Donald Barthelme are still read as examples of "experimental fiction."

• John Irving and Walker Percy recently joined Kurt Vonnegut, Joseph Heller, E. L. Doctorow, William Styron and Bernard Malamud as still very active writers with a large body of work that must be taken into account. But except for their early writing, Graham Greene, Norman Mailer, Saul Bellow and Isaac B. Singer are now little mentioned in the classrooms.

All of this is, of course, quite subject to change. "In academe," one observer told us, "writers' reputations go up and down like hemlines on Seventh Avenue."

Haute Cuisine: Unrequired Reading

January 24, 1982

Drop into half a dozen or so houses along Publishers Row these midwinter days and you'll find editors, promotion people and sales representatives hard at work on projects in which they take a great deal of pride. Most of the houses are children of the Paperback Revolution; a few are old-line trade publishers whose interest in softcover books is relatively recent.

Herewith some notes on what they're up to:

• Penguin Books has been publishing paperbound editions of fine literary works in this country since 1939, but only in the past several years have its British owners permitted its New York editors to give it an American look. Its new Contemporary American Fiction series includes such works as Jessamyn West's *The Life I Really Lived*, Wright Morris's *Plains Song*, Barry Hannah's *Ray* and Alice Adams' *Rich Rewards*.

Nor is Penguin neglecting contemporary writers from other parts of the world. In recent months it has brought out notable fiction by England's Iris Murdoch, Ireland's Benedict Kiely, Australia's Patrick White, Czechoslovakia's Milan Kundera and South Africa's Nadine Gordimer and J. M. Coetzee.

• Avon Books, the Hearst-owned mass-market house, is home to two literary imprints, Bard for fiction, Discus for nonfiction. The former, established in 1955, was accorded a rare honor in 1981—the Carey-Thomas Award for a project that "demonstrates creative book publishing at its best." Bard's 100 titles include fiction by writers as diverse as Thornton Wilder, Mary McCarthy, Christopher Isherwood, Heinrich Böll, Walker Percy, Reynolds Price and Vladimir Nabokov. But its most remarkable achievement has been its introduction to North American readers of such distinguished Latin American writers as Gabriel Garcia Marquez, Machado De Assis, Alejo Carpentier and Jorge Amado.

• Pocket Books' Washington Square Press imprint dates back to the '50's, but in recent years it has grown a bit lethargic. Now it's undergoing a reinvigoration, publishing essays like Joan Didion's *Slouching Toward Bethlemen*, novels like D. M. Thomas's *The Flute Player* and Russell Hoban's *Riddley Walker*.

• Bantam Books has started two series that mine the same lode. Its New Age Books offers nonfiction works like Lewis Thomas's *The Medusa and the Snail*, its Windstone imprint reprints of critically acclaimed novels by William Styron, William Golding, Margaret Laurence and Margaret Drabble.

• Dutton is launching a series called Obelisk, composed of books it deems "fine examples of distinguished writing, works that have never appeared in paperback or are no longer in print in any format." Typical titles: Noël Coward's only novel, *Pomp and Circumstance*; Calvin Tompkins' biography of Gerald and Sara Murphy, *Living Well Is the Best Revenge*, and Donald Barthelme's *Sixty Stories*.

• Dell Books is revamping its Laurel line to please "adult readers who wish to keep abreast of quality contemporary fiction and nonfiction." For example, *Irwin Shaw's Short Stories: Five Decades*.

The publishers involved in such programs are resigned to the fact that books like these won't displace the multi-million-copy blockbusters in popular favor. Nor do they count on having them adopted for college courses. They hope to make ends meet by choosing titles judiciously and marketing them carefully. They pay small advances—usually $2,000, rarely more than $30,000. They order small first printings—in the 15,000-to-35,000-copy range, rarely more than 100,000. They try to impress their sales reps with the enthusiasm they feel for their choices, hoping that in turn they will infect booksellers whose customers include people who seek relief from the tediousness of the workaday world in a book that is a work of art. Many of the bookstores are in college communities and most of their customers are students or graduates; but that is not always the case.

"This kind of publishing," says one editor who wishes to remain nameless, "has its own satisfactions. It's the difference between working in a grande-cuisine restaurant and a fast-food joint."

A Big Little Book

March 14, 1979

Many a college professor has written and self-published a "little book" designed to make his teaching more effective. Only one has ever made the best seller list and had a discernible influence on America's use of the English language. Therein lies a long, tangled and ultimately cheering tale.

Back in 1918, William Strunk Jr. of Cornell brought out a 43-page book called *The Elements of Style,* hoping that it would serve as a helpmeet to undergraduates taking his course English 8. It was, in the words of one student, "a summation of the case for cleanliness, accuracy and brevity in the use of English." Two years later, Harcourt Brace published it as a textbook. Revised editions followed in 1934 and 1935. Gradually the gospel according to Strunk acquired an influence on campuses far beyond Cayuga's waters.

But it wasn't until 1957, when the book was long out of print and Will Strunk had been dead for a dozen years, that *Elements* began to win glory outside the groves of academe. Jack Case, an editor at Macmillan, heard the professor and his precepts praised by E. B. White, Cornell '21, *The New Yorker* magazine writer whose style was the envy of the literary community. Mr. Case proposed that Mr. White prepare a revision of the *Elements.* Mr. White readily agreed. To Strunk's denunciation of "the vague, the tame, the colorless," he added his own prescription for potency, originality and effect.

The Macmillan version of *Elements* was published in a trade edition in the spring of 1959. It was reviewed enthusiastically. The Book-of-the-Month Club distributed it. It sold briskly in bookstores, made the best seller list for 34 weeks. Soon it had a devoted following not only among writers and editors but also among businessmen, engineers and housekeepers whose memories of English composition were distant and dim. A second Macmillan edition, published in 1972, removed what Mr. White had become convinced were "errors" and "bewhiskered entries." Last week Macmillan released a third edition that makes a few further concessions to changing times and tastes.

The records of Harcourt, Brace's version of *Elements* are lost in some corporate graveyard. Macmillan reports that the first two of its editions have sold more than four million copies, almost all in softcover. To date, the third edition has added 600,000 more. Not bad for what was intended to be just a help-meet for students.

Staples

October 19, 1980

"Backlist." Time was when mention of that word usually provoked yawns among paperbounders, for most were engrossed in the fortunes of the latest blockbuster best sellers. But in these nervous days, when new releases are being returned by many retailers if they don't sell briskly the moment they're placed in the racks, more and more publishing people are coming to regard older titles that sell steadily year after year as lifesavers. Recently a half dozen major mass-market houses calculated that between 30 and 50 percent of their total sales are of backlist titles—especially standard reference and how-to books bought by libraries and by customers of well-stocked bookstores.

Facts

February 12, 1978

Americans are a fact-happy people. Go into the reference section of any well-stocked bookstore and you'll find the fastest-moving, steadiest-selling paperbacks on display. Herewith a few facts about them:

• The world's all-time best-selling book (after the Bible) is *The World Almanac and Book of Facts*, first published in 1868. In recent years its sales have averaged 1,100,000 copies. Our source for this statement is *The Guinness Book of World Records*, begun in 1955, which last year sold 1,200,000 copies in the United States. It seems likely that *The Book of Lists*, with 2,000,000 copies in print only three weeks after publication, will become 1978's biggest-selling reference book.

• Some of the most successful fact books are designed to enable Americans to cope with their finances. Last year they bought 1,150,000 copies of that 50-year-old institution, *J. K. Lasser's Your Income Tax*. During the past 18 months they've bought 600,000 softcover copies of *Sylvia Porter's Money Book*.

• Some of the most successful fact books are designed only to entertain. At its start *The Guinness Book* was sponsored by the famous Dublin brewery as a promotion piece—a barroom argument settler. When millions of Americans began discovering it as a great source of amusement (the longest game of musical chairs, the longest unbroken apple peel) during the early '70's, many another fact-loving editor ventured into the sport. Of these, David Wallechinsky of West Hollywood, California, is by far the most successful. His 1975 collection of trivia, *The People's Almanac*, has sold 750,000 copies, his *Book of Lists* has already exceeded that. Even *The World Almanac*, which was originally designed as a working tool for journalists (election returns, names of public officials), have caught the spirit. Its latest edition lists such vital statistics as the age of Farrah Fawcett-Majors.

• The production of fact books often runs in families. *The Guinness Book* was edited jointly by twins Ross and Norris McWhirter until Ross's assassination by a political terrorist in 1975. *The People's Almanac* and *Book of Lists* are the collaboration of three members of the family of novelist Irving Wallace—son David Wallechinsky, daughter Amy Wallace and Irving himself.

• In producing a fact book, it helps to have friends. When Sylvia Porter of Manhattan's Park Avenue began assembling the data for her *Money Book*, she turned for assistance to folks at the stock exchanges, the Federal Reserve, the Social Security offices she'd come to know during her 43 years as a newspaper columnist. When Joe Graedon of Durham, North Caro-

lina, began compiling *The People's Pharmacy,* a layman's guide
to drugs and household remedies (400,000 copies sold to date),
he called on sources he had discovered during a lifetime
teaching pharmacy. Once a book is successfully published, its
author can count on receiving thousands of letters from readers with suggestions for future editions.
  • The production of fact books is essentially a cottage industry. *The World Almanac* has an all-year staff of nine based
in a Manhattan office, *The Guinness Book* 20 in a London
suburb, the J. K. Lasser guide five accountants and editors in
suburban Westchester County. For their fact enterprises, the
Wallaces, father and son, maintain a full-time staff of 14 who
work in 11 book-lined rooms of two homes a half-mile apart in
Hollywood. To produce Stanley R. Greenfield's just-published
National Directory, "the first and only book containing 50,000
most wanted addresses and telephone numbers," three women
worked regular hours around the dining room table of the
managing editor's Teaneck, New Jersey, home.
  • Every assembler of facts is apt to be overwhelmed by
them. Sylvia Porter ended up with more than two million words
of financial advice and her publisher had to excise 1,700,000.
For their upcoming *People's Almanac II,* the Wallaces have produced 1,250,000 words—and their publisher obviously will
have to do something about that.

November 23, 1980

Back in 1868, when Ulysses S. Grant was being elected President, *The World,* one of Manhattan's leading newspapers, began publishing an almanac listing election returns and public
officials to serve as a working tool for its own staff and other
journalists. *The World* has long since expired, but its offspring
is enjoying bounding good health. *The World Almanac and
Book of Facts,* a publication of the Scripps-Howard-owned
Newspaper Enterprise Association, is now distributed in a
paperback edition by Ballantine Books, in a hardcover edition
by Doubleday and in other editions by 131 American newspapers. Its total annual sales of 1,400,000 copies make it—in the
publisher's words—"the world's best-selling book, except for
the Bible."
  To win this readership, the almanac's scope has been greatly
expanded. A nine-member staff works throughout the year in a

large suite in the Pan-American Building in New York collecting data about political, economic and social conditions all over the world. In recent years, facts about such new concerns as nuclear energy, the environment and "influential women" have joined listings of information about sports events, show business and literary awards.

With all its expansion and prosperity, *The World Almanac* hasn't lost sight of its original *raison d'etre.* By the time election day came this year, all data for the 1981 edition except the returns were in type at the Buffalo printing plant. Just as soon as these started trickling in, the staff began tabulating them, county by county, and flying them to Buffalo. Within a week, 200,000 copies of the Ballantine paperback edition were en route to the bookstores, followed, at a more relaxed pace, by the other editions.

February 8, 1981

The current craze for facts overtook Americans early in the 1950's, spawned by a curious collection of curiosities from Britain. Guinness, the Anglo-Irish brewery, had commissioned Norris and Ross McWhirter, twins and onetime sportswriters, to prepare a tabulation of "world's records" that its customers could use to settle their barroom arguments. Copies of *The Guinness Book of World Records* went on sale in this country in 1956, but they reposed unsold on warehouse shelves until one fell into the hands of David Boehm, head of Sterling, a New York how-to book publisher. Mr. Boehm took over the distribution of the volume in the United States and arranged with Bantam Books to do a softcover reprint. Bantam sent the personable McWhirter twins on cross-country tours, and by 1963 *The Guinness Book* was the talk of every American bar and home. Ross McWhirter is dead now, the victim of an I.R.A. terrorist, but from offices in suburban London, Norris McWhirter carries on, revising the volume annually, publishing spin-off books and directing numerous enterprises that use the Guinness name.

Dictionaries

October 19, 1980

Stop in the section marked "Reference" in any well-stocked bookstore and you may find yourself a bit boggled. ("Boggled," according to *The Merriam-Webster Pocket Dictionary,* means "to overwhelm with amazement.") On those shelves you'll find an amazing variety of dictionaries, encyclopedias, thesauruses, synonym finders, and other books about words and their use, in both mass-market and trade paperback format, at prices ranging from $2.50 to $9.95. All are intended not as substitutes for their counterparts in hardcover, but as companions for everyday use, to be kept on your desk or carried in a large coat pocket.

To reduce your amazement, consider just the dictionaries, which consititute paperbacks' largest-selling category. There are six that stand apart from the crowd, each with its own claim for distinction:

• *The Merriam-Webster Pocket Dictionary* (Pocket) says on its cover that it "offers approximately 57,000 definitions." Since 1947, it's had more than 16 million copies in print, making it "the No. 2 all-time best-selling paperback, second only to Benjamin Spock's *Pocket Book of Baby Care*."

• *The New American Webster College Dictionary* (NAL/Signet) says that it provides "115,000 definitions of useful words." Dating back to 1955, it has "more than ten million copies in print."

• *Funk & Wagnalls Standard Dictionary* (NAL/Meridian) defines 82,000 words.

• *The Random House Dictionary* (Ballantine) has more than 74,000 entries.

• *The American Heritage Dictionary of the English Language* (Dell), with 60,000 definitions, is remarkable for its numerous attractive illustrations.

• *The Scribner-Bantam English Dictionary* (Bantam), a relative newcomer, first appeared in 1979.

Despite the claims of distinction, all six books have much in common. All are the works of professional lexicographers. All, except for the Scribner-Bantam volume, are abridgments of works that have long been American institutions. All carry on the tradition of the 19th-century Yankee Noah Webster, who believed that a dictionary, like an encyclopedia, should instruct as well as define. All adhere to the spirit of Webster and the 20th-century iconoclast H. L. Mencken, who felt that concern should be shown for the way that Americans, rather than the British, use their language.

Last week yet another, most remarkable, dictionary joined their company—the *Oxford American Dictionary*, published simultaneously in hardcover by the Oxford University Press and as a trade paperback by Avon Books. Two years ago, Walter Meade, Avon's editor-in-chief, learned that the publishers of the classic 13-volume Oxford English Dictionary was planning a desk dictionary designed specifically for American use. Anxious to strengthen Avon's already strong backlist, he bought the paperback rights for "a very respectable sum."

The provenance of the Oxford American is far more diverse than its competitors. It is essentially the work of Stuart Berg Flexner, Eugene Ehrlich and Gorton Carruth, three Americans who have made important contributions to other dictionaries, but as they prepared their material, they sent it for review to Joyce Hawkins of Oxford's dictionaries department. Miss Hawkins is frequently called "the lady lexicographer who has declared war on sloppy English."

So Avon has a fine new trade paperback for its backlist. Backlist? Ironically, none of the softcovered dictionaries define the word.

May 18, 1980

Paperback books are low-priced and easy to carry? Well, not always. Scribner's recently reissued *Dictionary of the History of Ideas*, an authoritative reference work tracing 312 ideas in philosophy, history, science, mathematics, art, literature and the social sciences, edited by Philip P. Wiener, in five boxed, softcovered volumes. Price: $100. Weight: 11 pounds, 14 ounces.

Tax Guides

February 21, 1982

Step into any well-stocked bookstore these midwinter days, and you'll be confronted by displays of two dozen new books with a variety of titles but a single theme: *Perfectly Legal: 275 Foolproof Methods for Paying Less Taxes, How to Use Inflation to Beat the IRS*. One is named, hyperbolically, *How to Pay Zero Taxes*.

Most books about taxes are bought by persons whose annual family income of $10,000 to $25,000 does not allow them the services of a year-around consultant and who, during a few frantic weeks before April 15, undertake to fill out their own 1040 forms. For help, they turn to the authors of four annually revised how-to books.

• Jacob Kay Lasser (1896–1954), a Manhattan accountant, is generally credited with creating the first practical do-it-yourself tax guide in 1939. Nowadays, his work is continued and regularly updated by the J. K. Lasser Tax Institute, a small group of lawyers and accountants based in Larchmont, New York. The Institute's head is Bernard Greisman, a tax lawyer who once worked for Lasser. Sales of the 1982 edition of *J. K. Lasser's Your Income Tax* (Simon & Schuster) are expected to reach 1,600,000 copies—by far the largest of any trade paperback in one year.

• Henry and Richard Bloch, brothers and accountants, founded H & R Block Inc. in 1955, at a time when the I.R.S. was beginning to diminish assistance to taxpayers. For business purposes, they spelled their name "Block" to avoid the suggestion that they might be responsible for "blotching" clients' reports. During the first 15 weeks of each year, the Kansas City-based firm now keeps 40,000 part-time employees busy in 8,500 offices across the country filling out forms for ten million Americans. To accommodate the hardy souls who prefer to do their own thing at tax time, in 1967 the Blochs began publishing their own guide. Sales of the *1982 H & R Block Income Tax Workbook* (Macmillan) will total 635,000 copies.

• Back in 1977, when he was 33, Barry R. Steiner, a former I.R.S. agent and Chicago accountant, bravely self-published a do-it-yourself tax guide. It was a sales disaster. Happily, a literary agent took the work to New American Library, which was looking for such a title to add to its list. Now, four editions later, Mr. Steiner divides his time between offices in Fort Lauderdale, Florida, and Chicago and, alone among the guide makers, tours energetically to promote his work at tax time. This year sales of his *Pay Less Tax Legally* (NAL/Signet) are expected to reach 400,000 copies.

• Sylvia F. Porter of New York is a household name across America, thanks to the column of advice on personal finance she's been writing for 47 years, which currently appears in 450 newspapers, and to several best-selling books on the same subject. Back in the late '40's, she collaborated with J. K. Lasser on several of his annuals. In 1981, with the aid of a small staff working in her Fifth Avenue apartment, she began producing *Sylvia Porter's 1982 Tax Book* (Avon). Its expected sales this second year: 365,000 copies.

Cookbooks

December 18, 1980

"That branch of American literature which has been sorriest is the literature of the kitchen. We need good cooking far more than we need novels. The old novels will do, new cookbooks we must have." But patience is necessary. "A belt of darkened kitchens 3,000 miles wide cannot be illuminated in a day." Such was the view of the editor of *The New York Times Book Review* in the issue of September 29, 1900.

How things have changed in the past 80 years! Today, there are some 3,500 cookbooks in print, dealing with every phase of the culinary arts—from traditional American cooking to ethnic cuisines from every part of the globe. Many bookstores report that these represent one-fifth of their annual sales.

Although the lights began turning on in American kitchens early in this century—such classics as *The Better Homes and Gardens Cookbook* and *The Joy of Cooking* made their appearance in 1930 and 1931 respectively—it wasn't until the end of World War II, when soldiers brought home an appetite for fare more interesting than grandma's old-fashioned home cooking that the cookbook came to be considered a necessity in every household.

In the culinary revolution that followed, the just a-borning paperback book played its part. First there was *The Pocket Cook Book* by Elizabeth Woody, a guide for beginners. It's still in print 38 years after its debut and has sold nearly five million copies. Later came updated versions of *The Joy of Cooking* by Irma S. Rombauer and Marion Becker (NAL/Signet), *The Better Homes and Gardens Cookbook* (Bantam) and *Betty Crocker's Cookbook* (Bantam), which regularly sell between 75,000 and 100,000 copies every year.

But these are mass-market, rack-size paperbacks, for which food critics rarely have a good word. "They're hard to use because they won't lie flat on the kitchen table" is a typical complaint. "They aren't packaged attractively enough to serve as acceptable gifts" is another.

Trade paperbacks meet such objections as these. Cookbooks in this format first became staples in American bookstores, particularly those in college communities and neighborhoods with a youthful population, during the 1960's. Since then, as Judith Jones, cookbook editor at Knopf, has observed, "Thanks to their attractiveness, relatively modest price and easy accessiblity, they have introduced several generations of Americans to the fun of culinary adventure."

January 4, 1981

Recently we've received five new trade paperbacks that all have one word in their title—"vegetarian." It would seem that America is being caught in a new movement. We queried Paul Obis Jr. of Oak Park, Illinois, publisher of the newsletter *Vegetarian Times*, about its extent and significance. He tells us that the present movement started in the early 1970's, when idealistic veterans of the Vietnam generation gave up eating meat because such fare necessitated the slaughter of animals, was not as good for one's health as natural foods and was relatively expensive. No one knows how many practicing vegetarians there are in the country today, but a notion is offered by the fact that last year 6,500 health food stores did a nearly $1.5 billion business.

There are now 60 books in print dealing with vegetarianism, but three have been doing more than their share in making converts:

• *The Vegetarian Epicure* by Anna Thomas (Vintage) is a collection of 262 recipes that promise "to bring cooking to new heights." It has sold nearly 700,000 copies since 1972, largely through word-of-mouth.

• *The Vegetarian Epicure Book 2* (Knopf) continues in the same spirit and has sold 300,000 copies since 1978.

• *The Moosewood Cookbook* by Mollie Katzen (Ten Speed Press) is a collection of recipes from the popular Moosewood cooperative restaurant in Ithaca, New York. Although it was first published in 1977, most of its sales—more than 250,000 copies—have been in the past 12 months.

Travel Guides

June 3, 1979

In summer, not all the best-selling paperbacks are light novels intended for poolside reading. Most booksellers report that some of their most sought-after wares are guides for travel here and abroad. Most well-stocked stores have shelvesful of volumes designed for every taste and destination. All are collaborative efforts, researched, written, edited and published in ways as diverse as two of the past season's top sellers—the *Rand McNally Road Atlas,* which for generations has been helping Americans discover the wonders of their own continent, and Harvard Student Agencies' *Let's Go! A Budget Guide to Europe,* the present college generation's favorite counsellor in coping with the ways of the Old World.

Rand McNally, the venerable giant of the travel-guide industry, watches the world from a sprawling six-and-one-half acre building in Skokie, Illinois, a Chicago suburb. There, 155 researchers, cartographic designers, writers and editors labor throughout the year, reinforced seasonally by more than 120 specialists, to update its several hundred atlases and travel books, including a popular campground and trailer guide and seven regional editions of the *Mobil Travel Guide.*

Travel has been Rand McNally's stock-in-trade ever since the business was founded in 1856 by two young newcomers to Chicago, William Rand from Boston and Andrew McNally from Ireland. Among the earliest contracts the firm obtained were for printing tickets and then travel guides for the railroads that were starting to span the continent. Since then, as Americans have traveled farther and farther and in more various ways, Rand McNally, still controlled by Andrew McNally's descendants, has adapted its map-making and publishing program to satisfy their needs, even as it ventured into other enterprises.

Harvard Student Agencies, the liveliest fledgling among the travel guide makers, looks out on the world through the single window of an office in the basement of Thayer Hall in the middle of Harvard Yard. It has just dispatched 16 university students, chosen from 100 applicants, to Europe and the farthest corners of the United States to research and write next year's edition of its Let's Go! series. The preparation of these publications is only one of the many ways by which Harvard Student Agencies provides part-time employment for 950 university students each year. Other services include catering, bartending, office clerical work and custodial care.

Harvard Student Agencies got into travel book publishing by chance. Back in 1962 it yielded to the requests of young people who were taking charter flights to Europe for printed advice about what to do once they got there. Over the years, the mimeographed booklet it supplied them has evolved into a printed book, then into the present annually revised Let's Go! guides—Europe, Britain and Ireland, France, Italy. Two additional volumes—one about the United States, the other about Greece and Israel—are planned for 1980–81. Since 1970, two New York houses—Dutton and St. Martins—have handled the series' bookstore distribution. This past year's sales totalled 130,000 copies.

But how well are travel guides selling during this year of galloping inflation and immobilizing gasoline shortage? We asked the buyers of several national book chains what was happening in their stores. "Sales began falling off in March," said one. "The situation's comparable to that during the 1973–74 oil embargo," said another. All agreed that the *Rand McNally Road Atlas* and the Let's Go! series have been holding up remarkably well.

At Harvard Student Agencies, the two professional administrators who oversee its operations were even more sanguine. "Inflation isn't affecting European travel this year," they told us. "Between one and two million college students are going abroad. Besides, our books emphasize what every traveler between 18 and 30 needs to know—how to get a lot for his dollar."

Word Puzzles

July 27, 1980

What's the name of the game—15 letters, beginning with "c" and ending with "e" that was born on December 21, 1913 in the "Sunday Fun" section of *The New York World?* Anyone who spends part of his Sundays with a pencil and eraser in hand should be able to shoot back the answer: crossword puzzle.

Who is widely known as the First Lady of the Crossword Puzzle, 14 letters beginning with "M" and ending with "r"? Answer: Margaret Farrar. As Margaret Petheridge, a secretary recently graduated from Smith College, Mrs. Farrar in 1921 assumed the responsibility of making *The World's* crosswords impeccably correct. It was she who, three years later, helped Richard Simon and M. Lincoln Schuster, two young men eager to get in the book business, assemble the 50 puzzles that composed their first publication, *The Cross Word Puzzle Book.* The book became an instant best seller, starting a rage that quickly spread to every part of the world, except the Orient, where the orthography of the local languages made it impracticable.

Today, in America, the crossword puzzle is among publishing's most dependable sub-industries, one of the most popular features in several thousand newspapers and magazines serviced by three large press services and the content of more than 125 paperbacks currently kept in print by 25 houses. The book publishers are especially fond of them because their devotees—people in every walk of life, in every section of the country—can be counted on to grab up a 25,000-to-50,000 copy printing within a few months. There are crossword puzzle books for every age and taste—children who are learning to read and spell, oldsters whose eyesight is failing, erudite scholars, Bible students, mystery buffs, lovers of British-style subtlety and innuendo.

Under the direction of Mrs. Farrar—with assistance in recent years from Eugene J. Maleska—Simon & Schuster and its affiliate, Pocket Books, still lead the crossword industry. But a close contender is Dell Publishing Company, whose 80 puzzle magazines and continuing series of paperbacks have been edited for the past 40 years by Kathleen Rafferty. Mrs. Rafferty's *The Dell Crossword Puzzle Dictionary* is considered by many fans to be the best of a half dozen such reference works for puzzle-solvers. In the last 30 years, it's sold nine million copies.

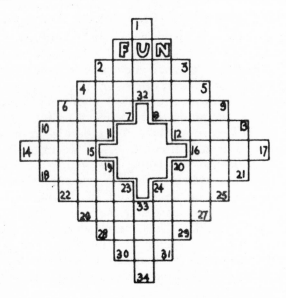

October 4, 1981

The diamond-shaped grid above is the first crossword puzzle ever published—the invention of Arthur Wynne, editor of the "Fun" section of *The New York Sunday World,* which printed it in its issue of December 21, 1913. So many readers said that they had fun figuring out its 31 clues—"1–32, to govern" to "33–34, an aromatic plant"—that it was made one of *The World's* regular features. In time, the rage for crosswords spread around the world—as *mots croisés* in France, *crucigramas* in Spain, *Kreuzwortratsel* in Germany, *krestoslovitsa* in Russia. It's estimated that today well over 30 million Americans are addicts, making crosswords this country's most popular armchair sport. Virtually every newspaper prints them as regular features and two dozen publishers periodically issue collections of them in paperback.

The history of the crossword puzzle, from such ancient antecedents as riddles, rebuses, anagrams and charades to such latterday offshoots as double-crosstics, Scrabble and the diagramless contrivances of the British, is told in lively, authoritative style by Michelle Arnot in *What's Gnu?* (Vintage). As a veteran constructor herself, Miss Arnot is able to serve up many a morsel of behind-the-scenes gossip. Throughout the text, 47 puzzles are reproduced to illustrate how the genre evolved. Of course, there are answers to them at the back of the book.

Incidentally, the answer to 1–32 in the first crossword puzzle is *rule,* to 33–34, *nard.*

Astrology

August 13, 1978

The racks filled with suspensers and historical romances aren't the only sections of the paperback shops where there's a lot of action these midsummer days. Take a look at the corner marked "Astrology," where clerks are busy unpacking books that promise to tell what next year holds for us all.

Since the early 1960's—the dawn of what astrology's true believers call the Age of Aquarius—interest in such publications has been at an all-time high. Thirty-two million Americans—women outnumber men more than two to one—say they are convinced that the positions of the heavenly bodies at the moment of a person's birth have a direct impact on his or her character and destiny. Columns of advice based on this credo appear in 1,250 newspapers. There are more than 500 books about astrology in print, half of them in softcover.

Nearly every paperback house has a few astrological titles on its list. Five—Ace, Dell, Pocket, New American Library and Bantam—publish dozens of volumes each year. Dell, publisher of *Horoscope* magazine since 1935, has an in-house editorial staff that commissions books from a pool of "qualified freelancers." Bantam distributes the works of Llewellyn Publications, a long-established astrological specialist in Minneapolis. The others are a bit vague about the creators of their lines, bearing such names as Zodiac International, Astroanalysis Institute and Constellation International.

A few astrological titles are staples, selling steadily year after year. Biggest all-time seller is *Linda Goodman's Sun Signs*, of which Bantam has sold three million copies since 1971.

The books the faithful will be grabbing up most avidly during the coming weeks deal specifically with the next calendar year. There are single volumes, such as *Sydney Omarr's Astrological Guide* (NAL), covering everyone's fate, and a half dozen series that treat the 12 zodiacal signs individually. By this time next year they'll have sold a total of 12 million copies.

How much stock should a rational soul place in the counsel they offer? Two years ago, 186 eminent scientists, including 18 Nobel Prize winners, issued a statement declaring that astrology has no scientific basis. One bookstore owner tells us that his clerks, one and all, agree that there's nothing to it, but as soon as the new guides arrive they hasten to consult them to see what the coming year holds for their sign.

Timely and Trendy

The People's Choice

Best Sellers of the 1970's

By its fourth decade, the Paperback Revolution had pro-foundly influenced not only the publishing industry, but indeed all of American culture, as a study of the best-selling books of the 1970's makes quite clear . . .

December 30, 1979

It began with the invasion of Cambodia and the bloodshed at Kent State. It is ending with an anguished drama in Iran. In between there have been half a dozen other traumas, including the evacuation of Vietnam that concluded the longest and most futile war in United States history and the Watergate affair that led to the first resignation from office of an American President.

During the turbulent 1970's, Americans bought more books, hardcover and soft, than during any preceding decade. What kind of books did they choose? Their selections were as varied as human taste, but the titles that attracted them most often were books that provided entertainment and escape, books that offered religious inspiration and hope, and books concerned with hedonistic impulses.

This generalization is based on an analysis of the titles that leading publishers report were their best sellers during the

'70's. To answer that question more specifically—which books Americans bought and why—we've analyzed the contents and publishing history of the 20 top-selling works of fiction and nonfiction, as well as those of other books that sold well enough to be counted runners-up.

As in the past, during the '70s Americans showed a marked preference for fiction. The top eight books on the fiction list sold more copies than any of the works on the nonfiction list.

Few of the best-selling novels were serious works of literature, the sort that will be studied in college courses in years to come. Nearly all had strong story lines and were crowded with action.

It is certainly no happenstance that half a dozen of these novels served as the basis of popular motion pictures and television shows. The decade's largest-selling work of fiction, Mario Puzo's *The Godfather,* sold 292,765 copies when it was published in hardcover in 1969. Following the release of the 1972 movie based on it, the number of copies in print rose to 13 million, an all-time record.

It is perhaps ironic that only a few years after the close of the '60's, a time when many youth leaders proclaimed that "history is irrelevant," millions of Americans chose to read books whose subjects were rooted in the past. Indeed, the word *Roots* was used by Alex Haley to describe his quest for his heritage, which led to a record-breaking television series and a best-selling nonfiction book.

The fascination that the past holds for Americans was again revealed in the reception accorded James A. Michener's fact-packed novels, his top-selling *Centennial* and his runner-up, *Chesapeake.* It was evident in the enormous success of Irwin Shaw's *Rich Man, Poor Man* and the multi-volume family sagas of Howard Fast, Herman Wouk and John Jakes. Nor was the interest of Americans in clans and bygone days limited to their own country. One of the most beloved novels of the '70's was Colleen McCullough's *The Thorn Birds,* which its fans often described as an Australian *Gone With the Wind.*

Americans also sought entertainment and escape through a number of other kinds of fiction:

• The spookiness and mystery of the occult in William Blatty's *The Exorcist* and a runner-up, Thomas Tryon's *The Other.*

- The menace of water-borne monsters in Peter Benchley's *Jaws*.
- Romantic sentimentality in Erich Segal's *Love Story*.
- The pleasure of sharing vicariously the glamorous lives of the international jet-set, as in Sidney Sheldon's *The Other Side of Midnight* and in such runners-up as Jacqueline Susann's *Once Is Not Enough* and Judith Krantz's *Scruples*.
- The fantasies and phobias of newly liberated women, as in Erica Jong's *Fear of Flying* and in a runner-up, Judith Rossner's *Looking for Mr. Goodbar*.
- Inspiration through a book that is truly a rara avis: Richard Bach's *Jonathan Livingston Seagull*, an allegory about a dauntless bird, received little attention when it was first published in 1970 but, thanks to readers' word-of-mouth enthusiasm, it became the first-ranking hardcover fiction best seller in 1972 and 1973.

One literary genre that enjoyed extraordinary popularity during the '70's, in films as well as in books, is notable for its absence from the list of top-ten fiction. Several books of science fiction/fantasy—most notably J. R. R. Tolkien's *The Silmarillion* and Richard Adams' *Watership Down*—sold well enough to be counted runners-up. The sales of one million hardcover copies of Tolkien's posthumous novel in 1977 is generally attributed to the loyalty of the readers who enabled his *Ring Trilogy* to make paperback history during the '60's.

Writers like Tolkien acknowledged that their work was fiction. In 1970, a Swiss hotelkeeper named Erich von Däniken appeared on the American scene with a curious book that professed to be factual. *Chariots of the Gods* expounded the theory that the earth had been visited in the remote past by men from other planets who interbred with early man. In support of his thesis he presented a number of "archeological finds." Scientists scoffed, but over the years the book has attracted several million credulous readers, making it the No. 2 best-selling nonfiction book of the '70's.

Americans found entertainment of a more believable sort through the humorous jabs Erma Bombeck took at the absurdities of middle-class life in two other top-ranking nonfiction books, *If Life Is a Bowl of Cherries—What Am I Doing in the Pits?* and *The Grass Is Always Greener Over the Septic Tank*.

Late in the decade, as the family of President Carter moved

to the forefront of the American scene, many usually well-informed people first became aware of the fact that the nation was in the midst of a great religious revival. If they had been watching the best seller lists, they would have known sooner, for a number of works by evangelists had been selling well for some time. None achieved the popularity of *The Late Great Planet Earth,* in which Hal Lindsey contended that the second coming of Christ was fast approaching. Published in 1970, it has gone through countless editions and remains the top-selling nonfiction book of the '70's.

Numerous social critics have been calling the '70's an age of hedonism, narcissism and "me-ism." Such a spirit would account for the appearance on the weekly best seller lists of books about diet, health, running and physical fitness during the past year or two. James Fixx's *The Complete Book of Running,* for example, has sold 771,140 copies in hardcover since its publication in 1977, but remains only a runner-up among the decade's best sellers because it has yet to be paperbacked.

Hedonism is also reflected in the enormous popularity of such books as Wayne W. Dyer's *Your Erroneous Zones,* "M."'s *The Sensuous Man* and Marabel Morgan's *The Total Woman.*

It could be argued that the book that has most affected the personal lives of Americans during the '70's was Alex Comfort's *The Joy of Sex.* This illustrated how-to book continued the sexual revolution begun by the Kinsey books of the late '40's and early '50's.

The most shocking political development of the decade, Watergate, occasioned the publication of two runners-up, Carl Bernstein's and Bob Woodward's *All the President's Men* and *The Final Days.* Several participants in the episode also published books, most of them thinly disguised fiction that sold well but not phenomenally.

At the outset of the '70's, when memories of the youth unrest of the '60's were still vivid, millions of readers turned to several books for insights into the future that then lay ahead. Among them was Alvin Toffler's top-selling *Future Shock,* a preview of a society founded on technology and broken up into many subcultures. In a runner-up, *The Greening of America,* Charles A. Reich assured his readers that the younger generation would make their country "livable." Some of these predictions have come to pass, many of them have not.

As we enter the 1980's books reassessing the legacy of Cambodia and Vietnam are beginning to reappear in the stores and even on the weekly best seller lists. It seems likely that the new role of women in society and the new shapes that family life is assuming will be among the subjects covered in the best sellers of the coming decade.

In the listing below, hardcover figures represent the number of copies sold, as reported by the publishers. Paperback figures represent copies in print, as reported by the publishers.

FICTION

1. THE GODFATHER, by Mario Puzo (published 1969).
   Hardcover: Putnam, 292,765.
   Paperback: New American Library, 13,225,000.
2. THE EXORCIST, by William P. Blatty (1971).
   Hardcover: Harper & Row, 205,265.
   Paperback: Bantam, 11,948,000.
3. JONATHAN LIVINGSTON SEAGULL, by Richard Bach (1970).
   Hardcover: Macmillan, 3,192,000.
   Paperback: Avon, 7,250,000.
4. LOVE STORY, by Erich Segal (1970).
   Hardcover: Harper & Row, 431,976.
   Paperback: Avon, 9,778,000.
5. JAWS, by Peter Benchley (1974).
   Hardcover: Doubleday, 204,281.
   Paperback: Bantam, 9,210,000.
6. THE THORN BIRDS, by Colleen McCullough (1977).
   Hardcover: Harper & Row, 646,503.
   Paperback: Avon, 7,405,000.
7. RICH MAN, POOR MAN, by Irwin Shaw (1970).
   Hardcover: Delacorte, 99,610.
   Paperback: Dell, 6,550,000.
8. THE OTHER SIDE OF MIDNIGHT, by Sidney Sheldon (1973).
   Hardcover: Morrow, 85,000.
   Paperback: Dell, 6,500,000.

9. CENTENNIAL, by James A. Michener (1974).
   Hardcover: Random House, 458,788.
   Paperback: Fawcett, 5,715,000.
10. FEAR OF FLYING, by Erica Jong (1973).
   Hardcover: Holt, Rinehart & Winston, 100,000.
   Paperback: New American Library, 5,700,000.

NONFICTION

1. THE LATE GREAT PLANET EARTH, by Hal Lindsey and
   C. C. Carlson (1970).
   Hardcover: Zondervan, 57,227.
   Paperback: Zondervan and Bantam, 7,229,542.
2. CHARIOTS OF THE GODS, by Erich von Däniken (1970).
   Hardcover: Putnam, 59,924.
   Paperback: Berkley, 6,298,000.
3. YOUR ERRONEOUS ZONES, by Wayne W. Dyer (1976).
   Hardcover: Funk & Wagnalls, 780,569.
   Paperback: Avon, 4,640,000.
4. THE JOY OF SEX, by Alex Comfort (1972).
   Hardcover: Crown, 1,000,000.
   Paperback: Simon & Schuster, 4,236,000.
5. FUTURE SHOCK, by Alvin Toffler (1970).
   Hardcover: Random House, 209,475.
   Paperback: Bantam, 4,795,000.
6. THE SENSUOUS MAN, by "M." (1971).
   Hardcover: Lyle Stuart, 410,000.
   Paperback: Dell, 4,500,000.
7. ROOTS, by Alex Haley (1976).
   Hardcover: Doubleday, 1,174,000.
   Paperback: Dell, 3,677,000.
8. IF LIFE IS A BOWL OF CHERRIES—WHAT AM I
   DOING IN THE PITS? by Erma Bombeck (1978).
   Hardcover: McGraw-Hill, 702,926.
   Paperback: Fawcett, 3,440,000.
9. THE TOTAL WOMAN, by Marabel Morgan (1973).
   Hardcover: Revell, 903,000.
   Paperback: Pocket, 2,700,000.
10. THE GRASS IS ALWAYS GREENER OVER THE SEPTIC
   TANK, by Erma Bombeck (1976).
   Hardcover: McGraw-Hill, 463,915.
   Paperback: Fawcett, 3,116,000.

Pop Psychology

How to Cope

November 9, 1975

Americans, it seems, are deep in a grand funk. Before this year is out, they'll have carried to the checkout counters well over three million copies of eight paperbacks that promise to tell them how to cope—with their spouses, their children, their bosses and customers, and themselves.

No matter what's getting you down, there's softcovered advice waiting for you on the self-help shelf. So what's your problem?

Everybody's manipulating you, getting what they want but keeping you from what's rightfully yours? Two "Assertiveness Training" books bear virtually the same firm panacea and title: *Don't Say Yes When You Want to Say No* by Herbert Fensterheim and Jean Baer (Dell) and *When I Say No I Feel Guilty* by Manuel J. Smith (Bantam).

You suspect that your troubles are more complicated than that, that you'll have to understand other people in order to make the most of yourself? *Born to Win* by Muriel James and Dorothy Jongeward (Addison-Wesley), combining the Transactional Analysis popularized by Eric Berne *(Games People Play)* and the gestalt experiments of Frederick S. Perls, has already sold one million paperback copies.

You're anxious to get along better with your kids, help them become mature, responsible youngsters? Thomas Gordon's *P.E.T.* (NAL/Plume) uses a technique that in some respects resembles Transactional Analysis to chart a course. Incidentally, P.E.T. stands for Parent Effectiveness Training.

Your marriage has lost its sizzle? *The Total Woman* by Marabel Morgan (Pocket) and *Fascinating Womanhood* by Helen B. Andelin (Bantam) are palpitating bags of sexy tricks and religious inspiration. Encouraged by the fact that *The Total Woman* was last year's No. 1 best seller in hardcover, Pocket has just sent out a two-million-copy printing.

You suffer a lot of internal stresses and strains? Transcendental Meditationists, disciples of the Indian guru Maharishi Mahesh Yogi, have a technique they believe will foster such things as contentment, health and efficiency. The movement recently acquired a university in Iowa, has 6,000 teachers in the United States and claims to be making 15,000 recruits a month. Among the celebrities now "into" TM are Joe Namath, Clint Eastwood and Merv Griffin. Its teachings are told in two books: *TM* by Harold H. Bloomfield, Michael Peter Cain and Dennis T. Jaffe (now available in paperback from Dell after 24 weeks on the hardcover best seller list) and *The TM Book* by Denise Denniston and Peter McWilliams (15 weeks on the trade paperback list; now available in a mass-market edition for which Warner paid $550,000 for reprint rights).

A few footnotes: most of these guides to coping serve as textbooks of well-organized movements that conduct classes throughout the country, frequently under the sponsorship of businesses and churches. Three were originally published by small, little-known firms and were picked up by the large paperback houses after they'd sold spectacularly well in hard covers. Four are by psychologists and psychiatrists. Seven of the authors are Californians.

Sons of Eric Berne
April 9, 1978

Among the many movements that cropped up on the shores of San Francisco Bay back in the hippyish 1960's and one of the few that continues to flourish as never before is one called Transactional Analysis. Its principal organization, the International Transactional Analysis Association, whose headquarters are in a Victorian house in San Francisco's Marina area, now has some 10,000 members—psychiatrists, psychologists, social workers, clergymen. The I.T.A.A. is not dogmatic in its credos—the headquarters bookstore stocks some 80 titles from 50 publishers.

One thing all TA-ers share is a respect for the teachings of Dr. Eric Lennard Bernstein (1910–70), who simplified his name to Eric Berne after leaving his native Montreal to practice psychiatry in the New York area, in the Army Medical Corps and finally in northern California. During the '60's, Dr. Berne formally dropped his allegiance to Freudianism and developed a psychological system of his own, one based on the notion that everyone has within him three ego states—child, adult and parent—and that he should come to terms with them through small group encounters.

Dr. Berne first set forth these ideas in popular style in *Games People Play*, a volume published quietly by Grove Press, a small New York house, in 1964. It was picked up by the youth underground from coast to coast; it appeared on the best seller list 111 times, the longest run in history.

Dr. Berne died eight years ago, but many of his books continue to sell briskly. This month Ballantine is bringing out a new edition of *Games People Play*, bringing its total sale to more than five million copies. The same house is issuing for the first time in paperback *Beyond Games and Scripts*, a posthumous collection of his papers and memorabilia. Bantam reports that in the past three years it's sold 1,380,000 copies of Berne's most ambitious work, *What Do You Say After You Say Hello?*

One criticism made of Eric Berne by other psychiatrists was that his TA lacks "any philosophical or religious perspective." That objection was met by one of his followers, Dr. Thomas Harris, a Sacramento psychiatrist, in a 1969 volume, *I'm OK—You're OK*. Dr. Harris, a practicing Presbyterian, suggested that the child's ego state bears the mark of original sin. Many church groups embraced the Harris version of TA, with the result that *I'm OK—You're OK* made the best seller list for 70 consecutive weeks. This week Avon is releasing its 32nd printing of it in paper covers, bringing its total to 5,515,000 copies.

Meanwhile, TA has been acquiring a devoted following among the management echelons of business and government. It was for this public that two California consulting psychologists, Muriel James and Dorothy Jongeward, wrote their 1971 book *Born to Win*. The James-Jongeward work combines Dr. Berne's TA with a version of Gestalt psychology developed by a now-deceased San Francisco psychiatrist, Dr. Frederick S. Perls. *Born to Win* was originally published by Addison-Wesley as a book for business people, but a year later the same house decided to make it available through general bookstores as a trade paperback. In the last six years it has sold 1,600,000 in that form.

Supersalesman: Dale Carnegie

Books proffering self-help advice are one of the hardiest staples of the paperback industry. The first one was published by Pocket Books during its first year in business . . .

September 5, 1982

How can I persuade people to like me? How can I win them over to my way of thinking? How can I get the job that I want and make it and myself amount to something?

Questions like that have troubled mankind from its beginnings. Answers to them have been offered in countless books, but few have been as successful as one created in the midst of the Great Depression—Dale Carnegie's *How to Win Friends and Influence People.*

The book was originally the inspiration of Leon Shimkin, one of the triumvirate of young men who made the fledgling house of Simon & Schuster one of the go-getting wonders of the publishing world in the late 1920's and 1930's. In 1934 Mr. Shimkin took one of the one-evening-a-week-for-14-weeks courses then being offered by Dale Carnegie (1888–1955), a Missouri farm boy, failed actor and salesman who had struck it rich by giving lectures on the art of selling oneself. Convinced that "there was a book in those lectures," Mr. Shimkin persuaded Carnegie to let a stenographer take notes on them to be revised for publication. Essentially they are shrewdly organized restatements in the vernacular of age-old truths. S&S ventured a first edition of 5,000 hardcover copies in 1936 and four years later, after it had helped launch Pocket Books, made it available in paperback. By 1954 it had sold 1,300,000 copies and it has never been out of print.

Last year, the powers-that-be at Dale Carnegie Associates—the organization in Garden City, New York, that continues to spread the founder's gospel to 2,100 students a week through 125 centers in 56 countries—came to the conclusion that, although the book's message remains as pertinent as ever, its language is getting a bit long in the tooth. A small staff went over it, systematically changing words like "man" and "salesgirl" to "clerk," dropping references to such fairly forgotten worthies as Henry Wadsworth Longfellow, Isadora Duncan and Douglas Fairbanks and substituting new anecdotes for those that time has withered. Pocket Books is about to launch an all-out promotion on behalf of the revised edition.

The new version of Carnegie's 50-year-old doctrines failed to create any excitement at the paperback racks—probably because in the late '70's two charismatic and very lively self-helpers had appeared on the publishing scene . . .

Cheerleader: Wayne W. Dyer

October 23, 1977

This week, for the second time in succession, one book holds a place on both the hardcover and mass-market paperback best seller lists—Wayne W. Dyer's *Your Erroneous Zones.* This is not unprecedented, but it's a rare enough occurrence to raise questions as to how it happened.

The folks at Avon Books, the firm that paid $1,100,000 for paperback rights shortly after its hardcover publication by Funk & Wagnalls early last year, say that of course the book's upbeat message—"you can control your own life, you are the sum total of your own choices"—has much to do with it. Every bit as important, they say, is the outgoing personality and tireless energy of the author.

Soon after the book was published, Mr. Dyer quit his teaching job at St. John's University in Jamaica, New York, and began touring the country coast to coast, border to border. He's been at it constantly ever since, submitting to countless radio and television interviews, answering questions, microphone in hand, from crowds that gather in large bookstores and shopping malls. Most authors aren't invited back to a show or a store until they publish another book, but Mr. Dyer is asked back repeatedly to satisfy what seems to be a growing loyal following—the women outnumbering the men, often twelve to one—who end up buying both editions of the book, hardcovers for themselves, paperbacks for friends. In addition, Mr. Dyer has made a number of lecture appearances at places like Carnegie Hall and the Westbury Music Fair.

Mr. Dyer's appeal is not limited to Yankees. This summer he made a tour of Australia and New Zealand in behalf of Avon's export edition and within weeks was the No. 1 bestselling author Down Under.

Now that Avon has 2,635,000 copies in print and it seems certain they'll have to go back to press for many more, they're glad that at the last minute they decided to put Mr. Dyer's picture on the cover of their edition. His face, with its bright blue eyes and jaunty blond mustache, is fast becoming one of the best known in the United States.

Before 1977 was out, Avon had 4,240,000 copies of *Your Erroneous Zones* in print. Since then, Mr. Dyer has published two more paperbacks with much the same theme,

Pulling Your Own Strings (Avon, 2,200,000 copies) and *The Sky's the Limit* (Pocket, 1,216,000 copies).

Meanwhile, the self-help bookshelf had acquired yet another star performer . . .

Dr. Love: Leo F. Buscaglia

May 16, 1982

"The greatest thing we have is life. And where there's life, there's hope. The old truisms about love and life—know thyself, love yourself in order to be able to love others, seize the day—are still entirely valid. Life is God's gift to you. The way you live your life is your gift to God. Make it a fantastic one."

Such is the message offered by Leo F. Buscaglia in his two books on this week's best-seller lists:

• *Personhood: The Art of Being Fully Human* (Fawcett paperback).

• *Living, Loving & Learning* (published in hardcover by Charles B. Slack, distributed by Holt, Rinehart & Winston).

A third book, *Love*, published four years ago, is now selling more briskly than ever; its Fawcett paperback edition is now a candidate for the mass-market best seller list.

All three volumes are collections of lectures that Mr. Buscaglia has delivered in crowded classrooms and auditoriums across the country and on television. None of the humanistic ideas they offer are new, but the colloquial, person-to-person style in which they are expressed is novel and winning.

This week Mr. Buscaglia will be in Wisconsin and Colorado, winding down his latest cross-country lecture tour. Wherever he goes, he creates a stir. When he was in Manhattan last month, more than 1,000 fans filed through B. Dalton's Fifth Avenue store to get his autograph. While he was walking up Third Avenue with a publishing executive, a woman who recognized him from his television appearances rushed up to embrace him with a warm bunny hug—which, according to Mr. Buscaglia's tenets, is the way people should behave when they care for each other.

Most of the Americans for whom Mr. Buscaglia is a cherished name came to know him through the **PBS** television series he has been making for the past three years. But his books sell everywhere in the country—even in New York and

Los Angeles, where the local PBS stations rarely air his shows. He's also a great favorite of the college lecture circuit. Indeed, a large cross-section of "typical Americans," from teenagers to octogenarians, are finding his answers to the narcissism of the "me decade" refreshing and appealing.

Just who is Leo F. Buscaglia? He's a bearded, ebullient man in his '50's whose official title is Professor of Education at the University of Southern California. He was born in California into a large, closely knit family from northern Italy and for many years was a public-school teacher and administrator, specializing in the problems of disadvantaged children. In the late '60's, he quit his job and spent two years traveling around the world. As his lectures make abundantly clear, he was greatly impressed by Eastern religions and philosophies. Back home, he persuaded the dean of USC's School of Education to allow him to give a course called "Love"—a course that has ten times as many applicants as can be accommodated. On campus, he's called "Dr. Love." Several times he's been voted USC's Teacher of the Year.

And how did he get started on the road to bestsellerdom? In 1972, Charles B. Slack, a Thorofare, New Jersey, publisher of professional magazines who was about to enter the book field, was so impressed by Mr. Buscaglia's performance at a conference on learning disabilities that he proposed issuing his lectures in hardcover. So far, to his profit, he's published five collections. In 1977, a Fawcett sales rep heard Mr. Buscaglia deliver a lecture and strongly urged his New York superiors to bring out *Love* in paperback. To date, it's sold 1,400,000 copies.

Mr. Buscaglia's form of love has enduring as well as endearing qualities. In the summer of 1984, when *Living, Loving & Learning* was enjoying a run on the mass-market best seller list, it was joined by a new edition of *Love*.

Comforter of the Elderly: Elisabeth Kübler-Ross

August 22, 29, 1976

With one-fifth of the U.S. population now over 55, the problems of the elderly are no longer unspeakable, but a Great National Problem. Little wonder that two books currently on the best seller list address themselves to what's on the minds of oldsters and their children:

Life After Death (Mockingbird Books, Covington, Georgia) is the work of Raymond A. Moody Jr., a young Georgia psychiatrist who's done research in an uncharted land—the experiences of men and women who have clinically died but were subsequently brought back to life. Published late last year, it at first sold exclusively in Mockingbird country. Then Midwesterners, attracted by a foreword written by Chicago's Dr. Elisabeth Kübler-Ross, began buying it. A news story in *The New York Times* in April widened the market. Soon the book was the talk of philosophical, medical and religious circles.

On Death and Dying (Macmillan) is the work of Dr. Kübler-Ross, a psychiatrist who has made the scientific study of the aging her concern for the past decade. *On Death and Dying* is the first—and probably the best of her three books on the subject. Swiss-born and 50, she's the wife of a neuropathologist, the mother of a pair of teen-agers. But she travels constantly, lecturing before large groups of nurses, clergy and others whose daily work is with the aging. Often when she returns to her motel she finds a long line of elderly people and their children seeking her counsel. Each year since its paperback publication in 1970, *On Death and Dying* has sold a greater number of copies.

By 1984, both *Life After Death* and *On Death and Dying* had sold well over one million copies.

Religion/Inspiration

• *Religion/Inspiration.* A term used by paperback publishers to categorize books that seek in the Holy Bible hope for escaping from the pressures of life, from the limitations of the natural world or from the world itself.

The Spirit of the '70's

October 31, 1976

You'll find few of them in the bookstores on New York's Fifth Avenue or on the main streets of America's big cities. You'll seldom see them mentioned in literary reviews. But the sales records that some of them have achieved during the past several years are truly extraordinary:

- In 1972, *The Late Great Planet Earth* by Hal Lindsey (Zondervan) outsold all books in all categories in the United States.
- In 1973, *The Living Bible,* a paraphrase of the Holy Bible in modern language by Kenneth N. Taylor (Tyndale and Doubleday) was the nation's top hardcover best seller.
- In 1974, *Total Woman* by Marabel Morgan (Revell) was the No. 1 nonfiction best seller in hardcover.
- In 1975, *Angels* by Billy Graham (Doubleday) headed the list. Within a year it had sold more than 1,600,000 hardcover copies.
- This year, *Born Again* by Charles W. Colson (Revell) is No. 4 on the best seller list.

These titles are all fruits of the fastest-growing segment of U.S. publishing—religious books. Of the more than 100 firms that are active in the field today, only two—Doubleday and Harper—are general trade houses. Since the start of the '70's, five firms that emphasize the evangelical and inspirational aspects of religion have been growing by leaps and bounds. The houses: Revell of Old Tappan, New Jersey, Logos of Plainfield, New Jersey, Tyndale of Wheaton, Illinois, Word Books of Waco, Texas, and Zondervan of Grand Rapids, Michigan. Their success, like the proclivities of Jimmy Carter and Gerald Ford, are symptoms of a prevailing spirit in the United States in this decade.

Most of their books are sold through some 3,500 Christian (i.e., evangelical Protestant) bookstores concentrated in the Deep South coast to coast and Mid-America north to south. But some are finding their way across the counters of some 530 Roman Catholic bookstores, most numerous in the Northeast and California, just as some books published by the few Catholic publishing houses that have survived the great changes that have overtaken the "unchanging church" since Vatican II are finding a welcome in Protestant bookstores. Some of the '70's spirit is ecumenical.

Thanks to the mass-market paperback houses, Americans no longer have to patronize religious bookstores to obtain inspiration founded on the Gospel. Bantam and Pocket Books led the way by publishing reprints of many volumes for sale in secular outlets—variety stores, stationery stores, general bookstores. Recently Warner and Ballantine have been following their example.

In several respects, the currently popular religious/inspiration books resemble those that were best sellers during America's last religious rage. In the 1950's, Norman Vincent Peale's *The Power of Positive Thinking* and Billy Graham's *Peace With God* were successful in no small measure because their clergymen-authors were charismatic figures who had become household names through their frequent appearances on radio and television. Both Mr. Peale and Mr. Graham recounted and extolled the Holy Scripture in their books — as did the writer-editor Fulton Oursler in another best seller of the period, *The Greatest Story Ever Told*.

Over the years since, Mr. Graham has continued to preach the Gospel to millions regularly on television, toured the world staging religious crusades and visiting the White House as a privileged guest of Presidents. This prepared the way for the extraordinary success enjoyed in 1975 and 1976 of *Angels*, his reassuring book about the role that "God's secret agents" play on heaven and earth. In 1977, after Doubleday had disposed of 1,600,000 hardcover copies, Pocket Books brought out a paperback reprint and disposed of 1,175,000 more.

Mr. Graham further demonstrated his influence with bookbuyers in 1977 when, as one of his guests on his television program, he presented pretty Joni (pronounced "Johnny") Eareckson, 27, of Sykesville, Maryland. Ten years earlier, when she was just out of high school, Miss Eareckson suffered a swimming-pool accident that left her paralyzed from the waist down. Undaunted, she learned to use her mouth to hold and guide a pen as she drew pictures and in time achieved something of a reputation as an artist. Within a few weeks of her appearance on the Graham program, 600,000 copies of *Joni*, her inspirational autobiography, were sold through secular bookstores and the volume has since become a steady backlist seller in a Bantam edition.

The inspiration that Americans currently find in the example of a person who puts her faith in God to work against formidable, evil forces has been demonstrated by an English evangelist named Corrie ten Boom. During World War II, Mrs. ten Boom was placed in a concentration camp for her role in helping Jews escape the Nazi dragnet in her Dutch homeland. Her account of that experience, *The Hiding Place*, sold more than 3,500,000 copies in softcover editions when Revell and Pyramid Books published it in 1975.

Equally appealing to Americans have been accounts of the experiences of celebrities who overcame crises in their personal lives by being "born again." Charles W. Colson, one of President Nixon's aides who went to prison for his role in the Watergate affair, recounted in *Born Again* (Revell and Bantam) how he put his life together again as a result of his conversion. Johnny Cash, the Nashville country singer, told how he gave up drugs for the Gospel in *Man in Black*, a best seller in Warner's paperback edition in 1976.

But authors need not have charismatic names nor extraordinary experiences for their books to sell well. This has been demonstrated by two women whose roles as wives and mothers were subjected to the common stresses and strains of the times.

In 1973, when women's liberation and the feminist movement were the talk of the land and one out of every four marriages was ending in divorce, Marabel Morgan of Miami, Florida, a onetime beauty queen, published a book in which she pointed out that the Bible declares that "you wives must submit to your husband's leadership in the same way you submit to the Lord." *Total Woman* described sexy tricks that true-believing women could use to "add sizzle" to their marriages. Revell sold 370,000 hardcover copies, Pocket Books disposed of 2,500,000 more in paperback. The folks at Pocket were surprised to find that the book sold well "everywhere, even in Manhattan."

Similarly, Helen B. Andelin of Santa Barbara, California, wife of a dentist and the mother of eight, felt that her marriage was becoming wobbly and sought help in the Bible. What she found there convinced her that woman's most satisfying role is satisfying her husband's needs. She assembled a collection of religious inspiration and popular psychology and in 1964 published it as a book called *Fascinating Womanhood* (Pacific Publishers, Santa Barbara, California). It became the textbook of a movement, with hundreds of branches that meet regularly in churches. Ten years and 400,000 copies later, Bantam brought it out in a mass-market edition and now has a big, steady seller on its hands.

Certainly the most extraordinary religious book phenomenon of our times is the work of Hal Lindsey, a California-based missionary, whose reading of the Scriptures has led him to publish some breathtaking predictions about what the future holds for mankind. To date, he has published four books, of which Bantam and other publishers have a total of seven million copies in print.

Millennialist: Hal Lindsey

April 6, 1980

When it came time, last December, to take a retrospective look at the book world during the 1970's, many a knowledgeable resident of Publishers Row was surprised to discover that the decade's best-selling work of nonfiction—accounting for 15.5 million copies—was *The Late Great Planet Earth* by Hal Lindsey.

The Late Great Planet Earth? Hal Lindsey?

The Late Great Planet Earth, published in 1970, predicts an international energy crisis and prophesies a great war in which Russia will become involved, ultimately followed by the second coming of Christ. This scenario, the author says, is based on a close study of the Old and New Testaments.

Hal Lindsey, a 50-year-old native of Houston, learned how to spread his message in the most practical way. Following hitches as a student at the University of Texas business school and as a tugboat captain on the Mississippi Delta, he was converted to fundamentalist Christianity. During the 1960's he rode the West Coast circuit for the Campus Crusade for Christ. The sermons he preached to young people at Berkeley, San Francisco State and other restive campuses became the basis for this, his first book. With visions of youthful audiences clear in his mind, he set down his chattily phrased ideas in longhand, then had Carole C. Carlson, a newspaperwomen active in the evangelical movement, shorten his sentences and tidy them up.

The Late Great Planet Earth was originally published by Zondervan of Grand Rapids, Michigan, for sale in both hardcover and paperback editions in the Christian bookstores that dot the Sun Belt and Middle West. "Nowadays, when you've got something to say to young people—the college generation—you must get the word to them through the kind of books they prefer—paperbacks," Mr. Lindsey told us the other day. "That's why I insisted that *The Late Great Planet Earth* and my later works be published simultaneously in softcover and hard."

The book caught the eye of Grace Bechtold, Bantam's veteran editor of "inspirational" books. Zondervan was willing to sell her reprint rights for a mass-market edition because it knew that Bantam's edition would not compete with theirs, for mass-market books regularly go into supermarkets, variety stores and newsstands, beyond the reach of a religious publisher.

March 12, 1978

During the '70's, Mr. Lindsey wrote five more books that followed the same publishing route and sold comparably well. In *Satan Is Alive and Well on Planet Earth* and *There's a New World Coming* he made predictions based on the Bible that, he says, have come true or are about to become true:
- The rebirth of Israel, "a sign that the countdown to Armageddon has started."
- The confederation of the Arab states.
- The Russian sweep toward the control of the Persian Gulf, begun in Afghanistan.
- "The decline of American power and morality."
- The increase of earthquakes, volcanoes and drought.

May 15, 1981

By the end of the decade Mr. Lindsey, the picture of a successful, with-it Southern California businessman, was operating out of an office in Santa Monica—Hal Lindsey Ministries—and still writing books about the approaching apocalypse. In 1981, he published *The 1980's: Countdown to Armageddon*, in which he made some more prophecies:
- The 1980's could well be the last decade of history as we know it. The leader in the final stage will not be the United States.
- The world is about to witness a close encounter of the third kind.
- The Chinese will spread a war to the rest of the world. Every major city will be levelled, and more than half the world's population will die during the coming battles.
- A ten-nation confederacy begun as a trade and economic organization (the Common Market) will spawn a political leader who will have powers of persuasion that no one in the troubled world of the future will be able to resist. This man, who is the Antichrist, is alive today.
- The second coming of Christ will follow.

Ecumenicalist: Thomas Merton

October 21, 1979

One day last week the mailman brought us packages from four different publishers containing handsome new paperback editions of five books written by a long-deceased author. Along with them came promises for more works from the same pen in the near future. Is this mere coincidence or a sign of a trend?

The author was Thomas Merton (1915–68), a convert to Catholicism, a Trappist monk, and the author of more than 50 books of poetry and essays on a wide range of topics. One of these, *The Seven Storey Mountain,* in which he tells the story of his conversion, was a best seller in 1948.

The five newly reissued books, their publishers—Houghton Mifflin and Harcourt Brace Jovanovich—tell us, are a response to a renewed interest in Thomas Merton. In the past year the man and his work have been reappraised in a number of American and British secular magazines. They were discussed recently at a two-week conference at Columbia University, and they have become the subject of several doctoral dissertations and college courses. A full-scale biography is in preparation. More than a dozen publishers have some of his writings in print, and most of those with whom we checked report there is a growing demand for them.

The five newly reissued books are:

• *A Hidden Holiness: The Visual World of Thomas Merton* (Houghton Mifflin), a collection of striking photographs that Merton and his friend John Howard Griffin, a novelist, took during Merton's last years.

• *The Seven Storey Mountain, The Waters of Siloe, No Man is an Island* and *The Sign of Jonas* (HBJ), autobiographical, religious and philosophical essays.

What explains the resurgence of interest in Merton? Robert Giroux, his contemporary at Columbia College and his editor first at Harcourt Brace and now at Farrar, Straus & Giroux, hazarded a guess: Merton was not narrowly Catholic or Christian in his religious vision; he sought to combine the best of Eastern faiths with those of the West; he was firmly opposed to violence in any form. In other words, he was a man for these times.

The Heritage of the Holocaust

November 7, 1976

And what of the Jews? Judaic publishing is steady and growing, but has been little affected by the ecumenical and charismatic spirits sweeping through Christianity. Accounts of the Holocaust and works of Yiddish literature continue to dominate the lists of the dozen principal firms in the field. There are some 50 bookstores located in large U.S. urban centers, but some brisk business is done through college and university stores.

May 28, 1978

Next Thursday, at New York's St. Regis Hotel, there'll be a reception to launch a new paperback series called The Holocaust Library. This is not, the host hastens to explain, a commercial enterprise designed to cash in on the popular interest in the subject whipped up by a recent television mini-series. It's a long-planned publishing project intended to keep succeeding generations aware of the lessons of Hitler's Holocaust, "so that the tragedy will never be repeated."

Chief among the project's movers is Alexander Donat, one-time Warsaw newspaper publisher, who described his family's experiences in the Nazi death camps in a well-received 1965 book, *The Holocaust Kingdom*. It troubled him when his and similar memoirs went out of print, and he found many fellow survivors who shared his concern. Several years ago he organized a six-man committee—among them the distinguished man of letters Elie Wiesel—to do something about it. Funds left by two old friends, Benjamin and Stefa Wald, financed the undertaking. To make the books available through bookstore channels, Mr. Donat's committee has turned to a general publishing house with an emphasis on Judaica, Schocken Books.

There are four titles in the Holocaust Library's first issues:

• Mr. Donat's own *The Holocaust Kingdom*.

• *Their Brothers' Keepers*, a reissue of Philip Friedman's 1957 book about "the Christian heroes and heroines who helped the oppressed escape from the Nazi terror."

• *The Death Brigade*, Leon W. Wells' 1961 memoir of his service in a corps assigned to obliterate traces of mass executions in Poland.

• Gideon Hausner's 1966 *Justice in Jerusalem,* a lawyer's brief on the Adolf Eichmann trial.

During the next half dozen years a score of other books were added to the Holocaust Library, much to the pride of the publisher, Schocken Books.

Popular interest in inspirational volumes with a Biblical orientation continued unabated well into the 80's, when Ronald Reagan occupied the White House. One of these was by a rabbi, Harold S. Kushner, whose 1981 *When Bad Things Happen to Good People* sold 332,000 copies in Schocken's hardcover edition, followed by 1,343,000 copies in Avon's paperback reprint. Another was the work of a charismatic new television evangelist, Robert H. Schuller, whose 1983 *Tough Times Never Last But Tough People Do!* sold 259,000 copies in Thomas Nelson's hardcover edition and later had 598,000 softcover copies circulated by Bantam.

Narcissism

"An age of narcissism, hedonism and me-ism" — such was the way many social critics described the 1970's and the early years of the '80's. And with good reason . . .

Diets

June 6, 1982

Eavesdrop on the conversations conducted beneath beauty-shop hair dryers, take a look at the covers of magazines on display at supermarket checkout counters, study the lists of best-selling books and you'll see that currently millions of Americans have a problem that troubles them as much as inflation and energy. They're anxious to take off some weight.

Consider how this mania has affected the sale of books:

• The biggest selling book of the past three years is *The Complete Scarsdale Diet,* by Herman Tarnower, M.D. and Samm Sinclair Baker, which offers a plan to lose up to 20 pounds within two weeks. The hardcover edition, published in January 1979 by Rawson, Wade, appeared on the best seller list for 49 weeks and sold 650,000 copies. The Bantam reprint, released a year later, broke all records for mass-market paperbacks by making the list for 70 weeks, with 4,250,000 copies in print.

But can't this success be attributed to what befell the book's author during the period copies were jumping out of the racks? As every headline reader knows, a Virginia schoolmistress named Jean Harris was being arrested, tried and convicted for shooting and killing Dr. Tarnower in his Westchester County, New York, home. The same woman who leads Dr. Tarnower's list of acknowledgements in the front of the volume: "We are grateful to Jean Harris for her splendid assistance in the research and writing of this book." The publishers insist that although some buyers may have first noticed the book as a result of the Saturday night affair, its huge sales over a long period are the result of word-of-mouth recommendations by satisfied followers of the regimen.

• Nearly as impressive is the record of *The Pritikin Program for Diet and Exercise,* by Nathan Pritikin with Patrick McGrady Jr. This plan, developed by a onetime inventor of electronic gadgetry who now operates several "Pritikin longevity rehabilitation centers" around the country, calls for an abrupt, drastic and permanent change in eating habits, including the avoidance of fats, oils, sugar, cholesterol, coffee and tea, supplemented by daily exercise, usually in the form of walks. Mr. Pritikin's book was published by Grosset & Dunlap in April 1979 and has sold 319,000 hardcover copies. A softcover reprint, issued the following year by Bantam, now has 1,300,000 copies in print.

• These come on the heels of a half dozen other diet books that sold hundreds of thousands of copies—in some cases, millions—during the past two decades. Among them: Dr. Herman Taller's 1961 *Calories Don't Count,* Dr. Irwin Maxwell Stillman's 1967 *The Doctor's Quick Weight Loss Diet,* Dr. Richard C. Atkins' *The Last Chance Diet* and Dr. Barbara Edelstein's *The Woman Doctor's Diet for Women.*

Diet books haven't always been such a bonanza for publishers. Back in 1864, a pamphlet called *Letter on Corpulence,* by William Banting, a British coffin maker, created a great stir throughout the English-speaking world. But it wasn't until 1922, when Lulu Hunt Peters' *Diet and Health With a Key to the Calories* made the best seller list and stayed there through 1926 (it was No. 1 from 1924–25) that such how-to books became part of the American way of life.

"The '20's, the '60's and the '70's were narcissistic decades," Theodore Berland, a syndicated science-medicine writer who has been watching the dieting scene for more than 20 years, told us. "Dieters are predominantly women, whose concern isn't for their health, but a desire to appear sexy—especially during the bathing-suit season."

Mr. Berland is the author of *Rating the Diets* (NAL/Signet), in which, with the help of the editors of *Consumers Guide* magazine, he analyzes and rates 75 currently popular diets. Twenty are "not recommended." He has one word to describe almost all of them: "Baloney!" Some are "positively dangerous." The dieter's real problem, as Mr. Berland sees it, is not taking it off but in keeping it off. Programs to cure alcoholics have a 33 percent rate of lasting success, those for the overweight only 3 percent.

Jane E. Brody, personal health columnist of *The New York Times*, recently made a similar survey, summarizing the findings of nutrition and obesity experts. Most of the diets prescribe high-protein, low-carbohydrate regimens that are fraught with many hazards to the dieter's health. After their use—which the books warn should be only for a short period—"80 to 90 percent of the dieters soon regain the pounds and then some."

Among the diets which Miss Brody's survey indicates are relatively safe and have much longer lasting results is that developed by Weight Watchers International. This emphasizes a reduction in calories consumed, but does not overemphasize any particular type of food. Over the past 20 years, four periodically revised Weight Watchers cookbooks, currently published by New American Library, have sold more than four million copies in hardcover and softcover.

Despite the warnings of experts, the approach of every bathing-suit season continues to bring a new crop of diet books that promise quick and visible results. Recently they are not the work of physicians, but of "celebrities," colorful men and women whose appearances on television, and in bookstores will attract wide attention to their book. Often they make much of the fact that the author was once fat and now is thin and fit. "If I could," they insist, "you can."

Two books that follow this form are now in the paperback racks:

• *The Beverly Hills Diet* is the work of Judy Mazel, a

38-year-old onetime secretary and model who now operates a clinic in the heart of Tinseltown. Her regimen, which she devised and which she says enabled her to lose 50 pounds, calls for six weeks of dieting, begun with ten days of eating nothing but fruit. Later, users are allowed to "acknowledge their food fantasies — pasta, popcorn, cheese cake, vodka, whatever — and fulfill them while losing weight."

The book's cover carries the enthusiastic endorsements of show-biz celebrities who patronize Miss Mazel's salon. But Dr. Philip L. White, director of the American Medical Association's department of foods and nutrition, has branded it "a terrible book." The controversy it has stirred has helped its sales. Macmillan's edition, published last year, sold 756,360 copies, the most of any hardcover book. Berkley's paperback edition has run up print orders of 1,600,000 copies.

• *Richard Simmons' Never-Say-Diet Book* takes into account the criticisms that have been made about the fleeting results of most diet plans and holds out hope for maintaining weight loss more or less permanently. Mr. Simmons, a bouncy, clownlike young man who runs a clinic in Hollywood and conducts a widely watched national television show, says that he has slimmed down from 268 pounds. His book professes to be "not really a diet book, but a plan to change your eating and exercise habits for life." Warner Books sold 570,000 hardcover copies last year and now has more than one million paperback copies in print.

> As the narcissistic spirit raged on, it developed that many Americans' concern about their physical appearance centered on particular parts of their anatomy . . .

Flat Stomachs

July 2, 1978

Every year a thousand brave souls publish books of their own composition and undertake to sell them by mail or on consignment through bookstores. Every year one or two of them have a stroke of luck and achieve bestsellerdom.

The latest lucky self-publisher is Jim Everroad of Columbus, Indiana. In 1974, after losing his job as a high-school athletic coach, Mr. Everroad thought he'd like to become a sportswriter. He spent the summer writing an article about something that had concerned him since he was a boy—his potbelly and the exercises he'd devised to flatten it. After selling it to a newspaper, he arranged to print an expansion of it in paperback—6,000 words illustrated with two dozen photographs—and sold out his 3,000 copies quickly. Euphorically, he then ordered 50,000 more copies, advertised the work more widely and persuaded a number of bookstores in his part of the country to stock it. After he had disposed of 35,000 copies he was compelled to take a number of odd jobs, such as driving a Pepsi-Cola truck.

Then came his stroke of luck. Late last year a new employee of Price/Stern/Sloan, the Los Angeles publisher, told its sales manager, Chuck Gates, about the many copies of Mr. Everroad's book she had sold while working in a bookstore back in Indiana. Mr. Gates investigated, found it to be just the sort of checkout-counter item that is P/S/S's specialty.

P/S/S published *How to Flatten Your Stomach* last January and promptly discovered that America is full of people worried about their potbellies. The book has now hopped onto the best seller list.

> Within the next half dozen years, Price/Stern/Sloan sold 1,500,000 copies of Mr. Everroad's book. Meanwhile, other writers and publishers moved swiftly to help women with one of their concerns . . .

Thin Thighs

September 19, 1982

Behind the book that occupies the No. 1 spot on this week's trade paperback best seller list is a story that shows how publishing continues to respond to widely felt popular desires. It began last March, when Betsy Nolan, who operates a Manhattan agency that conducts author tours and special promotion campaigns for book houses, was approached by two acquaintances with an unusual proposal. Would she join them in producing a book that would concentrate on women's most bothersome problem, the thickness of their thighs?

Miss Nolan had never acted as a literary agent or book packager, but the project as outlined by Wendy Stehling, vice president of a major Manhattan advertising agency, and John Olson, a freelance photographer, was irresistible. She promptly showed it to the major paperback publishers.

At Bantam Books, the third house to see it, publisher Jack Romanos and editor Brad Miner had some masculine doubts about the proposal, but when they showed it at a staff conference, every woman present was most interested.

What with the annual shaping-up-for-the-beach season fast approaching, Bantam put all its hands to work on the project. Within a few weeks 80,000 copies of a 64-page, profusely illustrated paperback called *Thin Thighs in Thirty Days* was placed on sale near the cash registers in stores across the country in early May.

Thin Thighs had been on the trade paperback best-seller list for four weeks when it received an unexpected boost from *People* magazine. To promote its August 2nd issue, in which an article about Miss Stehling and her book was featured, that magazine nationally televised a spot ad in which the pitchman held up a copy of the book. During August 400,000 copies were sold.

The summer beach season is over, but the end of the story of *Thin Thighs* is not yet in sight.

> Indeed, it was not. By the end of 1983, Bantam had sold 1,500,000 copies. The unexpected success of *Thin Thighs* led the same house to produce a companion volume in late 1982 — *30 Days to a Beautiful Bottom*. Within a year and a half 611,000 copies of it had been disposed of.
>
> Even as countless women were trying to reduce the size of their thighs and bottoms, great numbers of men and boys — and some women — were working hard to build up their physiques . . .

Body Building

February 14, 1982

Who in their right minds would want to buy an expensive book about men who obsessively spend most of their days in gyms, manipulating weights in order to build up their muscles? Who would want to read a whole book about the rigors these "muscle-heads" undergo while training so that they can compete for such titles as Mr. America and Mr. Universe?

Those questions were bandied about by members of the staff at Simon & Schuster when they returned from their summer vacations in 1973 and learned that while they had been away, one of the editors, Dan Green, had signed a contract with the novelist Charles Gaines and the photographer George Butler to produce a text-and-picture album exploring one of America's least appreciated subcultures, bodybuilding.

Inevitably, when the book was published in November 1974, the print order was for a modest 12,500 copies. And great pains were taken to explain that the title *Pumping Iron* was the phrase used by bodybuilders in Birmingham, Alabama, where Mr. Gaines grew up.

Nowadays the subject of bodybuilding is accorded far more respect in the halls of S&S. A thoroughly revised and updated paperback edition of *Pumping Iron* has just been published, bringing the book's sales in all editions to 258,500 copies.

The new edition of *Pumping Iron* records how Americans' attitudes toward bodybuilding have changed in the past six years. A 1977 film based on the book made the name part of the common vocabulary. Titleholders whose exploits the volume recorded, like Arnold Schwarzenegger ("The Best") and Lou Ferrigno ("The Incredible Hulk"), became national celebrities. "Your average stockbroker still doesn't put on skimpy little trunks on Sunday morning and hop onto a posing dais in a very public place," Mr. Gaines writes, "but the chances are very good now that he does exercises the way he has read that Arnold does them."

Mr. Gaines and Mr. Butler are about to honor the founding father of their cult. In May, S&S's Fireside line will be issuing their biography of Charles Atlas (1893–1973), the man who taught youths growing up in the 1920's how to develop "a perfect physique."

Recently, there's a growing interest in bodybuilding and physical fitness among women. Eight books bearing such titles as Arnold Schwarzenegger's *Bodyshaping for Women* have sold more than 1,500,000 copies. The film star and onetime political activist Jane Fonda has become a kind of guru, with a chain of exercise salons bearing her name. This week *Jane Fonda's Workout Book* is No. 3 on the hardcover best seller list. *Jane Fonda's Workout Book* sold 420,617 hardcover copies, making it 1983's No. 5 best seller. Later that same year, a trade paperback edition of it sold 179,734 copies.

Yet another form of exercise became a mania in the 1970's . . .

Running and Exercise

May 7, 1978

Look out the window almost anytime these spring days and you're likely to see a man or a woman go jogging by. A recent Gallup poll estimated that 22 million Americans now suffer from running fever—a form of mania that brings its victims a sense of salvation, improved health and relief from everyday tension through daily runs on rural roadways, indoor tracks and even city sidewalks.

Step into any bookstore and you'll find shelves full of evidence that, more than any other sport, running is particularly fascinating to readers. Several weeks ago the B. Dalton bookstore chain listed two dozen books that are making their cash registers whirl. Their No. 1 best sellers, in both hardcover and paperback, are about running.

Front-runner among the hardcovers is James Fixx's *The Complete Book of Running.* Published by Random House last October, it's been on the best seller list for 24 weeks and has 455,000 copies in print. This bonanza is keeping the people at Random from "even thinking about" selling paperback rights.

For the reader who prefers the price and the feel of a softcover book, Avon's trade paperback *The Complete Runner* may well be the answer. Although published only three weeks ago, it's already on the best seller list. This is no volume hastily thrown together to cash in on the success of Mr. Fixx's book. It's a compendium of essays covering the full range of runners' concerns—from choosing the right footwear to transcendental running—written by some of the sports' most illustrious names, drawn from the pages of *Runner's World* magazine. It is—in the words of Erich Segal, himself a born-again runner— "a major source" of Mr. Fixx's book. It sold 90,000 hardcover copies since it was published three years ago by World Publications.

What in the world is World Publications? In the answer to that question lies part of the explanation for the present popularity of the running life. Back in 1962, when he was still in junior high school in Overland Park, Kansas, Bob Anderson caught the bug: "I don't know why—I just started running and loved it." In January 1966, as a high-school senior, he started a small offset magazine that he moved with him to California in 1970. Today, *Runner's World* is a thick slick monthly with a

250,000 circulation, the chief clearing house for information about the world in which runners dwell. World Publications, of which Mr. Anderson is the sole owner, is a main industry of Mountain View, a town across the bay from San Francisco, employing 125 people, publishing three magazines and 80 books.

"I like to think I'm partially responsible for running's current popularity," Mr. Anderson says. "But we were helped tremendously by the 1972 Olympics, when millions of Americans watched Frank Shorter win the marathon on television." The rage surfaced first in California, then raced eastward, helped along by Y's, camps and sporting-goods stores.

In the offing are half a dozen other books about running. Will these soon sate the public's appetite? Not very likely, one bookseller assures us. "The true believers come in and buy five or six books at a time!"

> The true believers kept buying books so fast and furiously that by the end of the year they had bought 297,000 paperback copies of *The Complete Runner*, 543,500 hardcover copies of James Fixx's *Complete Book of Running* (none of Fixx's books has appeared in paperback), as well as such paperbacks as Dr. George Sheehan's *Running and Being* (Warner; 230,000 copies) and Bob Glover and Jack Shepherd's *The Runner's Handbook: A Complete Guide for Men and Women on the Run* (Penguin; 175,000 copies).
>
> Meanwhile, another softcover book has entered the race for runners' favor, with a slightly different prescription to achieve physical fitness . . .

May 28, 1978

If you should happen by the Peachtree Street side of Atlanta's Hyatt Regency Hotel early any morning this weekend, you'll see an odd sight—a cluster of bookish types attending the annual convention of the American Booksellers Association, decked out in T-shirts and track shoes, getting ready for a "fun run." It's part of a celebration Bantam Books is staging for three of its paperbacks about running. They're all the work of Dr. Kenneth B. Cooper, a Texas physician, and, with a total of 5,341,000 copies in print, are among the biggest sellers on the house's backlist.

Dr. Cooper, 47, an Oklahoma-born Baptist, is the chief

apostle of "aerobics," a credo which holds that life can be prolonged by systematic exercise that stimulates the heart, lungs and blood vessels. To document and refine his belief he operates the Institute for Aerobics Research on an estate in a Dallas suburb.

Bantam's association with Dr. Cooper long antedates the nation's current running mania. Nearly a dozen years ago Herbert M. Katz, editor at M. Evans, a small New York hardcover house, brought Bantam editor Marc Jaffe a manuscript that seemed to be what both were looking for—an American counterpart to the then best-selling *Royal Canadian Air Force Exercise Plan for Physical Fitness.* At Mr. Katz's suggestion, *Aerobics* has been written by Dr. Cooper, who at the time was a member of the Air Force assigned to develop a physical fitness plan for United States astronauts. The Air Force hadn't given aerobics its official seal of approval but, even so, the program was already winning influential followers, including Wisconsin Senator William Proxmire. Evans and Bantam decided to publish the book simultaneously in hardcover and soft in April 1968.

Helped by the book's informal style and Dr. Cooper's evangelistic promotion, *Aerobics* immediately got off to a running start in the bookstores. It was unusual in that it took the guesswork out of exercising: it listed numbers by which a born-again reader could measure his efforts in activities requiring lots of oxygen—running, walking, cycling, swimming.

In time Dr. Cooper came to realize that his book had neglected the special needs of men over 30 and of women. He corrected this with *The New Aerobics* (1970) and, with his wife Mildred, *Aerobics for Women* (1977). In September Bantam will publish *The Aerobics Way*, which claims to "bring together all the information the reader needs to tailor the exercise program to his or her personal needs."

Meanwhile, Dr. Cooper continues his research and proselytizing. To confute the lingering official skepticism of the American Medical Association, his Institute continues to compile more evidence to support the validity of aerobics. To win over the nation's booksellers, Dr. Cooper will be on Peachtree Street tomorrow morning personally leading the seven o'clock run.

The "fun run" proved to be so popular with jogging book-men that Bantam staged it at succeeding conventions of the American Booksellers Association.

The running-book craze took a tragic, ironic turn in the summer of 1984, when James Fixx—whose *Complete Book of Running* led the pack—died while jogging on a vacation in Vermont at age 52. A few weeks later, Dr. Kenneth Cooper signed a contract with M. Evans and Bantam Books to write a book to be called *Running Without Risk: How to Prevent the Jim Fixx Syndrome.* By this time, Dr. Cooper's books, according to his publishers, had sold "almost 13 million copies in 24 languages."

The dawn of the '80's brought Americans an increased concern about getting ahead in business and social life—and a need for yet another variety of how-to book . . .

Looking Good

October 18, 1981

What "season" are you? A "summer," like Princess Grace and Candice Bergen? A "winter," like Elizabeth Taylor and Jacqueline Onassis? An "autumn," like Katharine Hepburn or a "spring" like Zsa Zsa Gabor? Your season is determined by the coloring of your skin, hair and eyes and therefore is an invaluable key to the way you can dress most effectively.

The notion that everyone has a color season was conceived by the German Bauhaus teacher Johannes Itten. Now it's been elaborated upon and turned into a flourishing American business enterprise by Carole Jackson, operator of a Washington, D.C.-based "color consulting service." Mrs. Jackson's *Color Me Beautiful,* a Ballantine paperback that offers its reader help in finding her seasonal color and through it clothes that will "make her look great and feel fabulous," has sold 350,000 copies in the past six months. This week it's on the trade paperback best seller list for the 22nd time.

Mrs. Jackson's book is being joined in the bookstores this fall by a covey of paperbacks that raise and answer questions about clothes and grooming:

 • Are you a fashion-conscious woman who "wants to create the look that's just right for you"? Priscilla Hecht Grumet's *How to Dress Well* (Cornerstone Library) describes itself as a "guidebook of do's and don'ts."

• Do you want to "look up to 35 pounds thinner without losing an ounce?" Dale Goday and Molly Cochran's *Dressing Thin* (Fireside) details some tricks to accomplish it.

• Want to "dress in good taste without camouflaging your sexuality, no matter what your age and figure type"? See Brigitte Nioche's *The Sensual Dresser* (Perigee).

• Want to dress to that you'll "make conversations stop and heads turn?" Barbara Burgdorf and Sue Nirenberg's *Dressing Sexy* (Fireside) offers tips about clothes and makeup.

The male of the species isn't being forgotten:

• Are you a man who'd like to know where to buy and how to wear "quality clothing and furnishings"? Take a look at Alan Flusser's *Making the Man* (Wallaby).

• Are you a woman who'd like to be able to enable the man in your life "to look and feel as terrific as you know he is"? Study Charles Hix's *How to Dress Your Man* (Crown).

The effects of inflation are being reckoned with:

• Are you a woman who'd like to "dress smashingly on a shoestring"? Judith Keith's *I Haven't a Thing to Wear!* (Avon) undertakes to tell how.

• Want to dress smashingly, economically and perhaps make your own clothes? See Judith H. McQuown and Odile Laugier's *The Fashion Survival Manual* (Everest House).

• Want to know how and where to outfit the whole family "with label-name clothing at budget prices?" Consult Vicki Audette's *Dress Better for Less* (Meadowbrook Press).

Most of these books, you'll notice, are addressed to women. And with good reason. Not only are 60 percent of the books in this country bought by women, but—according to a study made in 1978 by the Menswear Retailers of America—80 percent of all menswear sales are made to women, 40 percent to men accompanied by women.

Advice on dressing right and looking good have been the staff of life of fashion magazines and newspaper sections for decades, but it's a relative newcomer to the world of books. Some social commentators say its appearance there is a manifestation of the "me generation's" narcissistic, success-oriented spirit, the spirit that's making volumes about diets and money so popular.

The first two books about clothes ever to achieve bestsellerdom, the work of John T. Molloy, a clothing consultant to the executive corps of large corporations, were published in paperback by Warner Books only a half-dozen years ago. The *Dress for Success Book* has sold more than 1,300,000 copies since 1976, the *Women's Dress for Success Book*, 650,000 copies since 1978. Two other fashion books have also done uncommonly well: Charles Hix's 1978 male-oriented *Looking Good* (Wallaby, 100,000 copies) and Emily Cho and Linda Grover's 1979 volume for women, *Looking Terrific* (Ballantine, 150,000 copies). Their publishers report that all four books continue to sell briskly.

The growing acceptance of trade paperback books has greatly enhanced the popularity of fashion books. Their large-format permits the profuse use of illustrations and graphic designs that a writer on clothing and grooming needs to tell his story effectively.

In promoting and selling this season's new books, the publishers will be making use of every technique developed in recent years. In this they find their writers most helpful. For example, as a syndicated fashion writer, Charles Hix knows his way around the nation's fashion establishment. With a record of more than 3,000 lectures on grooming in her past, Judith Keith knows how to give a professional performance when she visits television stations. As a veteran menswear designer who is opening a network of boutiques to handle his own "collection," Alan Flusser will be selling his book as well as his line of clothes when he makes personal appearances in department stores. All this, in the patois of the retail trade, is "cross-merchandising."

In 1982, *Color Me Beautiful* was one of the year's biggest-selling trade paperbacks, with 814,000 copies in print. As the decade rolled on, innumerable other books offering tips about looking good as a way to $uccess in the business world kept things lively at the checkout counters of bookstores, books bearing such suggestive titles as *Looking, Working, Living Terrific 24 Hours a Day, Firm Skin in 15 Minutes a Day* and *How to Clear Up Your Face in 30 Days.*

There was, however, also a spate of books of a quite different character whose popularity boded new roles and importance for women in American society . . .

Feminism

June 28, 1981

Back in 1963, a suburban woman, who took time out from her housewifely chores to write articles for the mass-circulation women's magazines, published a book with a theme that none of her editors, all of them male, had allowed her to present in their pages. The theme: a great many of the young women who had hurried to get married when Johnny came marching home from World War II were disconsolate now about their roles as housebound wives and mothers. The author: Betty Friedan of Grandview, New York. The book: *The Feminine Mystique.*

During the next several years, Mrs. Friedan's book sold more than two million copies. Dell Books has kept it in print ever since and continues to sell 25,000 paperbound copies a year. But today the volume is interesting mostly as a historical artifact, for most of its suggestions have become accepted parts of American life as a result of the social revolution that it triggered.

Nowadays the changes that *The Feminine Mystique* helped bring about are evident everywhere that books are sold. The racks are crowded with titles like these:

* *Back to Business: A Woman's Guide to Reentering the Job Market* by Lucia Mouat (NAL/Signet).
* *Winning at Work: The Essential Self-Help Guide to Every Woman Who Works* by Dr. Florence Seaman and Ann Lorimer (Bantam).
* *The Two Paycheck Marriage* by Caroline Bird (Pocket).
* *The Entrepreneurial Woman* by Sandra Winston (Bantam).
* *The Landau Strategy: How Working Women Win Top Jobs* by Suzanne Landau (Playboy Paperbacks).
* *Networking: The Great New Way for Women to Get Ahead* by Mary-Scott Welch (Warner).

But these are just the tip of the iceberg, the latest, trendiest expressions of a far-reaching movement. Under "women" in the current edition of *Subject Guide to Books in Print* are listed more than 1,500 titles in such categories as "biography," "economic conditions," "health and hygiene," "history" and "psychology." Many of these provide a longer view, offer a scholarly perspective. Some books of this type that have just been published:

- *Eve's Rib* by Marietta Nowak (St. Martin's).
- *The Ways of My Grandmothers* by Beverly Hungry Wolf (Morrow).
- *The Ideas of the Woman's Suffrage Movement 1890–1920* by Aileen S. Kraditor (Norton).

Some of the most interesting publishing in the feminist field is being carried on by small houses:

- The Crossing Press of Trumansburg, New York, has a lively line of fiction and poetry by contemporary writers.
- Academy Chicago Ltd. of Chicago is republishing many long out-of-print novels by such writers as George Sand, Alexandra Kollontai, Winifred Holtby, Olive Schreiner and Sylvia Townsend Warner.
- The Dial Press, the large Manhattan house that is a sibling of Dell Books, which has done so well with *The Feminine Mystique*, is releasing in this country a series of "lost women's classics," produced by Virago, a small London feminist publishing enterprise.
- The Feminist Press of Old Westbury, New York, has had notable success with modern editions of Rebecca Harding Davis's 1861 *Life in the Iron Mills* (70,000 copies in print), Charlotte Perkins Gilman's 1892 *The Yellow Wall-Paper* (78,000 copies) and Agnes Smedley's 1929 *Daughter of the Earth* (50,000 copies).

Much of the market for these books has been generated by academia's interest in feminism. There are 350 women's studies programs being conducted at colleges and universities across the country and some 20 research centers. Their activities, as one publisher puts it, "keeps us all hopping." But not all the sales are to students for assigned reading. The Feminist Press proudly points out that, although most of its publications are designed for academic use, two-thirds of its sales are through bookstores that serve the general public.

One feminist book stood out from the crowd . . .

May 9, 1976

This week's success story is about a book that was not really written, but rather evolved. Even its begetters—young women, married, single, in-between—are a bit hazy about the details.

They recall that their consciousness was raised at a Boston women's conference back in 1969, a time when the feminist movement was percolating furiously. Some time after that some of them began conducting a course on "Women and Their Bodies" and assembled a mimeographed study guide to go with it. Later, calling themselves the Boston Women's Health Book Collective, a dozen of them issued a revision of the material in printed form. They are definite about what started happening in 1971, when Simon & Schuster took over their publication. In the next five years 850,000 copies of *Our Bodies, Ourselves* were sold.

Nor is the end in sight. A new, greatly revised and expanded edition released a month ago has 150,000 copies in print and this week appears on the trade paperback best seller list.

In its latest form, *Our Bodies, Ourselves* is a 383-page, profusely illustrated, large-format book, written and edited entirely for women, that combines encyclopedic facts with scraps of personal reminiscence about such matters as female physiology, sexuality, child bearing, abortion, menopause and lesbianism.

It's been hailed as "the most important book to come out of the Women's Movement," "the Dr. Spock for grownups"—and chided for "embracing the idea that biology is destiny."

Parenting

Dr. Spock? One of the landmark names in one of the major concerns of Americans in the mid-20th century, the rearing of children—or, as it came to be called, "parenting."

Dr. Spock and His Heirs

Dr. Benjamin McLane Spock (1903–   ) first became a mentor, indeed a guru, to millions of young parents in the late 1940's. These extracts from a review by Catherine Mackenzie, printed in *The New York Times Book Review* on July 14, 1946, suggest why:

THE COMMONSENSE BOOK OF BABY AND CHILD
CARE. By Benjamin Spock, M.D. Illustrated by Doro-

thea Fox. 527 pp. New York: Duell, Sloan & Pearce. $3. Pocket Books, Inc. 25 cents.

Dr. Spock's book touches on practically every question likely to occur to parents from the time they expect a baby until they begin to worry about his (or her) radio-listening, comic-reading and progress in school. Writing in the easy, informal vein characteristic of his platform talks, he hews to his line of reassurance.

"Trust yourself" is the sub-heading in his first chapter "Preparing for the Baby"; "You know more than you think you do" is its opening statement. "Don't take too seriously all that the neighbors say. Don't be overawed by what the experts say. Don't be afraid of your own common sense." And again, "Better to make a few natural mistakes from being natural than to do everything letter-perfect out of a feeling of worry."

[Dr. Spock's] directions range from formula-making, weaning, toilet-training, to a discussion of vitamins, allergies and innoculations. A section on illness includes hints on how to handle colds, croup and nose-bleeds, when to take a temperature, what to do until the doctor comes in case of illness or emergency.

"Enjoy your baby" is his counsel. "You'd think from all you hear about babies demanding attention that they come into the world determined to get their parents under their thumb by hook or crook. This is not true at all."

Sociologists might read the book for its reflection of present anxieties in our contemporary culture. Dr. Spock deals with queries on spoiling, spanking, tantrums, thumb-sucking, punishment; on whether or not to pick up a baby when he cries, on queries about children's manners, their fears, jealousies. "Don't take it too seriously," he says again and again.

Especially helpful and timely are sections on nursery schools, on separated parents, on adopting a child, and on mothers who work. Dr. Spock interprets the best in modern thinking on these subjects, and underscores it with his own wide experience, kindliness and good sense.

Although it was not publicly acknowledged at the time, Dr. Spock's book had been inspired by that pioneer paperback house, Pocket Books. In 1941, its editor Donald Porter Geddes proposed to Dr. Spock, then an up-and-coming Manhattan pediatrician, that he write a vade mecum for parents that would encompass all the latest ideas of the pediatric fraternity on the subject of child rearing. The most recent widely used book was Dr. John B. Watson's 1928 *Psychological Care of Infant and Child*, which directed parents, in a stern, authoritarian style, to adopt a rigid, authoritarian manner in dealing with their offspring.

Dr. Spock wrote the book during wartime service in the Navy and it was published in 1946, soon after his return to private practice. Pocket Books arranged with Duell, Sloan & Pearce, a small trade house, to publish a hardcover edition simultaneously with its own. For its edition, Pocket shortened the title to *Baby and Child Care*.

It could not have appeared at a more propitious moment. The post-World War II baby boom was just getting under way and literally millions of young Americans were looking for advice about raising their children. Ten years later, more than eight million copies had been sold and—as one journalist put it—"nowadays one out of every four American babies is being brought up by Spock-doting parents."

By 1956, however, the pendulum had begun to swing again. That year Dr. Spock revised his book to emphasize, as he put it, "the limits of permissiveness." This note of moderation did not keep many publicists from blaming him and his book for the spirit of protest and the counter-culture movements that flourished during the 60's among the baby-boom generation, now old enough to attend college and join communes. Their case appeared even more compelling when Dr. Spock became a leading figure in the movements against draft registration and the Vietnam War.

By the mid-'70's the Vietnam War was over, the baby boom had long since ended and . . .

The Children Come Back

December 25, 1977

The birth rate is way down and likely to plunge further. With that bit of received wisdom firm in our mind, we were surprised the other day to find on our desk seven new books:

- *A Child to Change Your Life* by Thomas D. Murray (Grosset & Dunlap).
- *Making Love During Pregnancy* by Elizabeth Bing and Libby Colman (Bantam).
- *A Guide to Pregnancy and Parenthood for Women on Their Own* by Patricia Ashdown-Sharp (Vintage).
- *The Child Before Birth* by Linda Ferrill Annis (Cornell University Press).
- *The Birth Primer* by Rebecca Rowe Parfitt (Running Press).
- *Giving Birth* by Sheila Kitzinger (Schocken).
- *The Home Birth Book* by Charlotte and Fred Ward (Doubleday/Dolphin).

We've talked with the editors of some of these books to discover why, in the face of received wisdom, they are publishing them. Some points they made:

- The number of childbirths isn't declining, just leveling off.
- Members of the generation born during the post-World War II baby boom are realizing that they've been missing one of life's great experiences and that they should do something about it before it's too late.
- As parents who are more mature and better educated than in the past, today's women and their partners are naturally turning to books for inspiration and guidance.
- There'll always be a need for good books benefiting from the latest scientific research.
- During the past five years, the editors have observed a demand for books offering a far franker discussion of sex and childbearing than in the past.
- Ideas that were part of the counterculture of the '60's are part of the mainstream now. These days, couples who are about to have children want to use or at least know about midwifery, delivery at home and other practices that were pioneered and have gained wide acceptance in Britain and northern Europe.
- The fact that it's now quite usual for mothers to work and not unusual for single women to raise families has created a set of problems little known in the past. There's need for books that offer them counsel.

The editors assure us that we'll be seeing many more books like these during the coming years.

The editors were quite right. During the next several years there were many more books on parenting, covering every aspect of the child-parent relationship. Some sold remarkably well:

- *Pregnancy and Childbirth* by Tracy Hotchner (Avon, 1980). 105,000 copies.
- *The First Three Years of Life* by Burton L. White (Avon, 1978). 209,000 copies.
- *Feed Your Kids Right* by Lendon H. Smith, M.D. (Delta, 1980). 255,000 copies.
- *The Second Whole Kids Catalog* by Peter Cardozo and Ted Mentzen (Bantam, 1977). 185,000 copies.
- *The Read Aloud Handbook* by Jim Trelease (Penguin, 1983). 365,000 copies.

By the way, what's happened to Dr. Spock's *Baby and Child Care*, the bible by which the baby-boom generation was raised? Pocket Books reports that it's continued to sell a fairly constant 450,000 copies a year. In 1985, 39 years and 30 million copies after its publication, in the midst of a new baby boomlet, "the largest selling paperback in U.S. history" appeared in a fourth revised edition with a new name joining Dr. Spock's on the title page. In his 83rd year, Dr. Spock had engaged as his collaborator and successor Dr. Michael B. Rothenberg, 58, a Seattle pediatrician and child psychiatrist, a former student who had raised his own family according to Spock. The new edition included many changes that took into account the latest techniques and family problems, but opened with the same words of counsel to parents as the 1946 original: "Trust yourself. You know more than you think you do."

In the midst of this baby-book boomlet, a small mom-and-pop publishing house started up to specialize in the field . . .

All in the Family

April 2, 1978

What do you do if you're a boy from Scarsdale, married to a girl from Mount Vernon, with two small children, living in a pleasant suburb of Minneapolis, when you're suddenly fired from your job with the Pillsbury Company? Well, if you're Bruce Lansky, you set up a business at home and with help from your wife, your children and the part-time services of ten housewives from the neighborhood, within three years become one of the most successful book publishers in the Midwest.

To accomplish a miracle like this, it helps to have a wife like Vicki Lansky. Mrs. Lansky's the sort of woman who, coping with the problem of feeding a pair of infants, bones up on the subject and then writes a bright, informative book about the mysteries of baby and toddler foods for the Childbirth Education Association of Minnesota. It was the immediate sellout of *Feed Me, I'm Yours* (2,000 copies) that led Bruce Lansky to try to place it with a New York publisher (50 said, "No thanks") and finally publish it himself under the name of the Meadowbrook Press. Copies to date: 350,000 spiral-bound paperbacks plus 430,000 mass-market reprints recently issued by Bantam.

Meanwhile, to keep the family and the neighbors busy, if you're Bruce Lansky you take on five other books, all dealing with parent-child relations in a high-spirited style.

Last month Meadowbrook published a book that promises to be its biggest success to date. As Vicki Lansky's children, Douglas and Dana, climbed out of the playpen and into Sesame Street and the Saturday morning cartoons, she became concerned about their growing passion for anything sweet or salty that's advertised on television. Her answer is *The Taming of the C.A.N.D.Y. Monster,* "a moderate, realistic answer to children's longing for 'Continuously Advertised, Nutritionally Deficient Yummies.'" Nearly 100,000 copies have been ordered to date and the large national bookstore chains, Waldenbooks and B. Dalton, report it as one of their current top sellers.

Meadowbrook's Pop acknowledges that Meadowbrook's Mom deserves much of the credit for Meadowbrook's success. In guest appearances on such national television shows as the Today Show and the Phil Donahue Show, Vicki Lansky is the vision of the bright, concerned parent—not an expert but just a nice woman eager to learn the facts and pass them on to other nice, concerned women. On the days when she's not out plugging her books, Vicky Lansky can be found in Meadowbrook's office, helping her neighbors to pack the books she wrote.

April 12, 1981

Every year, more than three million American couples are faced with a difficult problem: what shall we name the baby?

Several hundred thousand of them—mostly those who are parents for the first time—seek assistance from one of a dozen paperbacks bearing such titles as *What to Name Your Baby* and *How to Pick the Right Name for Your Baby*.

The dozen have much in common. Their prices hover around $2.75 and $2.95. All give the meanings and historical associations of from 2,500 to "more than 10,000" names. All are the works of little-known freelancers, with the exception of *What Shall We Name the Baby?* (Pocket Books), the labor of love of a leading Broadway producer, Winthrop Ames, who died in 1937. Biggest seller of all is *Name Your Baby* by the late Lareina Rule, which has an unusual feature—a section on the horoscopic significance of various names. Bantam has sold 1,830,000 copies of it since 1966.

During the past two years, these hardy perennials have had stiff competition from a book bearing a nervy title, *The Best Baby Name Book in the Whole Wide World*. This is the off-spring of Bruce and Vicki Lansky, whose Meadowbrook Press specializes in books about parenting and housekeeping. In the case of their baby-name book, as with Meadowbrook's other publications, Mr. Lansky makes a point of employing the latest, "most sophisticated" marketing techniques. It is sold in baby-supply stores as well as bookstores. It uses the large format of the trade paperback, with many illustrations and graphic effects. The names in his competitors' books have an old-fashioned air, Mr. Lansky says, for they haven't been updated for years. He employs a research firm to make sure that every new trend in baby names is duly noted. As a result, his book now sells some 18,000 copies a month, nearly as many as Bantam's.

And what are today's most popular names for babies? For girls, Jennifer, Kristin, Amanda and Sara. For boys, Matthew, Christopher, Jason and David. What about Mary and Robert? They don't even make the top 20!

Remarkable Books

Every era has a number of books that, because of their special qualities and publishing history, stand out from the crowd. Among those in the 1970's and early '80's were eight . . .

Jonathan Livingston Seagull

July 23, 1972

To many outsiders, the publishing business seems as chancy as horse racing. Insiders know better. As astute observers of the trade have remarked, there are seven simple rules that, if conscientiously applied, are almost certain to induce a best seller. As a public service, we share them with readers.

1. Start with a writer already well known to the general public for his ability to entertain, instruct or shock. The great majority of novels on any best seller list are works by authors of previous best sellers.

Consider, for example, the case of Richard Bach. This mid-thirtyish native of suburban Chicago, onetime Air Force captain and latterday barnstorming pilot, was supporting himself in a way by editing and writing for flying fan magazines. He had published three books, the most successful of which, *Stranger to the Ground,* the reflections of a fighter pilot on a flight from England to France, sold a grand total of 17,000 copies.

2. Have him tell a story that enables the reader to (a) see how a glamorous industry or profession operates on the inside; (b) feel imperiled by unseen forces; or (c) live a raunchy life vicariously.

One foggy evening back in 1959, depressed by the fact that his writing was barely paying his rent, Mr. Bach took a stroll along a canal embankment in Belmont Shores, California, when he heard a crystal clear voice chant in his ear three words: "Jonathan Livingston Seagull." He rushed back to his lonely writer's room and, a man inspired, typed some 3,000 words. These told of a seagull who grew discontented with the life lived by the other birds of his flock, dreary creatures who flew merely to pick up scraps of food dropped from garbage scows. One day this seagull, whose name was Jonathan, soared up and away, determined to perfect his flying ability. Unable to think of a way to end his fable, Mr. Bach put it away.

Nine years and several editorial jobs later, Mr. Bach woke up early one morning in Ottumwa, Iowa. That crystal clear voice was dictating the next chapter. In perfecting his flying at high speeds, Jonathan had turned into a bird of another feather. By reaching for the impossible beyond the boundaries of time and space, he became a kind of divine teacher of other birds.

After a couple of tries, Mr. Bach placed the story with *Private Pilot Magazine,* for an honorarium of $200. So many fan letters flew into the editor's office that Mr. Bach obliged with two more installments. *Jonathan Livingston Seagull* was reprinted by other magazines here and abroad with thanks but no fee. Mr. Bach then asked his agent, Don Gold, if he could find a publisher willing to bring it out as a book.

3. *A work of fiction must run at least 50,000 words—preferably much longer—for book buyers demand a long, good read for their money. Short stories, even collections of short stories, never sell well in book form.*

All told, the saga of Jonathan Livingston Seagull ran less than 10,000 words. Mr. Gold decided to circumvent this obstacle by submitting it to juvenile-book editors. Short tales about animals, if profusely illustrated, are popular with children. One reply: "The personification of the seagull represents a grave problem. Jonathan's lucid analysis of a falcon's wing seems to suggest that birds really can analyze the physics of flight. There is no evidence that this can be true. Have you ever thought of doing a factual book for children that explains how birds fly?"

Two years passed. Then, in the summer of 1969, Eleanor Friede, senior editor at Macmillan and an amateur pilot herself, happened to have lunch with a friend of Mr. Bach. Mention of his name reminded her how much she had enjoyed *Stranger to the Ground.* She promptly launched a prescient letter off to Ottumwa: "I have a very special feeling about the subjects you write about that makes me think you could do a work of fiction that would somehow speak for the next few decades." Within a week tearsheets of *Jonathan Livingston Seagull* arrived in her office.

The text made Mrs. Friede's heart and imagination soar, but the stiff, scientifically accurate sketches sent along to illustrate it left her uneasy. Perhaps photographs would serve better. Mr. Bach, on a flying trip to New York, solved the problem readily. A friend and fellow flying nut, a professional photographer named Russell Munson, just happened to have in his files a thousand pictures of seagulls he had taken on a grant.

In a memo proposing the book's publication to the Macmillan management, Mrs. Friede projected more visions: "While the story has special appeal to pilots and seamen, its theme is a universal one, suggesting that through perseverance, ability and love of learning each of us can touch perfection every day of his life and in lives to come. I think it has a chance of growing into a long-lasting standard book for readers of all ages."

The Macmillan management was indulgent. A book of 93 pages, 40 of them text, the rest of them Mr. Munson's photographs, priced at $4.95, would pay for itself if 7,500 copies could be sold. But on their rounds of bookstores to take orders, the company's salesmen ran into apathy. "Wait until you see the finished copies!" they urged. "It's a beautifully designed book and the pictures are lovely." "Pictures!" said the booksellers. "It must be a children's book." On publication day, August 31, 1970, fewer than 3,000 copies had been ordered, most of them in California and the Midwest.

4. Before publication, have the book, or parts of it, published in a large-circulation magazine. Secure its adoption by one or more book clubs. This creates great expectations among book buyers.

No large-circulation magazine was interested, not even *Reader's Digest*, which had published articles by Mr. Bach and for which, it seemed to Mrs. Friede, Jonathan's inspirational overtones seemed especially appropriate. No book clubs were interested, not even the Book-of-the-Month Club, for which Mrs. Friede once worked as an editorial reader.

5. Advertise the book vigorously and prevail upon influential reviewers to give it major attention.

At publication time, Macmillan placed a small ad in *Publishers Weekly* and *The New York Times Book Review*. Mrs. Friede addressed personal appeals to old editor friends on magazines and newspapers. *P.W.'s* reviewer loved the pictures but found the prose "a mite too icky poo for comfort." Not a magazine or newspaper—including the *Book Review*—so much as mentioned it. The only reviews were in flying fan journals.

6. Arrange for the author's appearance on television talk shows.

Not a single television showman was interested in having Mr. Bach as a guest. "What kind of a guy would write a book like that, anyway? He must be too—well, shall we say too *sensitive* a type!" What would we talk about? I can't picture myself carrying on a very exciting half-hour conversation about seagulls!"

Once in the stores, *Jonathan Livingston Seagull* took flight, slowly at first, then ever higher and faster. The first printing was sold out by the end of the Christmas season, largely to flying fans. It made a fine remembrance for a friend for whom a card was not enough, a television set too much. The friends started coming into the stores for several copies for their friends. Enthusiasts of a great variety of persuasions — Christian Scientists, Yoga devotees, Buddhists, practitioners of Zen, existentialists, theosophists, followers of Karl Barth, Platonists, Christians who professed to find it an allegory of Jesus's life.

Booksellers, still believing that a story about a bird couldn't be fiction, didn't know where to place it in their stores. Some put it under Nature, some under Religion, some under Photography, some under Children's Books, some with the paperbacks, even though its covers were hard. "Put it next to the cash register," Mrs. Friede advised.

During 1971 there were eight more printings, for a total of 140,000 copies. But it was not until the spring of 1972 that the trade and press began to realize what an extraordinary phenomenon it had on its hands. Macmillan began to run large ads. A short interview with Mr. Bach in the daily *New York Times* led to a two-page picture spread in *Life* magazine. Publishers in half a dozen countries bought rights. A West Coast film maker who read the book in his barber's chair rushed to the telephone to buy film rights in a deal that gives Mr. Bach half the profits and collaboration in the production. A television showwoman in Pittsburgh ventured to book Mr. Bach on her show, found that the tall, rangy, mustachioed flier had the makings of a show-biz personality and has invited him to return again and again. A Chicago talkcaster had the same experience. A West Coast FM station that drew a record mail when the story was read on one of its programs, now styles itself "The Jonathan Livingston Seagull Station." The Book-of-the-Month Club offered the book as a dividend in April, 1972. *Reader's Digest* condensed it the next month. At the annual convention of the American Booksellers Association held at Washington in June, Mr. Bach attracted the most clamorous lines of any of the authors present to autograph their works.

Booksellers, resolving their doubts as to whether Jonathan is fiction, nonfiction or really a book at all, began to report it to the compilers of best seller lists. Its popularity in all parts of the country was demonstrated by its debut on the *Times* list on

April 30. Three weeks ago, 96 weeks after its publication day, with 440,000 copies in 14 printings, *Jonathan Livingston Seagull* finally alighted on the highest rung of the fiction list.

Now, let's see. Have we forgotten anything? Oh, yes . . .

7. *If neither the author nor his plot has proven ingredients for bestsellerdom, be certain that the book contains some special quality that will strike a responsive chord in the yearnings and aspirations of millions of people.*

The end of Jonathan's tale is not in sight. Even now the deep thinkers of the land are scanning Mr. Bach's misty, poetic prose and its parable "of one little seagull's search for freedom, his striving to attain perfection." They'll soon have figured out what all this reveals of the predicament of Western man in the afternoon of the 20th century.

All the pundits have not yet filed their reports, but the sales figures of *Jonathan Livingston Seagull* are in. By the end of 1972, 2,355,000 hardcover copies had been sold. Avon's paperback edition, issued the next year, accounted for 6,700,000 more copies.

The Whole Earth Catalog

June 5, 1977

With a dozen prominent writers analyzing and in some cases lamenting "the style of the 1970's" in this issue of the *New York Times Book Review*, it occurred to us that it might be a good idea to ask a number of bookpeople how they think that spirit is manifesting itself through the softcover book. Some of the most interesting comments came from the trade paperback buyers for two chains that together have more than 700 stores across the country: Tom Simon of Waldenbooks and John Schulz of B. Dalton Bookseller.

This is scarcely surprising, for today's trade paperback is a creature of the '70's. Back in the '50's and '60's, the trade paperback was a small subspecies of book, an academically oriented volume intended largely for campus reading. Today it is addressed to the great public and is the particular favorite of a whole generation, from teenagers to the under-30 set. It represents the fastest growing branch of U.S. book publishing.

In a sense, Mr. Simon and Mr. Schulz suggest, the new style trade paperback was born during 1968 in a converted warehouse in Menlo Park, a suburb of San Francisco. In this unlikely place Stewart Brand, 31, beneficiary of an Eastman Kodak legacy, alumnus of Stanford and the Band of Merry Pranksters that Ken Kesey led during Haight-Ashbury's early days, opened a counter-culturalish emporium called the Truck Stop Store. To promote its sales, Mr. Brand, with the aid of six ex-hippies, got together a thick pamphlet called *The Whole Earth Catalog.* On its large, eccentrically designed pages were offered services and advice, tools and techniques to anyone seeking escape "from the oppressions of post-industrial society" without resorting to "the Revolution" for which the hippies were crying so loudly.

The Whole Earth Catalog was an overnight success. The first 2,000 copies went so fast that Mr. Brand followed it with three more issues, each thicker than the last. To distribute it to the book trade, he turned first to a Berkeley firm, then to New York's Random House. The latter made it a best seller. The sixth issue, called *The Last Whole Earth Catalog,* sold 900,000 copies and was honored with one of the Literary Publishing Establishment's prized garlands, a National Book Award. "In 100 years," one of the NBA's judges predicted, "this probably will be the only book of 1971 to be remembered."

It certainly has not been forgotten. In many editions and under various names, Mr. Brand's "whole earth catalogs" have sold 2,100,000 copies and netted him more than $1,500,000, with which he has set up a foundation to further causes close to his heart.

Dozens of other publishers have hurried out with more books in the same style. There have been catalogues covering everything from bedrooms to children's games to Judaica.

The spirit of *The Whole Earth Catalog* lives on in other ways:

• It helped the off-sized, often profusely illustrated paperback gain wide acceptance.

• It led Americans to regard a book not only as an object to be read and then stored away, but as a tool to be used.

• It has helped bring many once off-beat subjects into the mainstream of U.S. life: ecology, interpersonal relationships, women's consciousness, to name a few.

• Its example encouraged the founding of a number of successful small publishing houses, often located far from Manhattan. At its recent convention, the Association of American Publishers reported 50 new members.

January 16, 1980

The times keep a-changing—as Stewart Brand, at age 41, realizes full well. Tomorrow he's releasing, through Random House, 150,000 copies of *The Next Whole Earth Catalog*. The new volume is even heftier than its predecessors: 608 14½-by-11-inch pages, weighing five pounds, two ounces. Of the 3,000 items listed, only 350 are carry-overs from the past, and even the evaluations have been completely rewritten to accord with what Mr. Brand considers the spirit of the '80's. "Today's whole-earth people are less concerned about countering culture than in surviving," he says. "The new catalogue pays less or no attention to such matters as "black interest," "China," "new foods" and "dope," much more to solar energy, computers, medical selfcare and—most important—political activism."

The Next Whole Earth Catalog was produced by Mr. Brand and a score of young men and women, working a 70-hour week for five months, out of a onetime luncheonette near the Sausalito waterfront of San Francisco Bay. He hopes that his changing concept of the whole earth will prove so popular that he'll have to issue a complete revision annually.

The times kept a-changing, but not in quite the way Stewart Brand had anticipated. Nearly 275,000 copies were sold of *The Next Whole Earth Catalog*, but only some 75,000 of a revision issued in 1981. However, the giant Manhattan house of Doubleday perceived enough popular interest in just one of the fields it treated—computers—to agree to pay him $1,300,000 to prepare a *Whole Earth Software Catalog*. The first edition of this paperback guide to the electronic marketplace—software, hardware, magazines, books, etc.—employing the fact-packed, anecdotal style that characterized Mr. Brand's earlier efforts, was published late in 1984.

Foxfire

December 18, 1977

Eleven years ago, when Eliot Wigginton, fresh out of Cornell, took a job teaching ninth- and tenth-grade English at Rabun Gap-Nacoochee School, deep in the mountains of northern Georgia, he was confronted with two problems common to teachers in these restless times: how to maintain a modicum of order in the classroom and how then to wipe the glaze from his students' eyes. The solution he contrived has since given him a niche in pedagogical and publishing history.

Mr. Wigginton's idea was that the students go out and interview the oldsters of the surrounding areas—many of them their own kinfolk—about the traditions, crafts and culture of their native Appalachia. What they brought back in notebooks, on tape and on film they would then write up and publish in a magazine of their own.

Foxfire magazine—the name comes from a phosphorescent glow to be seen in Appalachian forests—has accomplished far more than Mr. Wigginton hoped. It has induced the children not only to read, write and respect English, but to learn about and respect their past. With the aid of Government and private grants, it has become the keystone of a nonprofit enterprise that has charted, through video tapes and records, new paths in the teaching and the collection of folklore. Nowadays, Mr. Wigginton, still deep in the enterprise, is referred to by his students as "Wig."

The Foxfire idea might never have gotten out of the Appalachians if a college fraternity brother of Wig, who worked at Doubleday, hadn't received a copy of the magazine and seen possibilities.

Results: in March 1972 Doubleday published *The Foxfire Book*, a collection of pieces from the magazine. *Foxfire 2*, containing more of the same, followed in 1973, *Foxfire 3* in 1975. Last month came *Foxfire 4*, a volume dealing with "fiddle-making, spring houses, horse trading, sassafras tea, berry buckets, gardening and further affairs of plain living." Total sales of Foxfire books to date: 3,491,000 sales distributed evenly across the United States.

Wig himself is more interested in the influence of his experiment than in sales totals. As far as Foxfire country itself is concerned, he believes the popularity of the books has accomplished three things. It's encouraged the young people of the region to take a greater interest in writing—more and more of those who go away to college are enrolling in journalism and English courses. It has made its youth anxious to stay in or return to Appalachia, a reversal of the trends of the past. And it has increased the respect youth feels for the oldsters who brought them their heritage.

During the next five years, five more Foxfire books were published, with sales totalling well over half a million copies.

The Joy of Sex

January 7, 1979

The book that's been on the best seller lists longer than any other in American publishing history is about to pass another milestone. Five years ago this week, a how-to book that had already placed on the hardcover best seller lists 60 times, made its debut in soft covers. It's been a paperback best seller ever since. Its author: Alexander Comfort, M.B., B.Ch., M.A., D.C.H., Ph.D., D.Sc. Its title: *The Joy of Sex: A Cordon Bleu Guide to Lovemaking.*

That may seem an odd topic for a man whose career has been centered in medical practice and administration, but during his 58 years the British-born physician has often wandered down curious bypaths. Alex Comfort has published more than 40 volumes—not only medical textbooks and sociological studies, but novels, plays and poetry—and was a featured performer on BBC's cultural program Horizons.

Some ten years ago, when Dr. Comfort was in charge of a medical research group on the biology of aging at University College, London, he and his wife began making notes on their erotic relationship. His intention was to write a textbook on the ethology of human sexual behavior. At the time, an old publishing friend, James Mitchell, was about to launch a book packaging firm that would specialize in profusely illustrated, large-format books. He persuaded Dr. Comfort to turn his textbook into a form that everyone could read—and use.

The fruit of their labors was a dummy which Mitchell Beazley, Mr. Mitchell's firm, displayed to publishers from all over the world at the 1971 Frankfurt Book Fair. It consisted of short recipes for sexual encounters written by Dr. Comfort, illustrated with softly sketched drawings by a team of artists. (The photographs originally intended to serve as illustrations had been scrapped as "too harsh.") The publishers looked, fascinated, and turned away.

Undaunted, Mr. Mitchell soon after came to New York to show his dummy along Publishers Row. At Crown Publishers, one of the houses that had said no at Frankfurt, he received a qualified reception. Crown would take the book if some of the "strong stuff" were toned down. Mr. Mitchell and Dr. Comfort agreed.

When Crown's salesmen showed the dummy to American booksellers the next year, the reception was even more qualified. The first printing was only 15,000 copies. There were no reviews and little promotion. But book buyers began grabbing up copies so avidly that tens of thousands of copies had to be air-lifted from the printer in Holland to satisfy the Christmas trade. It became a regular on the *New York Times* best seller list between December 1972 and May 1974. To date it has sold one million hardcover copies.

This was only the beginning for Dr. Comfort's *Joy*. About the time Crown had its first copies ready, it routinely sold paperback reprint rights to Pocket Books, one of the leading mass-market paperback houses. But Simon & Schuster, Pocket's owner, felt that the effectiveness of the book's pictorial presentation would be lost if it were reduced to small rack size. With Crown's permission, it published 750,000 softcover copies in a large format on January 14, 1973. *The Joy of Sex* has been a trade paperback best seller continuously ever since, with a total of 3,927,000 copies in print. A 1975 sequel, *More Joy of Sex*, has sold 763,000 copies in paperback, a boxed set of the two 240,000 more. They are as openly displayed and eagerly grabbed up in the Bible Belt as in San Francisco.

What explains this phenomenon? Dr. Comfort, now a fellow of the Institute of Higher Studies in Santa Barbara, California, tells us he thinks there are two reasons. One was the timing—the book both accorded with and contributed to the revolution in sexual mores of the '70's. The other was the illustrated format, very much in the spirit of these times.

The Joy of Sex dropped off the paperback best seller list in October 1982, ending a nine-year run with total sales exceeding five million copies.

What Color Is Your Parachute?

August 13, 1978

The formula is simple: write a book jammed with information that many people are interested in. Xerox and bind 2,000 copies of your typed manuscript. Send sample copies to persons influential in the field it deals with. Place a few ads offering it for sale by mail. You're on your way to bestsellerdom.

Once in a blue moon it works. It's worked notably well for Richard Nelson Bolles, 51, a native of Teaneck, New Jersey, an Episcopal clergyman who moved to California in the mid-'60's. Half a dozen years later, at a time when most of "the established churches" were feeling a severe financial strain, he felt lucky to be working with students on San Francisco Bay area campuses for the United Ministries in Higher Education, an alliance of Protestant faiths. In his spare time, with the help of friends, he wrote a book designed to help the nation's many unemployed clergymen find new careers. In 1970 he published it himself according to the time-honored formula.

Then a series of minor miracles befell Mr. Bolles. He began receiving orders not only from churches, but from schools, colleges, corporations, the whole career-counseling and personnel establishment. They had found his book's advice and information as useful for laymen as the laity, for young people still in school as for midlife career-changers. They had learned about it through that most effective of promotion devices—word of mouth.

Among those who heard about it was Phil Wood, head of Ten Speed Press, an enterprising young publisher in Berkeley. In 1972, Mr. Bolles, tired of wrapping and mailing his own books, yielded to Mr. Wood's importunities and let Ten Speed publish the book in the conventional way. Since then, *What Color Is Your Parachute? A Practical Manual for Job-Hunters & Career-Changers* has sold nearly 800,000 copies, half by mail, half through bookstores.

The book is as winningly idiosyncratic as its title. In a style that blends the wisdom of the ages with the jargon of the '70's, illustrated with old prints and larded with self-discovery games for readers to play, it provides down-to-earth facts ("The best man doesn't usually get the job") and up-to-date lists of books and organizations worth consulting.

Ten Speed has just published what Mr. Bolles considers his second magnum opus—*The Three Boxes of Life and How to Get Out of Them*. It extends the techniques of *Parachute* to planning for life's three phases—education, work, retirement. (His advice about retirement: don't.) Mr. Bolles says he'd have finished it much sooner if he hadn't been shaken by the tragic death of a brother to whom he was most attached. Don Bolles was the *Arizona Republic* reporter who was murdered two years ago for discovering too much about the Arizona underworld.

What Color Is Your Parachute?, though born in the 1970's, turned out to be very much atune to the career-oriented early 1980's as well. Richard Nelson Bolles revised it annually to report changing conditions and Ten Speed Press sold between 250,000 and 300,000 copies of each edition.

The Teachings of Don Juan

September 21, 1975

It began, as many publishers' success stories do, with a quandary. The manuscript, by a Ph.D. candidate, was brought to the University of California Press by the author's academic mentor. Its significance as a scholarly contribution was attested to by a dozen leading anthropologists. Yet the style in which it was written was so much like fiction, its lack of conventional scholarly apparatus so conspicuous, the university pressmen wondered whether it belonged on their list. After much soul-searching, they ventured a 2,000-copy first printing in June 1968.

Word about *The Teachings of Don Juan*—this account of what Carlos Castaneda had learned about the karma of sorcery and peyote during an extended apprenticeship to a Mexican shaman—raced across the country on the anthropologists' grapevine. A review in the daily *New York Times* caught the eye of a Ballantine editor, who lost no time in arranging for a mass-market paperback edition. Within a year, Don Juan was the rage of the hippie underground. In academic circles debates raged as to whether the whole thing was fact or fantasy.

Certainly Don Juan has turned out to be no flash in the desert sun. Since becoming his principal publisher four years ago, Simon & Schuster has brought out three sequels in both hard and soft covers: *A Separate Reality, Journey to Ixtlan* and *Tales of Power*. With each volume, sales have mounted. *Tales of Power*, with 230,000 copies sold, was one of 1974–75's biggest hardcover best sellers. This week S&S is releasing a boxed set of the quartet in trade paperback format.

Now that there are upwards of four million copies of his

work in print in all publishers' editions, what of the sorcerer's apprentice, Dr. Castaneda? At 49, this native of Peru who worked his way through UCLA doing odd jobs, still lives in Los Angeles, frequently turns up to do research at UCLA's library, occasionally participates in meetings on "ethnomethodology." Those who know him describe him as small and swarthy, an irrepressible wit and storyteller. But few know him well: he's a very private person, a man in a Brooks Brothers suit, armored against the world.

January 11, 1981

Richard de Mille of Montecito, California, is a man with a mission. A former university psychology teacher, Mr. de Mille is determined to discover the truth about the life and works of Carlos Castaneda, whose five books— *The Teachings of Don Juan, A Separate Reality, Journey to Ixtlan, Tales of Power* and *The Second Ring of Power*— profess to report the author's conversations during an 18-year apprenticeship with a Mexican Indian named Don Juan Matus. These collections of "anthropological fieldnotes" have sold over ten million copies in this country and are among the most influential testaments of the youth culture of the past dozen years.

It bothers Mr. de Mille that these books, which Joyce Carol Oates and a number of other literary critics have said "read like fiction," have been taken so seriously by poets, scientists, philosophers, religious leaders and the press. It concerns him that one of them won Mr. Castaneda a Ph.D. in anthropology from UCLA and another was published as a work of serious scholarship by the University of California Press before the series was taken over by New York publishing houses, most recently Simon & Schuster and Pocket Books.

Mr. de Mille is convinced that Mr. Castaneda is "one of the great intellectual hoaxers" of all time. He has never succeeded in meeting the man face to face— Mr. Castaneda lives invisibly somewhere in the Los Angeles area— but during the past five years he has stalked his prey's persona in libraries. What he has discovered is presented in two books issued by two well-regarded Santa Barbara publishers: *Castaneda's Journey* (Capra Press) and *The Don Juan Papers* (Ross-Erikson).

The latter, a volume as eccentrically organized as Mr. Castaneda's "fieldnotes" and as intellectually stimulating, contains 44 essays by Mr. de Mille and 30 other scholars, detailed notes and a bibliography. Among its findings:

• Although Carlos Castaneda has said he was born in Brazil in 1935, according to immigration records, he was born Carlos Arana in a Peruvian mountain town 55 years ago. After emigrating to the United States in 1951, he held a variety of odd jobs and served a brief stint as a teacher while studying anthropology at UCLA. At one time he took a course in "creative writing." Pen sketches based on rare photographs illustrate Mr. de Mille's biographical essays.

• There is no evidence that a person named Don Juan Matus ever existed.

• The "sources" of some 200 passages in the Don Juan books are identified in detail by Mr. de Mille. These make it clear, he says, that Mr. Castaneda borrowed liberally from scientific and literary writers all over the world.

• Mr. Castaneda may be a "trickster-hoaxer," but he must be taken seriously as one of the important intellectual forces of our time. The ideas he has borrowed and popularized reflect the evolution of youth culture in recent years—first, a fascination with hallucinogenic drugs, later with Indian sorcery and mythology, then with witchcraft and metaphysics, and most recently with feminism.

While Mr. de Mille continues to stalk the man he regards as a "great trickster-teacher," Mr. Castaneda continues to write. His sixth book, *The Eagle's Gift,* will be issued by Simon & Schuster this spring. In it, according to the publisher, "as the inheritor of Don Juan's powers and tasks, Castaneda takes the reader into the very heart of sorcery, challenging both imagination and reason, shaking the very foundations of our belief in what is 'natural' and 'logical.' " After it has had its expected run on the hardcover best seller list, Pocket Books will bring out a softcover edition.

Last month, while Pocket Books was holding its seasonal sales conference at a hotel in San Diego, Mr. Castaneda unexpectedly drove up in a van, shared dinner and several hours of conversation with all the sales reps present, then disappeared into the night without permitting a single photograph to be taken.

Carlos Castaneda has never replied to Richard de Mille's charges, but he continues to please his loyal following with further accounts of magic and sorcery purportedly observed in remote Mexico. *The Eagle's Gift*, which sold 169,000 copies in hardcover, was followed by yet another best seller, *The Fire From Within*, in 1984.

A Confederacy of Dunces

March 22, 1981

The novelist Walker Percy was sitting in his office at Loyola University in New Orleans one day in 1976 when a 74-year-old woman, using a walker, hobbled in, followed by a chauffeur carrying a tattered manuscript. She said she was Thelma Ducoing Toole, a widowed retired schoolteacher, and that the manuscript, a novel by her deceased son, was "a masterpiece." She asked Mr. Percy's help in finding a publisher, something she had been unable to do despite years of persistent effort.

To get rid of her, Mr. Percy agreed to take a look at it, confident that he would have to read only four or five pages before returning it. At the end of five pages, he found that he couldn't stop. He found it "a fantastic novel, a major achievement, a huge comic-satiric-tragic one-of-a-kind rendering of life in New Orleans."

Mr. Percy set out to find a publisher. His own publisher rejected it on the grounds that a first novel without an author alive to help promote it had little chance in today's marketplace. Louisiana State University Press, about to embark on a publishing program of "worthy noncommercial fiction," was more hospitable. It agreed to bring it out, scheduling a first printing of just 2,500 copies.

A Confederacy of Dunces tells a story of a character who is not unlike its author John Kennedy Toole. Its hero, Ignatius J. Reilly, is a tubby medievalist who gets into a series of scrapes, some of them involving his oddball mother, in New Orleans' seedy neighborhoods. Toole wrote it in 1963, while serving a hitch in the Army. He made several ineffectual attempts to get it published before committing suicide in 1969 at the age of 32.

On its publication just a year ago, *A Confederacy of Dunces* was received with chortles of delight by literary critics. Some

typical expressions: "One of the funniest books ever written."
. . . "You laugh out loud until your sides ache." . . . "A masterpiece of comedy character." It is one of the nominees for the PEN-Faulkner Award for fiction.

Equally exuberant has been its commercial reception. To date, L.S.U. Press has sold 38,000 hardcover copies. The Book-of-the-Month Club made it an "alternate selection." Twentieth Century-Fox has bought film rights. And Grove Press reports that large orders are coming in for the 500,000-copy first printing of the paperback edition it will bring out next month.

How did a small house like Grove get a book that most of the major mass-market firms acknowledge they'd love to be reprinting? A Grove editor just happened to see a proof of the book before it was sent to the large houses and grabbed up the rights for $2,000.

Does L.S.U. Press now regret letting the book go for such a modest sum? L. E. Phillabaum, its director, tells us that he does not. "If it sells well in paperback—and we're confident that it will," he told us, "we'll get handsome royalties from it in due course. In the meantime, we haven't induced a paperback house to tie up a large sum in it for a long period, to the detriment of other worthy novels that lack large commercial potentialities."

April 26, 1981

Nobody was more surprised and pleased by the selection of *A Confederacy of Dunces* as the 1981 Pulitzer Prize fiction winner than the folks at Grove Press. They've been fervently fond of Toole's novel ever since they bought the reprint rights and sent hardcover copies to their wholesalers just as soon as they came off the press in the hope of spreading the faith. They had hoped that the novel would win a prize or two, but the Pulitzer Prize was beyond their dreams. They're already working on a second printing. Total to date: 545,000 copies.

Where's the Rest of Me?

July 12, 1981

During the past fortnight, more than five months after Ronald Reagan's inauguration, Dell Books has been slipping into the mass-market racks 100,000 copies of the only book ever written by the 40th President. *Where's the Rest of Me?* in collaboration with Richard G. Hubler, is considered by many political writers to be the best source of information about the first 54 years of Mr. Reagan's life. How it came to be written and what's happened to it since make a curious footnote to the ways of book publishing and its relations with politics.

In *Where's the Rest of Me?* (the title is borrowed from a line uttered by Mr. Reagan in the movie *King's Row*), the President tells in a chatty, anecdotal style about growing up in an Illinois small town; playing football at a small Midwestern coeducational college; serving as a sports announcer for a Des Moines, Iowa, radio station; acting in films and television for 30 years, often playing the role of the nice guy who doesn't get the girl; marrying twice, once infelicitously, once most happily; heading the Screen Actors Guild during a tumultous time; switching from liberal Democrat to conservative Republican. In an appendix, he crisply sets forth his views on such matters as taxation, housing, welfare, youth and foreign aid.

When *Where's the Rest of Me?* was first published in the spring of 1965 by Duell, Sloan & Pearce, a small, highly-regarded New York house owned by the Meredith Publishing Company of Des Moines, the reviews were so-so. The consensus was that it would be of interest largely to film buffs, to historians interested in its account of "Communist efforts to take over the film industry in the 1940's" and to political game-watchers curious about a man who obviously had ambitions to become a leader of the conservative wing of the Republican party. It was remarked that Mr. Reagan omitted all mention of his campaign on behalf of Helen Gahagan Douglas in her 1950 Senatorial race against Representative Richard M. Nixon.

In the next four years, during which Mr. Reagan served as Governor of California, *Where's the Rest of Me?* sold out four additional printings, largely in the author's home state. But when Meredith disposed of its Duell, Sloan & Pearce imprint in 1970, the book was allowed to go out of print.

Last fall, as the Presidential campaign warmed up, it occurred to the folks at Elsevier-Dutton, present owners of the Duell, Sloan & Pearce backlist, that *Where's the Rest of Me?* deserved a new life in paperback. There was only mild interest in the Manhattan headquarters of the mass-market houses. The fortunes of political leaders can change overnight, it was said, and so can the market for books about them. True, four years before, when Jimmy Carter was being elected, several publishers rushed out books by and about the Georgia liberal Democrat. But a California conservative Republican—that was something else again.

Dell, the only house to show real enthusiasm for the book, bought reprint rights for what buyer and seller describe as "a more than respectable sum." Then Dell approached Nancy and Ronald Reagan with the suggestion that they might like to update the book. They did not. So the book appears exactly as it was when first published 16 years ago, except that on the cover the legend "Ronald Reagan Tells His Own Story" is printed in much larger type than the title.

And what of Richard G. Hubler, who wrote the book with Ronald Reagan? We tracked down the veteran freelancer at his home in Ojai, California, not too far from the Reagan ranch. He had learned only two days before that *Where's the Rest of Me?* is being paperbacked and had not yet seen a copy.

He recalled that the idea for the book had been sparked by a group of "California native sons" who were urging Mr. Reagan to run for office. Duell, Sloan & Pearce had brought it to him because he had published a number of books with them, some of them collaborations with celebrities. He accepted the assignment on a 50-50 royalty sharing basis.

For two months in late 1964 he put in long days at the Reagan ranch taking notes in longhand. "Reagan's very fluent," he told us. "I didn't have to do much prompting or ask many questions. When I finished the manuscript, he went over it with a fine tooth comb, cutting out parts he had second thoughts about."

Mr. Hubler added that he hasn't talked with Mr. Reagan in ten years. Nor has he reread the book. With 30 books to his credit, he doesn't dare look back. Now he's at work on his 14th novel.

Richard G. Hubler died shortly after we talked with him, but his collaboration lives on, an indispensable source book for anyone curious about the first 54 years of the 40th President.

The Instant Book

Once upon a time, well before World War II, the world of books was an unhurried place, rarely concerned with subjects of fleeting interest. Authors conceived and wrote books at their leisure. After they delivered their manuscripts to their editor, at least six months—usually many more—passed before the finished books reached the stores.

Many things helped quicken the pace of that world, but none more dramatically than the Paperback Revolution. Since its birth, the modern paperback has had a close affinity to magazine publishing. As a result, since the 1960's, most of the significant trends and fads have been reflected in—and often nurtured by—best-selling softcovered books.

Nowhere has the publishing industry's concern with matters of the moment been more evident than in a genre called, variously, "the extra," "the fast book" or "the instant book."

On the afternoon of Friday, April 13, 1945, a time when U.S. soldiers were within 50 miles of Berlin, the Russian army was engaged in fierce battles east of the German capital and the Nazi Minister of Propaganda Joseph Paul Goebbels acknowledged that "the war can't last much longer," President Franklin D. Roosevelt died of a cerebral hemorrhage at Warm Springs, Georgia.

To Donald Porter Geddes, editor-in-chief of Pocket Books, a five-year-old firm that was prospering by publishing 25-cent papercovered reprints, the death of the only American elected to four Presidential terms seemed a challenge and an opportunity. Assisted by three students lent by the Columbia School of Journalism, by Professor Henry Steele Commager of Columbia University, Robert Van Gelder of *The New York Times Book Review* and William Rose Benet of *The Saturday Review of Literature*, and using the resources of the Columbia Broadcasting System, Geddes spent a long weekend gathering and editing the text—biography, tributes, poetry, photographs—for a book to be called *Franklin Delano Roosevelt: A Memorial*.

By Monday morning Geddes had all his copy at the Clinton, Massachusetts, plant of the Colonial Press. The printer had rearranged his schedules for the occasion and during the following week produced 340,000 copies of a 249-page paperbound book. Nine days after Roosevelt's death, it was on sale in New York at 25 cents a copy. Along Publishers Row it was said that "literally millions of copies" could have been sold if paper had been available, but paper was hard to come by because of wartime rationing. A few months later, several other publishers that had paper issued editions in hardcover.

All this was, as the "People Who Read and Write" column in *The New York Times Book Review* observed, an extraordinary event, "not merely for the book's excellence as a record and a tribute, but for the speed with which it was assembled and distributed. Nothing like it has ever been done before; now publishers are wondering if it hasn't ushered in a new and significant chapter in bookmaking."

Geddes and Pocket Books repeated the feat only four months later. On August 10, four days after the U.S. Air Force dropped an atomic bomb on the Japanese city of Hiroshima, a staff was assembled to produce a second "fast book": *The Atomic Age Opens.* An account of the research that had made the event possible was prepared under the direction of Gerald Wendt, science adviser for Time-Life, Inc. The War Department's lengthy statement, selections from the press services and the radio networks, and President Harry S. Truman's speech announcing the event were assembled and edited.

Four days later the complete 75,000-word manuscript was at the printing plant in Chicago. On April 17, 250,000 copies were being shipped to every part of the country. The press hailed the book as "a most useful summary of what had been taking place behind a thick curtain of secrecy and of the recent announcements about the bombing."

Once America returned to peacetime normalcy and a score of new mass-market paperback houses sprang up on Publishers Row to compete for readers' favor, the pioneering exploits of Donald Porter Geddes and Pocket Books were almost forgotten.

The game of fast-book making resumed, suddenly and spectacularly, in September 1964, when copies of the eagerly awaited *Report of the Warren Commission on the Assassination of President Kennedy* was put into the racks within a week of its release by two houses, Bantam Books and Popular Library. Of the two, Bantam's achievement was the more remarkable. Its 500,000-copy edition was rounded out with appraisals written by two *New York Times* correspondents and edited by three *Times*men holed up in a Washington hotel, proofread and indexed at a Chicago printing plant, and put on sale in Washington within 80 hours.

During the next 15 years other houses joined in the game. New American Library issued volumes on the 1965 night when New York City's lights went out and on the 1967 Arab-Israeli war; Ballantine offered several, including one on the 1969 Apollo moon landings; Dell one on the Watergate affair.

Bantam, however, remained the leader, with more than 60 "extras," as it termed them, covering a wide range of topics, including Pope Paul VI's visit to America in 1965, the moon landings, the Pentagon Papers and Richard M. Nixon's resignation from the Presidency.

Most successful of all, as far as sales were concerned, was one about the Israeli commando raid that freed 102 skyjacked hostages in Uganda in the summer of 1976. For this, Bantam commissioned William Stevenson, the Canadian author of a bestselling book about espionage, *A Man Called Intrepid,* and Uri Dan, military correspondent of Israel's largest newspaper, to collaborate on a hot-off-the-presses account. The two men settled into a Tel Aviv Hilton Hotel room and, a little more than a fortnight after the raid, trucks from Bantam's Chicago printing plant were carrying copies of *Ninety Minutes to Entebbe* to stores across America. In all, 1,100,000 copies were sold.

Two years later, Bantam found it had competition in covering an equally dramatic episode . . .

December 10, 1978

When an extraordinary event shakes the Western world, the residents of Publishers Row don't react merely with wonder or horror as do you and I. If they're paperbounders—especially if they've worked for Bantam Books—they're apt to get out an "extra" telling "the full story" within a fortnight. Consider the cases of Judy Hilsinger, a former Bantam staffer in Manhattan who now runs her own publicity firm in San Francisco, and Victor Temkin and Rena Wolner, who not long ago moved from Bantam to Berkley Books.

Three weeks ago, in San Francisco, Miss Hilsinger spent a most disturbing Saturday night. Arriving at a party at a friend's house, she watched as Mrs. Ron Javers, wife of a *San Francisco Chronicle* reporter, left for the airport under armed guard. Mrs. Javers was bound for Puerto Rico to join her husband, recuperating in a hospital from wounds he had suffered while accompanying Representative Leo J. Ryan on his visit to the Peoples Temple colony in the South American republic of Guyana.

Within the next few hours Miss Hilsinger heard many more frightening things about the way the Rev. Jim Jones's sect had harrassed California's press and intimidated its politicians before it moved to the jungle of Guyana. In the wee hours of Sunday she telephoned a Bantam editor in New York, proposing a book about the still unfolding horror that was to end in the ambushed death of the congressman and four others and the mass murder-suicide of 911 members of the cult. She then air-freighted a bundle of news stories, many of them written by Mr. Javers and Marshall Kilduff for *The San Francisco Chronicle.*

On Monday Bantam began moving fast, following its long-practiced routine. By phone Marc Jaffe, Bantam's president, arranged with the *Chronicle's* management to set up a team of 20 to assist Mr. Javers and Mr. Kilduff. Mr. Javers tape-recorded his contributions in his hospital bed. A Bantam editor flew west to oversee the work. As quickly as it was completed, the manuscript was flown to Nashville to be typeset, the type was flown to Chicago to be printed, finished books were flown to principal distribution centers. Thanks to a round-the-clock effort, maintained even on Thanksgiving Day, some 350,000 copies of Bantam's *The Suicide Cult: The Untold Story of the Peoples Temple Sect and the Massacre in Guyana* were in racks across the nation early this past week.

Meanwhile, at Berkley Books . . .

Berkley is a small paperback house that has never caused much of a storm during its 25 years. Things began to change there last year when Victor Temkin, who spent 11 years at Bantam, became its president. They took an even more tempestuous turn on the Monday Bantam was arranging to publish its book on Guyana. On that day Rena Wolner, who had worked with Mr. Temkin at Bantam, moved to Berkley as the house's new publisher. Later the same day Esther Newberg of the ICM literary agency came to them with a proposal for an instant book about the Peoples Temple cult and massacre prepared under the direction of *The Washington Post.* Its byliners: Charles A. Krause, who had been in Guyana with Congressman Ryan, and Larry Stern, the *Post's* assistant managing editor.

It was an offer that the two former Bantamites couldn't refuse. While Berkley made production and distribution arrangements in New York during the week that followed, a *Post* staff of 20 worked around the clock in a suite in the Madison Hotel, across the street from the *Post's* offices in Washington. Just about the time the *Chronicle's* team was getting its manuscript off to Nashville, the *Post's* crew was sending its copy off to a printing plant in Dallas, Pennsylvania. Last week some 400,000 copies of Berkley's *Guayana Massacre: The Eyewitness Account* were being stuffed into the racks.

Who won the race—Bantam or Berkley, *The San Francisco Chronicle* or *The Washington Post?* We'll report on that just as soon as the public has had a chance to decide.

December 24, 1978

It's scarcely five weeks since that ghoulish drama unfolded in the Guyanan jungle, but it's not too soon to appraise the performance of publishers who rushed instant books into the paperback racks, for it's a publishing truism that a book written, edited, printed and distributed with the speed of a newsmagazine has a life only slightly longer.

Thanks to the expertise that paperbounders have acquired in producing quickie books, 650,000 copies of Bantam's *The Suicide Cult* and 500,000 copies of Berkley's *Guyana Massacre* were on sale in New York and Washington bookstores on the morning of November 30, 12 days after the last of the events they chronicled. Thanks to airfreight, they reached the remotest part of the country by the official publication date, December 4.

There was also a third, little-heralded challenger: *Hold Hands and Die,* issued by Dale Books, one of the new, lively Lilliputians of paperback publishing. Sixty thousand copies reached its newsdealer outlets, most of them in the upper Middle West, about the same time as the Bantam and Berkley titles did.

Bantam's entry is particularly strong on the California background of the Peoples Temple sect, as befits the work of two staff correspondents of *The San Francisco Chronicle.*

The strength of Berkley's entry is the "I-was-there" reportage of *The Washington Post's* Charles A. Krause, who acknowledges that he had never heard of the Rev. Jim Jones and his cult "until a few days before the holocaust."

Dale's entry is the work of John Maguire and Mary Lee Dunn, a husband-and-wife team from Springfield, Massachusetts, where Miss Dunn is feature editor of *The Springfield Union.* They had access to wire-service copy and are adept at the journalistic rewrite.

How did the books fare in the marketplace? "They didn't jump off the racks," as one paperbounder put it. They did surprisingly well in rural areas, out of reach of the big-city newspapers with their exhaustive coverage. In each case the publisher made a profit and says he enjoyed the feeling that he was there when history was in the making.

Just a year later, a religious man of another stripe claimed the headlines as the leader of the movement that led to the ousting of the Shah of Iran . . .

February 10, 1980

What is the Ayatollah Ruhollah Khomeini's legacy to Iran and the Islamic world? Two new paperbacks offer answers in his own words:

• *Sayings of the Ayatollah Khomeini* (Bantam) is a selection of provocative passages from three books published during the Imam's 16 years' exile, maxims and mandates ranging from governmental matters ("Islamic government is a government of divine right, and its laws cannot be changed, modified or contested. . . . If a competent man, combining in himself supreme virtues, appears and founds a true Islamic government, it is the people's absolute duty to follow him") to personal hygiene ("One should wash one's head and the back of the neck, then the right side of the body, followed by the left side. . . . If this precise order is not followed, whether deliberately or out of ignorance, the ablutions are not valid").

• *Islamic Government* (Manor), described on its cover as "Ayatollah Khomeini's Mein Kampf," is the full, leaden text of a series of lectures he delivered ten years ago. Some notable passages: "Missionaries [of Christians and Jews], who are the lackeys of colonialism, have spread throughout the country, and have aimed their efforts at children, juveniles and youths and have misled them. . . . If we attain power, we should not be content with improving the economy and ruling justly among the people, but must make these traitors taste the worst torture for what they have done."

How did these two books get from the Imam's prayer rug to America's mass-market racks? Both are enterprises of book-men who became concerned with the Ayatollah three months ago, when his name was becoming a household word in the West.

Paul Tobey, son of Dell Publishing Company's president Carl W. Tobey, and in his own right publisher of a Philadelphia-based magazine called *House Plants & Gardens*, discovered that xeroxed copies of a C.I.A. translation of the Ayatollah's lectures on Islamic government were to be had from a satellite organization of the intelligence agency in Arlington, Virginia. He approached five publishers with the proposal that they issue the collection as a paperback quickie. All showed interest at first, then backed away, expressing fear that the national rage against the Imam would lead to protest demonstrations within their organizations. Finally he got Manor Books, one of the Lilliputians of Publishers Row, to take on the project. Early last month, 175,000 copies of *Islamic Government* were on their way to the stores.

Tony Hendra, a freelance writer and editor whose projects include the current best seller *The 80's: A Look Back*, a satirical remembrance of things to come, learned from a television news show that a "little green book" made up of morsels from the Ayatollah's published works had become a best seller in France. He convinced the editors at Bantam, one of Publishers Row's giants, that they ought to lose no time in publishing it here. Rights were acquired from the French publishers, the text was checked against the Persian original, and last week 140,000 copies were being stuffed in the racks across America.

Such ventures are risky, for the Ayatollah's health is precarious, the future of Iran uncertain and quickie books seldom become multi-million-copy best sellers. But, Mr. Tobey says, both books deserve publication for they can help Americans judge for themselves what prospects the Islamic world holds for them.

Americans' curiosity about the Ayatollah's beliefs was quickly satisfied. Both books were soon allowed to go out of print.

July 27, 1980

The current word along Publishers Row is that, although instant books are a lot of fun to get out, they're not very rewarding at the cash register.

Now, from out of the West, comes an instant book that is making its tiny publisher a lot of money. A few weeks ago Madrona Publishers was a mom-and-pop enterprise run by Daniel and Sarah Levant, Easterners who'd lost their hearts to the Pacific Northwest, out of a brick warehouse overlooking the Farmers' Market in Seattle, Washington. During the past five years the Levants and their staff have published 40 books, many of them with a regional touch.

Then, last March, 100 miles to the south, a series of tremors gradually developed into a geophysical catastrophe. Mount St. Helens, a 9,677-foot peak off the interstate highway connecting Seattle with Portland, began erupting ash at a volume that placed it among the eight most active volcanos in recorded history. Reporters and photographers from two nearby Washington state newspapers—the *Longview Daily News* and the *Bellevue Journal-American*—rushed to cover the blow-up and its effects on the people in the neighborhood. Sam A. Angeloff, former editor at *Life, People* and *Us,* who is now on the staff of the *Longview Daily News,* suggested to Mr. Levant that they all join hands and produce an instant book.

Volcano: The Eruption of Mount St. Helens, a large-format paperback, was rushed through Seattle's largest printing plant in nine days. To look at it, you'd never suspect that it was a quickie. The paper is excellent, the color illustrations handsome and the text, placing the event in historic context, is professional. To date, it's sold 170,000 copies in bookstores across the country.

One publisher saw the election of 1980 as the occasion for an instant book . . .

November 23, 1980

Scarcely two years ago, Victor Temkin and other executives of Berkley Books shuttled down to the nation's capital to toast Laurence M. Stern and other members of *The Washington Post* for their roles in producing, in ten days, an "instant book" about the Guyana massacre. As cocktail conversations in Washington usually do, the talk turned to politics. Would Teddy run in 1980? Could Jimmy be reelected? Who would the Republicans put up?

As soon as the Berkleymen got back to Manhattan, they started making plans for a book that would report and appraise the 1980 election, to be published a few days after the event. A dozen *Post* political writers, including David S. Broder and Haynes Johnson, would write it as the campaign progressed, under Larry Stern's direction.

A couple of hitches developed. Larry Stern died unexpectedly and his responsibilities were assumed by Richard Harwood, the *Post*'s deputy managing editor. ("I had some doubts about the project," Mr. Harwood acknowledges, "but I felt I owed it to Larry's memory. A really great guy.") As the spirit of the campaign ebbed and flowed, changes were made in the working title—from *We, the People* to *None of the Above* to *The Pursuit of the Presidency 1980*.

Between last April and Election Day, more than three-quarters of the 125,000-word manuscript was written and set into type—surveys of the demography of contemporary America, the roles played by the media and industry, the state of the parties; accounts of "the scramble of the primaries"; profiles of "the ordinary men" who were candidates. Once the final returns were in, Mr. Harwood settled down at his "magic lantern"—as *Post*men call the computer terminals that have replaced typewriters in most newspaper offices—and for three days pounded out the final chapter of his long survey of "the race."

Five days after Ronald Reagan's election, 225,000 copies of *The Pursuit of the Presidency 1980* began rolling off the presses in Dallas, Pennsylvania. Late last week, first copies of the $3.95 paperback, 416 pages plus a 16-page photo insert, went on sale in bookstores in Washington and New York. Next week, they'll be showing up at stores across the country. "It may become one of the historical documents of our time," says Mr. Temkin. "An on-the-scene, at-the-moment view of the event by a team of accomplished reporters." "Despite my first misgivings," says Mr. Harwood, "I think it's turned out all right."

Rages and Crazes

The young people of every generation are entranced by idols and activities that a few years later seem quaint or flaky. During the 1970's and the early '80's they exhibited their enthusiasm for such passing fads and fancies by purchasing millions of copies of paperbacks about them.

Elvis Presley and Pop Music

September 4, 1977

It was late in the afternoon of an August dog day when the word reached Manhattan. The King of Rock-and-Roll had died in Memphis, Tennesee, at the age of 42. Naturally, the news stirred up a great storm in Recordland, where 500 million Elvis Presley albums and singles had been sold during the preceding 20 years. Along Publishers Row things were calmer. No book about the Memphis Myth had ever reached the national best seller lists. Only four books about him—all paperbacks—were in print, and their sales were far from phenomenal. But by the next morning the whirlwind had reached the four publishers' offices.

• Warner Books five years ago issued a softcover reprint of Simon & Schuster's *Elvis: A Biography* by Rolling Stone editor Jerry Hopkins. A "star story" strictly for the fans, it narrates the singer's life competently—heavy on details, short on interpretation. Its sales averaged 125,000 copies a year, but Warner, seeing no great future for it, had allowed its stock to dwindle to 6,000 copies. The morning after the news came from Memphis, the publisher's telephone started ringing constantly, with orders from all over the country, especially from the South and West. During the next business week, orders for the book—which hasn't a word to say about Elvis's career after

1971—averaged 120,000 copies a day and the presses had to run around the clock to fill them.

• Grosset & Dunlap just a year ago published *The Illustrated Elvis,* a large-format paperback remarkable only for its 400 photographs obtained through the cooperation of the Elvis Presley Appreciation Society, a British fan club. ("Presley's management refuses to cooperate 'as a matter of policy' in 'any literary endeavour'," a note of acknowledgment explained.) The book had earlier been published in England, where the Memphis Legend has a huge following. At the time of Elvis' death, G & D had sold nearly 40,000 copies; within the next week it had to order a print run of 500,000 more to satisfy the demands of variety stores and bookstore chains.

• Pocket Books last October published *Elvis and the Colonel,* a gossipy reconstruction by journalist May Mann of Presley's life based on interviews with people who remembered him when. The publisher routinely disposed of 110,000 copies and had pretty much forgotten about it until reorders started rolling in on the frantic morning after. Pocket quickly ordered a new printing of 500,000 copies, added Molly Ivins' *New York Times* obituary and retitled it *The Private Elvis.*

• Ballantine Books just a month ago published *Elvis: What Happened?,* an account of Presley's life, with emphasis on "the dark late years" told by three former bodyguards and longtime friends, Red West, Sonny West and Dave Hebler. It is a product of Rupert Murdoch's World News Organization, a specialist in "inside stories," which offered the paperback rights to Ballantine to tie in with serialization in Mr. Murdoch's *National Star, New York Post* and *San Antonio Light.* From 300 hours of taped interviews with the three former bodyguards, one of Mr. Murdoch's star reporters, Australian Steve Dunleavy pieced together an often confusing, almost constantly startling picture of Elvis as a slave to uppers and downers, a womanizer, an insatiable buyer of automobiles, airplanes and firearms, a man who revered his mother's memory and the old-time religion but frequently indulged in spasms of selfishness and violence.

Ballantine's initial print order was a cautious 400,000 copies. By happenstance a few hours before Elvis' death, Hollywood gossip Rona Barrett gave the book a plug on the Good Morning America television show. Orders started pouring in—

3,500,000 in a single week, two million of them from the K·Mart variety store chain, the largest single order in paperback history. Ron Busch, Ballantine's president, stopped the print orders from going higher, for paperbacks are fully returnable.

Will the 5,100,000 books ordered in a single week sate the public's passion for Elvis? Stay tuned . . .

August 16, 1981
Four years ago this afternoon, an event in Memphis, Tennessee rocked America as it has never been rocked before. As one historian of pop culture has observed, no entertainer alive or dead—not Rudolph Valentino or Marilyn Monroe, not the Beatles and the Rolling Stones lumped together—has generated and maintained such a following over two decades as did Elvis Presley.

Presley's death has had a comparable effect on Publishers Row. To satisfy public demand, the four publishers who had books about him in print—they were all paperbacks—sent out 8,875,000 copies within the following few weeks.

Still more remarkable, Elvis's legend continues to bloom within book covers. The four titles are still in print and have been joined by 33 other paperbacks and ten hardcover books from 38 publishers—gossipy reminiscences by friends, albums of pictures and posters, data about his music and films, quiz books, even biographies for young children. The attention paid him far exceeds that accorded other youth heroes of the period, including the Beatles.

Nor is the end in sight. Avon Books has just paid $1 million for reprint rights to *Elvis,* described as a "warts-and-all biography" by the rock music historian Albert Goldman, which McGraw-Hill will bring out in hardcover this fall. Avon's edition will appear late in 1982.

Albert Goldman's biography turned out to be something of a disappointment for both the publishers and Elvis Presley's fans. McGraw-Hill's edition appeared on the best seller list for 14 weeks (134,000 copies sold) and Avon's only four weeks (1,015,000 copies in print). Perhaps the fans were put off by the stance Mr. Goldman assumed: a critic steeped in old-world traditions condescendingly discussing a late-20th century, very American subject.

September 13, 1981

Not long ago, the world of music and the world of books were light-years apart. Most music and record stores refused to stock books about even the most stellar performers because they could use their floor space more profitably by displaying merchandise on which the markups are high—guitars and other instruments, sheet music and record albums. Many booksellers, accustomed to catering to the genteel "carriage trade," were reluctant to carry books that would attract the sometimes obstreperous youngsters who lived by rock and roll. The few books published about pop music sold poorly.

The times began to change in the late '70's. More and more bookstores adopted the open supermarket style and began displaying large numbers of paperbacks. The rock generation grew older, more sedate, affluent enough to indulge in nostalgia. In the summer of 1977, four publishers, much to their surprise, disposed of 8,750,000 copies of mass-market paperbacks about Elvis Presley within a few weeks of his death. In 1979, three trade paperbacks about rock luminaries were best sellers: *Up and Down With the Rolling Stones* by Tony Sanchez, *The Bee-Gees: An Authorized Biography* by David Leaf, and *Born to Run: The Bruce Springsteen Story* by David Marsh.

Publishers Row has finally gotten the message. This fall 15 houses are bringing out books about rock, its stars, lore and trivia. The favorite subjects: the Beatles (3 books), David Bowie (three), Elvis Presley (two), the Rolling Stones (two).

Publishers of books about rock music have a means of promoting their wares not available to other genres—the hundreds of radio stations whose disk jockeys are eager to discuss books about the stars and popular groups while playing their records.

Cats

August 10, 1975

Are you an ailurophile? (To save you a trip to your classical dictionary, that's a cat-lover.) If you are, have we got a book for you! It's a small, oblong paperback named, very succinctly, *Cat.* In 152 line drawings B. Kliban, who's a *Playboy* cartoonist when he's not watching his pets, discloses the fantasy life not only of cat-lovers but of cats themselves. The sketches defy description, but the one reproduced here will give you an idea.

Workman Publishing Company, a small New York house, published *Cat* very quietly five months ago and to date it's sold, without any promotion, 65,000 copies—enough to make it a candidate for the trade paperback best seller list. Sales are especially strong in college and with-it bookstores. At the Harvard Coop one browser spotted a poster advertising the book—"CAT One hell of a nice animal, frequently mistaken for meatloaf"—and mused audibly, "Let's see, was it G. B. Shaw or Bertrand Russell maybe?"

Here at the *Book Review* office we tested it on the staff. The non-cat-lovers studied the pictures in stony silence. The ailurophiles broke up. Rate it four long, loud purrs.

December 2, 1979

For centuries, mankind regarded the dog as his best friend, extolling its virtues in countless stories and pictures. Then, in March 1975, something curious happened. Workman released an album of drawings that lured so many ailurophiles out of the closet and into the bookstores that it is now one of the biggest all-time trade paperback best sellers, with 717,000 copies in print.

If B. Kliban, (he pronounces it "Klee-ban") the begetter of the sketches, has become something of a guru, he has traveled a roundabout route to accomplish it. He is a Connecticut boy who tarried in Manhattan just long enough to study at Pratt and Cooper Union. Twenty years ago he took a cross-country motorcycle trip to California and liked what he found there so much that he never went back. Now in his mid-40's, he lives in Marin County.

For a long time he supported himself largely by work for *Playboy* magazine, and it was a *Playboy* editor who started him on the road to his new role. While Michelle Urry was visiting his studio he showed her the dozens of sketches his four cats had inspired him to make when he was not busy with an assignment. Miss Urry liked them so much that she found him an agent. The portfolio that became *Cat* was turned down by many editors ("Personally I love them, but I don't think they'd go as a book") until it found a happy home at Workman.

Mr. Kliban's cats are now a multimillion-dollar industry. They're to be found padding across more than 50 products, including posters, greeting cards, T-shirts, tote bags, aprons, throw pillows, note pads, autograph books, photograph albums, address books, scrapbooks, sheets, bedspreads and one of the largest-selling calendars (400,000 copies in 1978).

Those four cats that inspired Mr. Kliban to crosshatch the felines in the paperback that not only stirred the passion of ailurophiles across the land but inspired a flood of other books about felines—did they live happily ever after? Alas, not completely. One "just disappeared" from Mr. Kliban's home, he told a *Rolling Stone* magazine reporter the other day. One died of "feline leukemia." His ex-wife got custody of the other two. "I hope they're okay. I get very sentimental about pets. That's why I don't want another one."

February 15, 1981

According to the *Guinness Book of World Records*, the United States now has a cat population of 23 million—a statistic that suggests feline fanciers are one of this country's fastest growing minorities. The rage has been accompanied by a rapidly lengthening shelf of books—200 at last count—that deal with the lovely, lovable, often vexingly independent creatures. Some are designed to provide information, others merely to amuse. Three of the latter sort, collections of cartoons, have brought their authors overnight fame and fortune.

If any one book can be said to have triggered the current craze, it's B. Kliban's *Cat*, which has made its author the owner of a $50-million industry, so comfortably fixed that he says he'll never produce a sequel. Mr. Kliban's *Catcalendar* was this year's No. 1-selling calendar and his drawings of cats now adorn scores of products from bath towels to beer mugs. He swears he'll never produce another cat album.

The feline furor was intensified by the appearance in 1978

of a daily comic strip depicting the antics of a fat, pasta-loving cat named Garfield. This is the creation of a 35-year-old Muncie, Indiana, man who hasn't a cat to his name. James Robert Davis, who signs his work "Jim Davis," served an apprenticeship as assistant to the cartoonist of the "Tumbleweeds" strip before sensing that there was a bounding future in cat lore. A paperback collection of the strips, published just a year ago by Ballantine Books as *Garfield at Large* has sold 440,000 copies. The fat cat now appears regularly in more than 400 newspapers and is fast spawning its own brood of commercial spin-offs.

That other minority of Americans who dearly hate cats are getting their fair turn too—through *The Official I Hate Cats Book* (Holt). Published last September, this collection of cartoons showing the little beasts receiving their comeupance from outraged humans now has 200,000 copies in print. It's the work of Skip Morrow, 28, whose formal name is Dennis Morrow. Until recently Mr. Morrow eked out a living doing guitar gigs in New England's off-ski-slope bars. A year ago, he walked into Holt's New York offices with a portfolio of his sketches and got a warm welcome. At home in Wilmington, Vermont, he maintains a tentative relationship with a cat recently given him by a friend.

September 12, 1982

Today there are four cartoon books about Garfield the gluttonous cat on the best seller list. If that isn't enough to satisfy you, cheer up—more cat books are on the way. Two of the comers are also by Jim Davis: *Garfield Takes the Cake* in black-and-white cartoons and *The Garfield Treasury*, cartoons in color.

How do you look at cats? As objects for punning humor? There's *Purrplexities: A Book That Gives You Paws* by Don Grant. As objects for tender loving care? There's *The Good Cat Book* by Mordecai Siegal. As subjects for paper dolls to be cut out and dressed up? See *Cat's Closet* by Patty Brown and Jay David. As subjects for a pop-up book? Open up *Cat's Up! Purring Pop-ups* by Ray Marshall and Korky Paul. You're "into" astrology? There's *Cat Sun Signs* by Vivian Buchan. You're sentimental? See *Pritt: The True Story of a Deaf Cat and Her Fam-*

ily by Susan E. Moon and Susie Tracy. In all, 18 books from 12 publishers.

> Americans' appetite for books about cats became sated during 1983, but they made an exception in the case of the ravenous Garfield. By the end of that year, Jim Davis had published 11 albums with total sales close to seven million copies. During 1984 more Garfield albums continued to occupy high rungs on the best seller list. Mr. Davis hazarded an explanation for this phenomenon: "Garfield has antihero qualities that people find appealing in an animal." The folks at Ballantine Books thought it equally significant that the cartoons appealed to both cat lovers and cat haters.

May 30, 1982

By the bye, what about *Old Possum's Book of Practical Cats*, the 1939 collection of verse by T. S. Eliot that served as the inspiration for the current London musical hit *Cats*, which is headed for New York's Broadway?

Four times during his long and distinguished career, the American-born English poet-critic T. S. Eliot (1888–1965) tried his hand at writing for the theater—with results that intrigued literary critics, but created no sensations at the box office. But, ironically, in 1939, soon after finishing *The Idea of a Christian Society*, Eliot quietly published a slender volume of nonsense poems that serves as the libretto for *Cats*.

As a tie-in to the show, Harcourt Brace Jovanovich has just issued a new edition of the book. The felines of Mr. Eliot's 15 verses have nothing in common with those that dwell in children's books or, perish the thought, cartoon books. They are, as Delmore Schwartz put it back in 1939, "practical cats, cats engaged in getting something purposeful done or undone," and they owe much to the inspiration of Edward Lear. Edward Gorey, who a few years ago illustrated the works of Lear, provides 32 drawings.

Preppies

August 30, 1981

Just a year ago, at a small publishing house on the edge of Manhattan's Garment District, a quartet of talented young people and the publisher's staff of experienced editors, graphics designers and promotion people were joining hands and working long hours to produce a book about a style of life that they believed would shortly be very "in." The creative quartet: two men and two women, recent graduates of Brown, Princeton and Columbia. The publishers: Workman Publishing Company, which had turned out a number of best sellers in its ten years' existence. The book: *The Official Preppy Handbook*.

In 160 pages, the *Preppy Handbook* charts and illustrates, in somewhat tongue-in-cheek fashion, the proper behavior for anyone who'd like to look, act and feel as if his forebears had always been part of the Eastern Establishment from silver spoon to obituary in *The Times*. Along the way it offers counsel on how to bear up under a legacy of good taste and breeding, how to get into a good school and how to get out, how to dress and behave with members of the opposite sex, what games to play and where to "waterhole," what to do at a reunion.

The *Preppy Handbook* has far exceeded its begetters' highest hopes. Since its publication last November, it has sold more than one million copies, doing well everywhere except on the West Coast. It's been on the best seller list for 39 weeks, 17 of them in the No. 1 spot. It has generated good sales for a number of "preppy" products, including a book bag, a stationery kit, an apron, a tote bag and a desk diary that notes such historical milestones as February 17, 1951, the day J. D. Salinger delivered the manuscript of *The Catcher in the Rye* to Little, Brown.

What explains this outbreak of oldstyle manners? One of the four authors, Lisa Birnbach (Brown, '78), puts it this way: "In this time of jittery economics, shifting values and uncertain self-identities, it's nice to feel you belong to something enduring, secure, top-drawer, outstanding—like the world of preparatory schools that date back to the mid-18th century."

Rubik's Cube

June 21, 1981

The sketches below depict an innocent-looking toy that is currently causing millions of Americans to go quietly crazy. "Rubik's Cube," as it's called, is a 2⅛-inch-by-2⅛-inch plastic cube composed of 28 small blocks that can be moved about or rotated on a spindle inside. When you first get your hands on a

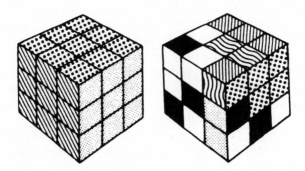

Cube, it looks like the first sketch, with each of its sides a different color—blue, white, yellow, green, red and orange. Once you start moving its parts, it will assume quite different looks, one of which is shown in the second sketch. By being twisted and moved about, the parts of a Rubik's Cube can be made to assume as many as 43,252,003,274,489,856,000 positions. That's right—more than 43 quintillion positions. No wonder that, once you start playing with a Cube, it may take you months to restore it to its original appearance.

This maddening puzzle is named after Erno Rubik, a Budapest teacher of architecture who obtained a Hungarian patent on it in 1975. (Apparently by pure coincidence, a Tokyo engineer named Terutoshi Ishige received a Japanese patent for the same idea in 1976.) In 1980, the Rubik Cube became a craze in several European countries. Last fall, several American companies began to market it here. The Ideal Toy Corporation alone sold more than nine million Rubik's Cubes. As a result, a malady called "cubitis" is affecting large segments of the population, particularly the scientifically and mathematically minded.

Help for sufferers from cubitis is now available between the covers of two paperback books: *Mastering Rubik's Cube* (Holt) by Don Taylor, an Australian mathematician, and *The Simple Solution to Rubik's Cube* (Bantam) by James G. Nourse, a Stanford University chemist. Neither is as simple to follow as ABC, but the latter is a bit more accessible because of its Yankee origin. Both will enable an assiduous reader to reduce greatly the duration of the delicious torment.

August 16, 1981

It looks as if Don Taylor, the Australian mathematician whose *Mastering Rubik's Cube* and James G. Nourse, the Stanford

University chemist whose *The Simple Solution to Rubik's Cube* now have a total of 2,300,000 copies in print, are about to have some competition from an extraordinary quarter. The book: *You Can Do the Cube* (Penguin). The author: Patrick Bossert, a 13-year-old schoolboy who lives in suburban London.

Patrick's book is a 112-page paperback filled with diagrams and text describing three dozen "tricks" by which this summer's most baffling problem may be solved in as little as 90 seconds; it offers directions for keeping your cube "in healthy working order." Several friends who are not manually dextrous tell us that it is easier to follow than its predecessors.

How did Patrick come to write the book? Last winter, he caught his first sight of a Rubik's Cube in the hands of a schoolmate who had received one from America. Always fascinated by "three-dimensional objects and puzzles," he tried unsuccessfully to find one on sale in Britain. He had better luck while on holiday in Switzerland. While recuperating from a skiing accident, he and a cousin spent long hours figuring out ways to conquer it. Then, when he got back to school, he and some classmates worked up a set of instructions. A copy of it fell into the hands of a boy whose father works for Penguin in London.

From then on, things have moved fast. Penguin helped him to develop his instructions into a handy little book. Fifty thousand copies, with a photograph of Patrick's beaming, bespectacled face on the cover, arrived by air freight in New York last week. Additional printings are expected to roll from American presses soon.

January 10, 1982

The midwinter gloom pervading Publishers Row was broken last week by a cheery publicist asking an arresting question: "Who do you suppose was the author of 1981's best-selling book? Sidney Sheldon? Richard Simmons? V. C. Andrews? Stephen King?" Stuart Applebaum of Bantam Books answered his own question. "It was James G. Nourse. His *The Simple Solution to Rubik's Cube* has had printings totaling 6,300,000 copies and helped make last November and December the best two months in Bantam's 36-year history.

Just who is James G. Nourse and how did he achieve the heights of bestsellerdom? This time a year ago Mr. Nourse, who is 34, was little known outside the Stanford University community, where he's a research associate in chemistry. Just before Christmas he had bought a Rubik's Cube—the diabolical Hungarian invention first reached this continent on the West Coast by way of Australia—intending to give it away as a present. The puzzle fascinated him so much that he spent the holidays working out the solution, which he then published as a 32-page pamphlet to be sold at the university bookstore.

Some time later, a copy fell into the hands of a Stanford alumnus and entrepreneur named Paul N. Weinberg. From then on, things moved fast. Mr. Weinberg hurried east to show it to Jack Looney, whose responsibilities at Bantam include puzzle and game books. Mr. Looney had been intrigued by Rubik's Cube ever since reading an article about it in *Scientific American*, but Mr. Nourse's was the first solution that seemed very practicable. He hurried west and for a week holed up with Mr. Nourse and Mr. Weinberg in a Stanford laboratory, elaborating and refining the pamphlet into the 64-page book that Bantam published in June.

Mr. Nourse's *Simple Solution* immediately became the fastest-selling book in publishing history, helping and in turn being helped by the Cube mania that was overwhelming America. To help game-players solve the numerous puzzles that were spawned by the Cube, in November he published a sequel, *The Simple Solutions to Cubic Puzzles*.

Mr. Nourse made two short tours to promote his books, pausing in New York long enough to show his ways of solving puzzles seated in the window of a Fifth Avenue bookstore and on several national television shows. A pleasant, low-keyed man, he is defter at demonstrations than at explaining the social significance of the puzzles' popularity. He leaves the latter to Mr. Looney, who says that cube games have a particular appeal to a generation anxious to understand space relationships, molecular structure and movements of particles—important concepts in the dawning age of the computer.

The past year's success has changed Jim Nourse's life style only a bit. He regards it as "pure luck" and says that he won't write another book about it unless the puzzle fad continues—and he very much doubts that it will. He continues to work in the Stanford laboratory. Several months ago he married a Stanford colleague, a neuro-physiologist. The other day, when she was told that there were now seven million copies of her husband's books in circulation, Mrs. Nourse exclaimed delightedly, "Great! Now we can afford to buy a bed!"

A Year of Crazes

December 27, 1981

By the general reading public, 1981 is likely to be remembered most vividly for three crazes that found expression through a dozen best-selling paperbacks:

- Cat lovers and cat haters have vented their feelings through seven cartoon books: *Garfield at Large* (909,000 copies), *Garfield Bigger Than Life* (850,000 copies), *Garfield Gains Weight* (825,000 copies), *101 Uses for a Dead Cat* (795,000 copies), *The Official I Hate Cats Book* (375,000 copies), *The Second Official I Hate Cats Book* (325,000 copies) and *Cat's Revenge* (225,000 copies).
- Preppies have been targets for *The Official Preppy Handbook* (1,233,725 copies) and *The Official I Hate Preppies Handbook* (180,000).
- We've lost track of all the books that promise solutions to Rubik's Cube, but three have achieved best-sellerdom: *The Simple Solution to Rubik's Cube* (6,308,000 copies), *Mastering Rubik's Cube* (2,005,000) and *You Can Do the Cube* (500,000).

How long can these crazes continue? Will they last long into the new year or will some other mania appear to take their place? Publishers can only hope. . .

Videogames

August 29, 1982

Last December a half dozen houses on Publishers Row began to look hopefully at a new kind of book to lift their sagging fortunes. Across the nation, hundreds of thousands of young people were congregating in arcades, bus terminals, gas stations, pizza parlors and delicatessens to take turns stuffing quarters into electronic contraptions that flashed colored lights and emitted sounds like "Pop!" "Ka-boom!" and "Zap!" The frenzy for "videogames" bearing bizarre names like Pac-Man, Berzerk, Gorf, Asteroids, Space Invaders and War Lords had almost overnight created an industry that was taking in close to $5 billion, twice as much as motion pictures, three times as much as major professional sports.

Of the 30-odd games being played, the most popular—and the only one to win feminine favor—was Pac-Man. Amateur Freudians attributed its popularity with women to the fact that, unlike the other games, where shooting is the thing, the objective of Pac-Man is to engulf. To win points, a player must keep an open-mouthed circle moving across the screen gobbling up small objects while avoiding being eaten by roving "monsters."

Many stores—even some bookstores—started to sell cassettes that would make it possible for enthusiasts to play the games on their television screens at home. Publishers figured that this development might create a huge demand for books that explained how to play—and win—the games.

What's the situation now that 1982 is two-thirds over? Piled atop our desk are more than a score of videogame books, the ventures of nine publishers, ranging in price from $1.95 to $5.95.

• Nearly half the books promise readers aid in "winning all the major games." As many as 20 games are named on their covers. The best seller is *How to Master the Video Games* by 19-year-old Tom Hirschfield, who wrote it during a year off from Harvard. Bantam has sold 926,000 copies to date.

• Of the books that focus on particular games, half a dozen take on that great favorite, Pac-Man. The biggest seller of these is *Mastering Pac-Man* by Ken Uston, a Yale Phi Beta Kappa, Harvard M.B.A. and former vice president of the Pacific Stock Exchange, who likes to be called "the foremost blackjack player in the world." NAL/Signet has distributed 1,500,000 copies.

• Books about such other currently popular games as Donkey Kong, Defender and Centipede have more modest sales, ranging from 125,000 to 225,000 copies.

• Like such other recent crazes as cats, cubes and preppies, the games have been lampooned in a number of books. There are, for example, *I Hate Videots* (Fireside), *The Official I-Hate-Videogames Handbook* (Pocket) and *Pac-Mania!* (Pinnacle). These afford a few smiles, but have yet to set many bookstores' cash registers tinkling.

Although videogames have yet to prove a bonanza to the book business, as many in the industry had hoped, they should be watched closely. Such is the message of a paperback just published by Pocket Books, *Video Games* by David Cohen, a onetime science magazine editor. Although the publishers say it is "for readers aged 9 to 13," their elders will benefit from its history of the games and the industry that manufactures them and from its discussion of the current controversy over·the social dangers of a youth's spending his free time in arcades. Most important, Mr. Cohen insists, is the fact that videogames provide an easy introduction to the computer age we're entering.

Although Publishers Row hadn't paid it much attention, the computer age had been dawning for a number of years . . .

Computer Books

September 18, 1977

The sentinels who scan the horizon for signs of approaching trends have been talking the past several months about a mind-boggling phenomenon: the microcomputer, the home-size version of those electronic machines that keep industry running. Some of the signs:

• Last April 13,000 persons attended a "West Coast Computer Faire" in San Francisco. Three weeks ago 9,000 persons attended a similar fair in Atlantic City, 4,000 another in Boston. Late next month fairs are scheduled in Chicago and in New York.

• Several large retail chains are planning to display personal computers, priced $500 and up, in their stores beside their hi-fi's and stereos.

• Some micro enthusiasts are predicting that within five years 90 percent of all American homes will have at least one computer.

What will the microcomputers be used for? The easy answer: to perform chores around the house, like controlling the lights, heat and air conditioner, and figuring out what's owed to the I.R.S.

Enthusiasts whose vision is longer believe microcomputers hold an infinite number of possibilities that will take several generations to realize fully. They may be used to play games—not only family pastimes, but sophisticated exercises like the creation of other worlds and alternate civilizations, à la Frederik Pohl and Isaac Asimov. They may help their users learn more about his own body and psyche. They may be used to create new forms of art and music. "The boob tube puts the mind to sleep," one leader in the field declares. "The microcomputer is the first new device in years that allows its user a chance to give his intellectual muscles a workout."

Although the personal computer is barely five years old, it has already created a world of its own. There are nearly 200 fan clubs in the United States, most of them concentrated in areas where industries employ numbers of young, well-trained technicians: the San Francisco Bay area, Southern California, New Jersey, Boston.

There are ten firms that issue magazines about home computers. Of these, two publish paperbacks that many general bookstores are beginning to stock: Creative Computing Press of Morristown, New Jersey, and People's Computer Company of Menlo Park, California.

So far the microcomputer bookshelf is small, but there are enough paperbacks to challenge anyone's intellectual muscles:

• For starters, there's *PCC's Reference Book of Personal and Home Computing*, edited by Dwight McCabe (People's).

• For a sampling of what's been written about the microcomputer's present and possibilities, there are two volumes of articles and essays: *The Best of Creative Computing* (Creative).

• For games to play: *101 Basic Computer Games*, edited by David H. Ahl (Creative) and *What to Do After You Hit Return* (People's).

• For those with artistic visions: *Artist and Computer*, edited by Ruth Leavitt (Harmony/Creative).

Within the next three years, the computer world and its relationship to books grew greatly . . .

December 21, 1980

Recently we've had a number of occasions to mention Santa Clara County, California, south of San Francisco, the home of hundreds of thriving computer firms whose fondness for books makes it a favorite place of the publishing industry. West Coast wits call it "Silicon Valley" in honor of the crystalline element used to make the transistors and other semiconductors by which computers work their miracles.

But Santa Clara County is by no means the only part of the nation that thrives on silicon. There are also large concentrations of computers and people whose life work is making them in Southern California, in the metropolitan areas of Phoenix, Houston, Dallas, Minneapolis and Chicago, near Florida's Cape Canaveral and, of course, along the East Coast between Washington and Boston. The proliferation of such communities accounts in part for the popularity of a book like the Pulitzer Prize-winning *Gödel, Escher, Bach* by Douglas R. Hofstadter, a professor of computer science. This "metaphorical fugue on minds and machines" has been on the trade paperback best seller list for ten weeks and has sold 128,000 copies.

In Silicon Country U.S.A. one generation of computers replaces another so quickly that publishers have all they can do to report the situation of the moment. Nearly 50 firms, bearing names as familiar as McGraw-Hill and as unfamiliar as dilithium Press, are currently issuing magazines and books. Some 75 books, with subjects ranging from overviews of the computer's influence on society to directions for using particular programs, are on sale in 1,500 independently owned technical bookstores, many of Radio Shack's stores, and more and more general bookstores, including the Walden and Dalton chains.

During the last five years, it has become increasingly evident that the electronic computer isn't just a tool for industry. Personal or microcomputers, priced as low as $500, are now available for use at home and in school. At present, half a million such devices are in use across the country; by 1985, it's predicted, there will be 12 million.

How can an ordinary householder, interested in buying and using a personal computer, find his way through the silicon wonderland? Two recently published paperbacks point the way:

• *Owning Your Home Computer* by Robert L. Perry (Everest House) is an illustrated guide book for neophytes. After describing the gadgets now on the market in their more than 1,000 varieties, it explains how they can be useful around the house, help children learn and enable the handicapped and elderly to perform useful work.

• *More Basic Computer Games* edited by David H. Ahl is a sequel to *Basic Computer Games* (Workman), which has sold 350,000 copies, making it the largest-selling work on personal computers. Both books explain 84 "mind-boggling games" that the whole family can play.

Mr. Ahl, now a senior statesman in the computer world, started Creative Computing in the basement of his Morristown, New Jersey, home in 1974 when he was only 35. Today the enterprise occupies extensive facilities in Manhattan and in Morris Plains, New Jersey.

By the spring of 1982, the changes were coming fast and furiously . . .

May 23, 1982

It sounds, from all you hear about it, like a wonderful yet slightly frightening place. A land crowded with contrivances whose green-lit screens resemble those of television sets and whose banks of keys are quite like those of typewriters—contrivances that the small businessman can employ to make a living, the householder can use to perform all manner of chores, the whole family can repair to for fun and games. The land of the personal or home computer.

These contrivances bear strange names like Atari, Apple II, TRS-80, IBM and PET. Scarcely a month passes that another brand name doesn't join the scene. Those pieces of "hardware" make use of something called "software" and communicate in languages called Basic, Cobol, Fortran, Forth and Pascal. A year ago their prices were astronomically high; now many can be bought for less than $1,000.

It's observed that kids, 15 and younger, understand almost instinctively how to cope with these mysteries. But many of their elders will find answers to their quandaries in those time-honored purveyors of information, books.

There are now some 700 books in print designed to help travelers find their way through computerland. Almost all are paperbound, because they're designed to be consulted rather than treasured on a shelf. They're issued by long-established general publishing houses like Addison-Wesley, Hayden, McGraw-Hill, Prentice-Hall, Sams, Wiley and Van Nostrand and by such relative newcomers and little-known specialists as dilithium, IJG, Que, Sybex and Tab. Every month another house or two enters the lists. The books have to be revised frequently because of the volatile popularity of the various types of computers. Addison-Wesley recently began converting some of its titles into a series called "Micro Books" to make them more accessible to readers lacking a bent for technology.

A number of these books may be found on display behind the counters of the 2,000 stores that currently sell computers. However, relatively few of them—100 to 200—carry large stocks. "The trouble with computer stores," one publisher told us, "is that while their owners know about hardware and software, they don't know much about books. But that may change as computer retailing becomes more stabilized."

Many general bookstores now have or soon will have special departments devoted to computer books and are training clerks who can help customers find the ones they need. This trend was pioneered by Kroch's & Brentano's, the Chicago-area chain which has been featuring them for a dozen years. Ingram Book Company, the giant wholesaler, is making preparations to supply a wide variety of titles to the 7,000 independent bookstores it services across the country. The nationwide B. Dalton and Waldenbook chains are opening computer sections at a lively clip.

By 1985, many a publisher and bookseller was wondering if he hadn't been carried away by his heady expectations for computer books. Many of the paperbacks that had been rushed into print—there were now more than 3,000 such titles—were languishing on store shelves. Especially disappointing was the reception of those about home computers.

The reason for this became clear when sales of micro computers were tallied. They had levelled off dramatically. Only 2,500,000 home computers had been sold. Families used these almost exclusively for entertainment and, after two or three months of playing "mind-boggling games," tired of them as they had videogames and Rubik's Cube. A number of publishers cut back on their computer book lines, in some cases discontinued them entirely.

Did a real future await the computer book once the whole computer industry went through a great shake-out and achieved more realistic goals? The denizens of Publishers Row wished they had an unclouded crystal ball to provide the answer.

Making and Selling Books

Acquiring Manuscripts

January 6, 1980

For many years, along Publishers Row, the mass-market paperback houses were often referred to, somewhat condescendingly, as "the reprinters." They were usually content to buy reprint rights to a promising work discovered, developed and promoted by a trade publisher and, a year after its hardcover publication, fill the softcover racks with what was, essentially, a pre-sold package.

The times are changing fast. Of the 83 titles that found places on the mass-market best seller list last year, 20 of them—all fiction—had not been previously published in any form. It looks as if the proportion of originals will be even higher in 1980.

The reason most paperbounders give for the change is the "astronomical" sums that have become routine at auctions for reprint rights. A new high was reached last fall when Bantam Books paid $3,200,000 for *Princess Daisy*, a novel still in manuscript. An Avon Books executive recently told a *Publishers Weekly* writer: "The advance we paid on one of the originals we now have on the best seller list was in the low six figures. We may ultimately pay a million dollars or more in royalties. But if we kept the money we saved on the advance in the bank, the interest alone would have paid for our publicity campaign."

August 1, 1976

In the last several years paperback publishers have been issuing more and more originals. How do they find the manuscripts? Do they pay any attention to those that come in unsolicited? A quick check along Publishers Row produced some answers:

- All large firms, except Dell and Bantam, say they welcome unsolicited manuscripts. Rejection or acceptance is likely to take many weeks, even months.
- All invite letters of inquiry with an outline.
- At some houses, all editors take turns reading the "slush." At others, the pile is doled out among young editorial assistants. Often an assistant who spots a manuscript that his superiors agree to take on is given charge of its publication. At New American Library, the assistant is given a bonus.
- Of all fields, science fiction has the largest welcome mat out to new writers. There isn't a veteran editor who isn't inclined to brag a bit about the big-name writers he's discovered.
- Fawcett's Gold Medal division began its policy of taking on unsolicited manuscripts 25 years ago, and has been most successful with Westerns and mysteries.
- In the last several years Avon Books has scored phenomenal successes with women's romances by the likes of Kathleen E. Woodiwiss and Rosemary Rogers, whose first work came in with the slush.
- Although fiction originals are most talked about, some of the biggest successes have been topical works of nonfiction.

May 22, 1977

Just what elements must a novel possess to start readers' word-of-mouth recommendations? Most veterans of Publishers Row confess that they don't know for sure. However, one editor told us the other day, the large, commercially-oriented house he works for has its own way of forecasting a book's fate. "If Gloria doesn't like a manuscript, even if it's by a Brand Name author, we know we're in trouble." Gloria is a high school grad, with a medium I.Q., whose title in the office is stenographer-clerk. As far as popular taste is concerned, she's a living piece of litmus paper.

We've told the story to several editors at other houses.

They listen with embarrassed smiles. "We've got our Glorias too," they acknowledge.

March 21, 1982

You're a young writer from the Midwest whose autobiographical first novel about your relationship with your father has just been brought out by a respected hardcover publisher. Several Big Literary Names have provided nice quotes for the jacket, and it's getting good reviews. What are its chances of being bought by a paperback house?

That was one of the hypothetical cases that engaged a representative panel of publishers during a clinic for writers recently held in New York. The panel included Robert Wyatt of Avon Books and Susan Ginsburg of Pocket Books: a trade-paperback editor, Sam Mitnick of Putnam's Perigee line; and the subsidiary rights director of a hardcover house, Irene Skolnick of Harcourt Brace Jovanovich. The audience consisted of members of the PEN American Center, a division of an international writer's organization.

The panelists didn't hold out much hope for the first novel. If its hardcover publisher was exceptionally high on it and was ordering a large first printing, they'd be happy to take a look at the manuscript. (Mr. Wyatt says that he regularly reads five to ten manuscripts a day.) But they were unimpressed by the blurbs from Big Literary Names and "good reviews." If they saw promising talent in the novel, they'd follow its author's work closely and, if and when he produced his "breakthrough" book, buy it—and perhaps rights to his earlier novels as well.

You've published several novels that sold 100,000 copies in hardcover and reached the No. 4 or No. 3 rank on the best seller list. Now you've completed something Really Big—"The Maranos," a saga about three generations of a Sephardic Jewish family that runs nearly 2,000 manuscript pages. The Literary Guild has made it a dual selection, and the publisher plans to spend $50,000 promoting it. Do the paperbounders have any questions before bidding for it?

Yes, indeed. The book's title isn't too good. Can a more attractive one be substituted? Does the story have a strong female character—or, better yet, several? As it stands, the book runs 1,000 printed pages. With paper so costly these days, it will have to be priced far beyond the average paperback buyer's reach. Is the author willing to cut it? Are the author's previous novels available for reissue in softcover at the same time this is published? How well has the author performed in the past on television talk shows like Good Morning America and The Donahue Show? Can the reprint purchase price be paid in installments rather than in one lump sum? In these days of tight money, this is an important consideration.

Throughout the discussion, the phrase "middle-list book" kept cropping up. A middle-list novel is one that falls between a "blockbuster" and a "category" book. A blockbuster is a novel whose author has such a loyal following that it is certain of a sale of one million copies. A category book is one with a certain sale of 50,000 copies or more—Westerns, science fiction, mysteries, women's romances and young-adult fiction.

Book Producers and Packagers

November 1, 1981

What do these books, now in the bookstores or soon to arrive, have in common?

- *The Book of Rock Lists* by Dave Marsh and Kevin Stein (Dell).
- *Al Ubell's Energy-Saving Guide for Homeowners* (Warner).
- *Desire's Legacy* by Elizabeth Bright (Pocket).
- *Cat's Revenge: More Than 100 Uses for Dead People*, produced by Philip Lief (Simon & Schuster/Wallaby).
- *American Film Now: The People, the Power, the Movies* by James Monaco (NAL/Plume).
- *The Skyscraper* by Paul Goldberger (Knopf).

All these books are the creations of "book packagers"—or, as they prefer to style themselves, "book producers"—tiny firms that assume responsibility for the writing, editing, layout and, in some cases, printing of a book for distribution by the well-known company whose name appears on the title page as "publisher." They are typical of the more than 200 book projects exhibited at a trade show, well attended by representatives of major publishing houses, that the American Book Producers Association recently staged in Manhattan. Their subjects suggest the diversity of books currently being created by producers—reference works, how-to books, popular fiction, cartoon humor, illustrated works of scholarship.

Book producers have been part of the American publishing scene for a quarter of a century, but it's only in the past ten years that they've become a force that deserves to be closely watched. It's impossible to say how many there are or how many books they create a year. Most are clustered in California, New England and, of course, the New York area. Usually their permanent staffs consist of three or four people working in a one-room office; freelance specialists—researchers, writers, editors, designers and the like—are hired only when they're needed.

To hear some of the ABPA's sanguine members tell it, book producers are riding the wave of the future. They recall that 30 years ago the great film studios like 20th Century-Fox and Universal stopped being involved in every step of film production and contented themselves with providing financial backing and distribution for the work of "creative people"—directors, actors, writers and cameramen. In the years to come, they predict, more and more publishers, beset with rising overhead costs, will depend upon producers to create books for them and concentrate their attention on the problems of production, warehousing and marketing. Sometimes the original idea for the book will come from the publisher; just as often it will be the inspiration of the producer.

That prospect, we're told, is beginning to intrigue many book people who now occupy editorial sanctums on Publishers Row. The chance to "do their own thing," to work as members of a small team on projects that are close to their own emotional and intellectual interests instead of putting in time on ever-lengthening lists of books to which they have been assigned at the behest of their employer's marketing staff—that, the current word is, "would be living again."

The number of book producers continues to grow. The 1983 edition of *Literary Marketplace*, an annual directory of organizations and individuals in publishing, listed 70, the 1985 edition 132.

As diverse as the books they produce are the ways they operate, as this sampling suggests:

Chanticleer Press

January 15, 1978

The name on the cover, *The Audubon Society Field Guide to North American Birds,* suggests that it is the creation of the prestigious wildlife conservation society. The title page states that it is published by Alfred A. Knopf. You must turn to the last page, where a statement appears that the work was "prepared and produced by Chanticleer Press, Inc.; Publisher: Paul Steiner," to discover the name of its begetter.

Paul Steiner is an old hand at producing books incognito. When he came to New York back in 1941, he brought from his native Vienna a kind of know-how then in short supply in this country — how to produce a well-made book containing many illustrations in color. For more than a quarter of a century now, his Chanticleer Press has been packaging such books, usually on natural history subjects, for distribution by a score of leading publishers.

Three years ago Mr. Steiner conceived of a way to increase the pleasure of those millions of Americans who enjoy watching and identifying birds. This was a set of guidebooks — one for North America east of the Rockies, the other west — that would list the birds not according to the customary scientific, ornithological principles (by families and species) but by the characteristics watchers observe in the field (color, shape, song, habitat). They would be shown not through drawings, as in most guides, but through color photographs, just as they appear to the watcher's naked eye or through his binoculars.

When Mr. Steiner took the idea to Knopf, for whom he'd produced a number of successful book packages in the past, he got a warm welcome. The house agreed to underwrite the high start-up cost. For editors, he found three scientists willing to overcome their original misgivings about abandoning ornithological principles for the convenience of bird watchers. For a title that would give the volumes a touch of prestige, he turned to the Audubon Society, for whose magazine he had been supplying sections of color photographs for a number of years.

Like his many associates in this far-flung project, Mr. Steiner is delighted but not surprised by the reception the two volumes have had to date: Eastern edition, 160,000 copies; Western, 110,000.

Book Creations, Inc.

November 18, 1979

From Manhattan, drive up the Taconic Parkway for two and a half hours, turning off as if you were going to Tanglewood. Shortly before you reach the Massachusetts line, in a village called Canaan, you'll come upon a small cluster of Tudor-style buildings amid snow-covered fields in which a herd of deer roam. This is Book Creations, Inc., a fiction factory operated by Lyle Kenyon Engel, 63, who, with the help of his wife, son and a staff of 23 editors and promotion people living in the neighborhood, will create during 1979, 75 plump novels for publication by ten leading paperback houses. Every one will sell in the hundreds of thousands of copies.

Don't look for Mr. Engel's name on any of their title pages. In the past 15 years, he has fathered more than 5,000 books, but their bylines have usually been the pseudonyms of some 80 professional writers, living in all parts of the country, whom he's engaged to flesh out story outlines he concocted and sold in advance to publishers.

Mr. Engel brings to the collaboration a sense of fiction derived from years of reading as a youth in Manhattan, bedridden with osteomyelitis. His best friends were Victor Hugo, Alexandre Dumas, Jules Verne, James Fenimore Cooper and Edgar Rice Burroughs. His contributions don't end with the outline. He keeps in close touch with his authors by phone as they write. Before forwarding a manuscript to the publisher, he and his staff go over it carefully to "maintain rigid quality control." The result may not be great literature, he says, but it certainly isn't junk.

Mr. Engel concentrates on series. ("If you please a reader with one book, he'll stay with you for the whole series.") At first he created men's action stories—Nick Carter, Richard Blade and the like. In 1973 a publisher's request for something to celebrate the American Bicentennial led him to his richest lode—the fat historical, crowded with characters and events as it traces a family through several generations. To date, 30 million copies have been sold of the seven-volume Kent Family Chronicles by John Jakes—which, incidentally, is not a pseudonym. Very much in the same spirit is the Wagons West series, recently launched by Bantam, the work of the pseudonymous Dana Fuller Ross.

Unlike most other book producers, Mr. Engel remains concerned with his packages even after they're published. Years ago, he served time as a magazine publisher and public relations consultant. He calls on that experience constantly. When *Texas!*, one of the Wagons West volumes, was published, for example, his office deluged every disk jockey, book editor and bookstore owner in the Lone Star State with promotional gimmicks on its behalf. His office also worked closely with Bantam's field representative to keep the orders flowing.

Mr. Engels estimates that it costs him $1 million a year to meet his high overhead. This, he says, makes it necessary for him to require that royalties be divided equally between his authors and Book Creations, Inc. All of his usually pseudonymous authors have written many books under their own names, some have even won literary prizes, but few have prospered as well without his unique collaboration. As one of them puts it, "Fifty percent of $1 million is far better than ten percent of $100,000."

Yolla Botty Press

March 18, 1979

From San Francisco Bay, drive up Route 101 for three hours, turn off to the right and for another hour follow a winding road into sparsely settled, mountain-enclosed Round Valley. There, just beyond the village of Corvello, deep in a cow pasture across which goats sometimes wander, you'll find a cluster of small buildings and a large redwood building. This is the Yolla Botty Press, a book farm operated by Jim and Carolyn Robertson, with the help of eight people from the neighborhood. This year Yolla Botty Press will produce ten imaginatively conceived, attractively designed paperbacks for release by Anchor, Bantam, Clarkson Potter, Little, Brown, the Sierra Club and Morrow.

In the four years since the Robertsons escaped from the high-rent Bay area, they've been making publishing history. Reviewers called their 1974 Sierra Club book, *Mind in the Waters: A Book to Celebrate the Consciousness of Whales and Dolphins*, one of the year's most beautiful. Last year the National Book Award went to another Sierra Club book, *The View From the Oak: The Private Worlds of Other Creatures*.

Jim Robertson, 42, prefers to think of what he and his wife are doing as "collaborative publishing." Yolla Botty conceives a book idea, finds an author to do it—usually on the West Coast—develops it to the finished-plate stage before sending it off to the East to be printed. Graphic design is his forte, editorial detail his wife's.

When Mr. Robertson first ventured into collaborative publishing, his book projects were intended for school use and were financed by foundations. He's moving on from that now. Clarkson Potter's just-published *Cold Comfort* is a jaunty self-help book about colds and the flu.

And what is Yolla Botty? It's the Indian name for those snow-capped mountains out yonder.

Associated Features

April 5, 1981

Next Wednesday afternoon, at Cincinnati's Riverfront Stadium, the Phillies will meet the Reds, and the 1981 baseball season will officially begin. From then until the World Series in early October, literally billions of words will be printed about America's favorite sport. Many of them will be published in newspapers and magazines—but for the real fan, the sort who treasures legends and statistics, the best will be preserved within book covers. This spring, as every spring, bookstore shelves and newsstand racks are crowded with volumes to satisfy this nostalgia and curiosity.

Many are products of book packagers. The most prolific in this field is Associated Features, which over the past 15 years has produced some 200 volumes for a dozen publishers, particularly New American Library.

Associated Features is a mom-and-pop enterprise run by Zander and Phyllis Hollander out of an office around the corner from Grand Central Station. Its two small rooms are lined with shelves of books about every sport and with file cabinets chock-full of photographs. This is not the extent of the Hollanders' resources. Over the years, they've created a nationwide network of sources of information and of writers able to turn out publishable articles on short notice.

For Zander Hollander, sports became a way of life four decades ago, when he was sports editor of his high school newspaper in Far Rockaway, Queens. He continued to live it as a sports writer for several Manhattan newspapers; as the *World Telegram* slowly expired, he devoted more and more time to book packaging. For Phyllis Hollander, sports have been fun ever since she played basketball at Hunter High; after her marriage, she happily turned out a book of her own on that apple-pie-American pastime, cheerleading.

Most of Associated Features' income is from its half-dozen annual handbooks about popular spectator sports. Baseball is by far the most popular, followed closely by football, with pro basketball a poor third. Sales run in the neighborhood of 100,000 copies. Some titles produced for special occasions have sold 200,000 or more.

Their production schedule keeps the Hollanders so busy that they seldom get a chance to go out to the ballpark any more. They do watch the little tube at critical moments and keep in touch with their contributing writers in all seasons.

The 1981 baseball season opens this week, but the Hollanders' preparations for it are long past. Half of the copy for *The 1981 Complete Book of Baseball* was ready last December 15. After the major leagues held their big meetings, the Hollanders had just four weeks to complete the rest in order to make the book's March publication date. And right now? They're gathering statistics about the current pro basketball season so that a complete book for the 1981–82 season can be delivered to NAL, ready for printing, early in July.

Richard Gallen & Co.

December 13, 1981

Even the most knowledgeable residents of Publishers Row are apt to look a bit blank when you mention the name of Richard Gallen. "Richard Gallen? Oh, yes—Richard Gallen Originals. Women's romances."

Since 1978, Mr. Gallen has been producing two historical romances and two contemporary romances a month for distribution by Pocket Books. They are, however, only a fraction of the activities he carries on from the no-frills offices of Richard Gallen & Company, on the Fifth Avenue edge of Manhattan's Garment District. He considers himself an entrepreneur who provides financial backing and counsel to veteran editors who wish to set up their own imprints for books distributed by major houses. "As publishing now operates," he says, "the editor is the last person to reap the rewards of his own creativity."

The enterprises in which Mr. Gallen has a stake keep 30 people busy full time, dealing with authors and agents, editing manuscripts, designing covers and, in some cases, handling publicity and promotion. Mr. Gallen now owns a share of Bryans Books, distributed by Dell, and Tor Books, distributed by Pinnacle. In addition, he's involved in a number of "one-book deals." During 1981, he has helped produce 100 titles; in 1982 it will be twice that number.

At age 48, Mr. Gallen is a man who prefers to maintain a low personal profile ("I put my name on the Originals only because Pocket Books' publisher Ron Busch insisted"), but the other day he was willing to try to analyze how he got involved in his present activities. As a boy growing up across from Brooklyn's Ebbets Field, he haunted the nearest Womrath's bookstore. After graduation from the Yale Law School, he became general counsel for Dell Publishing Company. After quitting to practice law on his own, he couldn't resist getting involved in partnerships to publish such books as *The Autobiography of Malcolm X* and *Games People Play*. For a time he was involved in a Wall Street corporation whose specialty was raising venture capital. "Finally, four years ago, I set up Richard Gallen & Co. to combine my two abiding interests—books and investing. My associates and I participate in all phases of publishing except distribution. I feel sick when I see books come back unsold."

Mr. Gallen won't predict where his passion for books will take him next. Most of his present ventures are in original paperback fiction. "But with more and more publishing houses, hardcover and soft, reducing their creative staffs to reduce their overhead, new opportunities keep arising. The editing and promotion of books could well become a land of cottage industry. I want to be in the middle of it all."

Yet another important book producer is Cloverdale Press, run by two brothers, Jeffrey and Daniel Weiss, out of an aging commercial building on Manhattan's West 20th Street. Both of the brothers Weiss worked as editors for major publishing houses before setting up their own business in 1981. Today they have a staff of 30 and use the services of many freelancers to produce some 100 books a year for a score of publishers. Their practice is to pay a flat fee to nonfiction writers, give a percentage of royalty to fiction writers. A number of their creations have claimed places on the national best seller lists: for example, Alfred Gingold's *Items From Our Catalog*, *30 Days to a Flatter Stomach* in versions for both men and women, and the Sweet Valley High series of young adult novels.

Packaging the Product

Cover Designs

July 17, 1977

"Don't judge a book by its cover!" That's an adage in which most mass-market publishers put little stock. They know of many undistinguished books whose covers impelled bookstore browsers to pick them out of the rack and carry them to the checkout counter and many good books that languished in the racks because their covers did not. Hence it's no surprise that among the most influential residents of Publishers Row are the art directors of the major houses—a dozen men and one woman whose mission in life it is to create covers that impel. This baker's dozen of "art directors" has just had an unaccustomed experience.

The American Institute of Graphic Arts, whose annual book design show is more highly esteemed than any other in the U.S., decided this spring to broaden the show's scope by including many varieties of bookmaking. An invitation went out to the mass-market art directors to submit examples of their work of which they were particularly proud. Several hundred mass-market paperbacks were entered. The 24 covers that won a nod from the judges—there were no prizes as such—were exhibited at the AIGA's Manhattan quarters last month.

After the show closed, we paid visits to the two men who

judged the mass-market entries to discover their reaction to the experience. Both are veterans: Leonard Leone, who's been Bantam Books' art director for 21 years, and Milton Charles, who's been at Pocket Books for the past four. Both acknowledged that they found it awkward to have to pass judgment on submissions from their own houses. However, they added, the paperback business is such a tight little world they don't know how that could have been avoided. All the directors have similar educational and professional backgrounds and watch each other's activities like hawks. They know each other, but when they get together socially they talk about everything except what they're up to at the office.

In their workaday routine Mr. Leone and Mr. Charles follow procedures common throughout the business. Each has a half dozen staff assistants. Eight or nine months before a book is scheduled for publication, they read it in manuscript or synopsis, then rough out sketches to be considered at meetings with the heads of their firm's other departments. When a design is agreed on, they call in one of the freelance illustrators with whom they regularly work to execute it. All in Mr. Charles' stable work at their homes in suburban New York. Recently, to add fresher touches, Mr. Leone has been recruiting talent as far away as California and England.

Both Mr. Leone and Mr. Charles agree that what they need most in their designs is originality. When a cover seems to have contributed greatly to a book's sale, there's a temptation to imitate or repeat the pattern. This is self-defeating, they feel, for the public senses the absence of creative spark.

An exception must be noted in the case of certain genre books. A cover showing a pair of lovers locked in an overarching embrace lets the fans know that the volume is womens' historical romance. A single light in a castle window is a summons to gothic fans. But even here a touch of originality is desirable.

Another exception is sometimes made in the packaging of books by the same author. Mr. Leone has designed a cover for the works of Philip Roth that varies from volume to volume only in coloring and textual detail. Mr. Charles is at work on a similar scheme for the novels of Morris West.

Both art directors are unenthusiastic about cover tricks. Psychedelic colors, silver and gold stamping, embossing, flocking (the overlay of a wool-like substance) may attract browsers' eyes and fingers for a book or two, but such gimmicks quickly lose their magic. Even die-cuts — holes in the cover through which faces peer from an inside page — ought to be used sparingly and only when they jibe with the book's theme.

Are there any tricks worth using frequently? Both directors like back covers that expand on the theme of the front, for the opportunities are innumerable. Mr. Charles is proud of his design for Pocket's edition of Joan Didion's *A Book of Common Prayer*. A hand holding a flame is shown on the front, but when the book is flattened out so that the back may also be seen it is evident that the hand belongs to a woman and the flame to a cigarette lighter. Mr. Leone is much taken with the stepback and gatefold, devices by which pages of inviting illustrations are revealed when a browser opens up the front cover.

February 2, 1975

The largest-selling paperback since its launching last November is *Fear of Flying*, a first novel by the poet Erica Jong. At last count, New American Library had two million copies in print. When published in hardcover in 1973, it received so-so reviews, never reached the best seller list. Bookfolk who profess to have all the answers attribute its softbound success to a teasing cover and the tale itself, which invites readers of both sexes to discover through four-letter prose what befalls a liberated woman's physique and psyche as she is doing her thing. Perhaps most important is the author's tireless touring: wherever she goes, through campus lectures, press interviews and television appearances, Miss Jong raises eyebrows and makes headlines — even in the shadow of the Smithsonian Institution.

June 1, 1980

Among the most highly paid residents of Publishers Row are the art directors of the mass-market houses — highly paid because their challenging job is to design copies that will impel browsers to pick copies of their latest publications out of the racks and carry them to the checkout counters. It's not hard to concoct a design that will captivate fans of genre books — an embracing couple for lovers of romance, a screaming child for addicts of the occult. But what of the book whose appeal is wide and diverse?

Four of the six covers designed by Milton Charles to illustrate the diverse appeal of War and Remembrance.

The cover that helped Erica Jong's tale of a liberated woman achieve best sellerdom in 1974 and 1975.

Some art directors attempt to solve that quandary by crowding their 7-by-4¼ inch covers with type and pictures describing a book's varied attractions. Pocket Books' Milton Charles, a believer in the "neat, clean look," took another approach in packaging Herman Wouk's best-selling (1,600,000 hardcover copies) novel of World War II, *War and Remembrance*. He designed six different covers, each emphasizing one of the book's appeals. Four of these are shown here—as a story of Navy life, a love story, a story of mother-and-child, a story of the generations on the home front. Two others conjure up thoughts of military action and of family sagas. When six covers are displayed side by side in the racks, even the hastiest browser is quick to get the point.

Mr. Charles' formula seems to be paying off. This is the second successive week *War and Remembrance* is No. 1 on the mass-market paperback best seller list. Formula? Mr. Charles would protest that word. Every week, he says, an art director faces a new batch of challenges and must find fresh ways to solve them.

August 10, 1980

Never underestimate the lengths to which an art director will go to create a cover that will make one of his paperbacks stand out from others in the racks. As of now, the ultimate dazzler is Pocket Books' *Fever Pitch*, a family saga by Betty Ferm. The glowing blue title is in what the trade calls "metallic stamping," the glittering red background is in "day-glow," and there's a face peering out through the gash in the cover. Put on your sunglasses when you approach it.

Blurbs

January 20, 1980

What about the words printed on the front and back covers and on the first inside pages of paperbacks, words that may induce browsers to buy them?

Those words—"blurbs" in the jargon of the trade—are the responsibility of one of publishing's unsung functionaries, the chief copy editor. Often he and his aides write the blurbs in the office. Often, like the art director, he turns to freelancers to help out. As an occupation, blurb writing is neither so well paying nor so soul-satisfying that anyone tries to make a career of it. Most blurb writers move on to jobs as editors just as soon as possible. A few have even become successful writers of books.

In the fluid society of blurb writers, Lester Schulman is something special. During four years as an in-house editor and 13 years as a freelancer for ten large houses, he has written blurbs for more than 6,000 books.

The pattern of Mr. Schulman's life is deceptively simple. In between daily visits to the tennis court to keep in shape and annual visits to Europe to keep intellectually stimulated, he periodically calls at his clients' offices, fills up a big bag with manuscripts and hardcover books scheduled to be published in paperback five months later and carries them back to his apartment on Manhattan's Upper West Side. Evenings, before going to bed, he reads; he's trained himself to read fast and can finish almost any book within an hour. His subconscious goes to work while he's asleep. In the morning he produces a blurb—sometimes several hundred words long, sometimes just a few snappy phrases—within two or three hours.

While writing, Mr. Schulman is not concerned with the writer's vision of his own work. Rather, he keeps in mind what the average paperback buyer—the majority of whom are women—might seek in it. If the book has been a hardcover best seller, he tells how many times it was on the list, for the buyer will be anxious to keep up with his or her friends and the times. If critics have used piquant phrases in reviewing it, he quotes them. Most often, especially if the book is a romance, he hunts for words that will stir up the reader's subliminal feelings, words such as "valley," "towering," "thrusting." "I knew Erica Jong's *Fear of Flying* would be a success even before I read it," he says. "A book with a title like that couldn't miss."

Mr. Schulman has no illusions about his work. "It's a skilled craft, like carpentry." He never goes around to the racks to see how publishers have made use of his creations and says he hasn't done any blurbs in which he takes particular pride. He looks forward to the day when he can devote himself to writing fiction. His all-time favorite author is Proust, his lone contemporary favorite V. S. Naipaul.

Collectors and Antiquarians

December 31, 1978

A year ago we had a visit from a young Dutch architectural student named Hans Oldewarris. Like a number of other Netherlanders, he collects covers of "antique American paperbacks"—those published before 1955 that are prized for their attempts to abandon the macho look of pulp magazines for styles of their own. What we wrote about Mr. Oldewarris at that time put him in touch with a number of American artists and collectors willing to share their memories and hard-to-come-by covers in preparing for an exhibition to be held at Utopia Rotterdam, a center for cultural activities in which he's a partner. The exhibition is still in the offing—"it's a lot more work than we expected"—but the center has just issued as a preview a special issue of its magazine, *Utopia*. In 32 large oblong pages it provides a history of early paperback publishing in the United States, based on original research and interviews with pioneers. Unfortunately only one-third of the text is in English, but the many illustrations, including reproductions of some 60 covers, speak a language all fans can understand.

July 4, 1982

The story of Americans' taste in reading since World War II largely parallels that of the mass-market paperback, a fact that is currently tempting a number of students of popular culture to write histories of softcover publishing. The latest scholar to respond to this challenge is Thomas I. Bonn, a librarian at the State University of New York College at Cortland, whose *Under Cover: An Illustrated History of American Mass-Market Paperbacks* has just been published by Penguin.

Mr. Bonn's long essay begins with summary accounts of the "penny dreadfuls" and "dime novels" that flourished in the United States during the 19th century, the Tauchnitz editions that made good English and American literature available in soft covers in Europe well before World War I, and the numerous experiments in mass-marketing merchandising of books that were made in this country during the 1930's. The burden of his story, however, is what followed the founding in 1939 of Pocket Books, which began the modern Paperback Revolution as we knew it, and the circulation of the paperbound Armed Services Editions in World War II. During the '60's and '70's, all-time sales records were achieved by more than a dozen

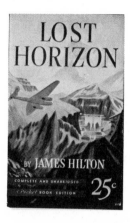

The changing nature of covers for mass-market paperbacks is illustrated by these editions of Lost Horizon. *From left to right, 1939 (by Isadore Steinberg), 1959 (by Tom Dunn), and 1974 (artist unknown). Reproduced from* UnderCover *by Thomas L. Bonn, courtesy of Penguin Books.*

houses, and the field was invaded by the conglomerates. Though far from definitive, Mr. Bonn's history is welcome as an introduction to the subject for newcomers, and it is a nostalgic memento for those who lived through it all.

Mr. Bonn's chief interest is in what was most original and creative in these modern paperbacks — their covers. As the two pictured here indicate, they ranged from the realistic to the suggestive. Much of Mr. Bonn's volume is devoted to discussions of cover artists and the continuing craze for collecting notable examples of their work. More than 70 covers are reproduced rather fuzzily in black and white, 100 others more satisfactorily in full color.

Promotion and Sales Campaigns

January 30, 1977

It's 10:15 on a Thursday morning in a windowless room on the fifth floor of a building across from the United Nations. Around a long table 20 men and women are huddled. At one end sit the chairman and the president of the company, at the other end two art directors. Between them are editors, advertising and promotion directors, other sales persons.

One by one the art directors present the designs they propose be used on the covers of the paperbacks the firm plans to issue six months hence—first routine reissues, then category titles, finally the "leaders." While each one is passed around, its editor explains why it is being published. The sales persons offer estimates of its likely sale based on past experience and their knowledge of current market conditions, then suggest an initial print order.

Sometimes, for the leaders, as many as four possible cover designs are circulated. Suggestions are offered from the circle—a girl ought to be added to the picture or her hair recoiffed to make her look sexier or more refined. Finally the chairman and the president rule which cover shall be used and what the print order shall be. An average of five minutes is spent on a title.

This ritual was enacted last Thursday in the office of Dell Books, where the destiny of 16 books to be released next August—from Mary Roberts Rinehart's 1937 *Married People* to William Goldman's 1976 *Magic*—was weighed. It's a ritual that is performed every month at virtually every mass-market house in the land.

December 25, 1977

The shows go on every year, during the first and second weeks of December. Their settings are usually a sunshiny place— Puerto Rico, the Bahamas, Miami Beach, Key Biscayne, Scottsdale, San Diego. Center stage are large resort hotels with many conference rooms and restaurants to offer liberal quantities of all-American food. Just offstage are beaches, swimming pools, tennis courts, golf links, cocktail lounges, sometimes cabarets and casinos. The shows' casts number 100 to 150, most of them sales representatives from every part of the United States, the rest editors and company executives from New York.

The shows are the annual (sometimes semi-annual) sales conferences of such mass-market houses as Avon, Ballantine, Dell, Fawcett, New American Library and Pocket Books.

When the performers return home, after a three-to-five-day run, they're apt to talk most about the tan they almost acquired, how they made out in the tennis or golf tournament, how much they lost at the casino. This year, if they're Bantam folk, they're likely to smile over memories of the amateur cabaret show staged by Esther Margolis and Fred Klein. If they're Pocket people, they may recall Peter Mayer's and Charlie Williams' running gag about a cricket.

But it was by no means all fun and games. No matter what late hours they kept, they had to be up and bushy-tailed early every morning to attend the long daily sessions at which editors, sales and promotion people presented the coming season's line, title by title. Many found the "work sessions," in which the sales reps meet people from New York in small groups or even one-to-one, especially useful. Now the field men feel they know someone they can get in touch with at headquarters if need be, while the Manhattanites feel they have friends who can keep them informed about what's going on "out there."

Everyone seems confident that next year is going to be a great year for paperbounders. To hear the people at Bantam talk, there's no doubt about it—they're going to remain No. 1. At Ballantine they're convinced that, thanks in part to Judy-Lynn del Rey's fine science fiction line, they're now No. 2. At Pocket Books, they'll tell you that after a long hiatus, they're again a major major. And so it goes—at Avon, Dell, Fawcett, NAL and all the others.

April 11, 1976

Total Release! Super-Release! Blockbuster! Under such exclamations major paperback houses several times a year stage all-out efforts to make one of their promising titles the year's biggest seller. Typical is the campaign currently being staged by Pocket Books in behalf of *Looking for Mr. Goodbar,* Judith Rossner's chiller about the disastrous fate of a New York single girl.

Ever since Pocket's executives sat down to set the strategy six months ago, their prevailing spirit has been urgency. Using the records kept by Simon & Schuster during *Mr. Goodbar's* 36-week-run on the hardcover best seller list, they zeroed in on the likeliest markets. They ordered 1,500,000 copies printed, later upped it to 1,800,000. Their salesmen began touting the novel to their more than 100,000 dealer outlets.

Shipments started moving from their Buffalo printing

plant on March 15—first to the West Coast, then progressively eastward, with an interruption for New York, the communications capital. Instead of relying on parcel post, as is done with run-of-the-mill titles, truckers and United Parcel were hired for the occasion. Instead of being packed in the same carton with a variety of titles, *Mr. Goodbar* was given whole boxes of its own bearing urgent inscriptions that shippers and dealers could not fail to observe.

Meanwhile, intensive promotional ploys were set to work: $100,000 worth of TV spots, bus and subway ads in New York and Chicago, two nationwide author's tours, banners and gimmicks to be displayed in stores, teasing slogans to be stenciled on city sidewalks. Since no store likes to run out of copies when its competitor down the street still has a stock, Pocket maintains an 800 toll-free telephone number a dealer can call for "immediate processing."

How is all this effort paying off? It's still too early to tell for sure, but *Mr. Goodbar* has made the best seller list this week.

Pocket Books' promotional efforts paid off. By the end of the year, *Looking for Mr. Goodbar* had 3,030,000 copies in print, a figure exceeded by only four other paperbacks.

April 15, 1979

Turn on your radio, open your local newspaper or favorite magazine, ride a midtown bus this week and you'll find yourself being teasingly invited to discover something called *Garp*. Stroll along a suburban lane or hang around a corner sandlot and you're apt to see young people wearing T-shirts bearing the declaration: "I Believe in Garp." Look in almost any bookstore window and you'll see piles of a paperback that has covers in six different colors.

What gives? It's all part of one of the most intensive book-promotion campaigns in years, staged in behalf of one of the most unusual books in a long time. *The World According to Garp* is a highly praised novel by John Irving that encompasses such topical themes as feminism, homosexuality and the problems that a man named T. S. Garp has as a writer and family man.

The folks at Pocket Books, the book's publisher, are practicing what they preach—they believe in *Garp*. They've been converts ever since the manuscript was submitted to them late in 1977, the work of a 34-year-old New Englander whose three previous novels had had good reviews but small sales. There have been many staff changes at Pocket Books since then, but the house's faith in *Garp* has continued unabated.

Convinced that the book had a particular appeal for readers under 25, they're spending $100,000 on the current promotion campaign.

Thus far, their faith seems well-placed. *Garp's* hardcover edition, published just a year ago by Dutton, has sold more than 100,000 copies. It was a runner-up for this year's National Book Critics Circle Award and is now spoken of as a real contender for the National Book Award. The book's official publication date is today, but the Pocket people have been stuffing copies into the racks for the past month. To date, they've disposed of 1,700,000 copies.

Unlike most book-promotion campaigns, the hyping of *Garp* is centered on the work rather than on the personality of the author. Mr. Irving has limited his personal appearances in its behalf to two—a reading before the PEN Club in New York and an interview on the Today television show. Now he's back at his Vermont home, typing away on his next novel, *Hotel New Hampshire*.

Pocket Books' belief in *Garp* paid off in the marketplace. It disposed of 2,755,000 copies in 1979, a figure exceeded by only a dozen other mass-market books.

August 28, 1977

"I think," writes Robert Louvis of the Dupont Plaza Newsstand in Washington, D.C., "that a good subject for 'Paperback Talk' would be a discussion of how mass-market publishers are trying a circus-like approach in merchandising and promoting books. The dump display of the Warner book *This Loving Torment* I believe will lead to much success in sales of the book. (In a two-week period I sold almost 30 copies, which in my store is a good figure for a romance book.) In September New American Library will have a romance called *Alyx*, and the floor displays will be scented to smell flowery and will have bottles of perfume for in-store giveaway. What will be next?"

We've just conducted a canvass along Publishers Row to find some answers for Mr. Louvis. Even the oldest oldtimers aren't sure how or when it all began, but all agree that sales-promotion gimmickry is now at an all-time high. NAL and Fawcett are especially active.

Much of the publishers' current effort is aimed directly at wholesalers and retailers. Only if these key men are convinced of a book's potential and order large quantities and display them prominently is it likely to become a best seller.

• Useful gifts festooned with blurbs for new books are being distributed with a lavish hand — to wholesalers, to bookstore owners, to librarians, sometimes even to favored customers. Once it was mostly bookmarks, tote bags and posters. Now it's T-shirts (to advertise Fawcett's *Sports in America*), ladies' garters (Pocket's *Fire in the Blood*), handcrafted porcelain roses (Avon's *Mystic Rose*), jigsaw puzzles (NAL's *The Domino Principle*, Fawcett's *Making Ends Meet*), lace handkerchiefs (Pocket's *Forbidden Rites*), perfume (Berkley's *Indigo Nights*).

• Bookstore clerks whose chore it is to unpack cartons of NAL's *Desires of The Heart* may find a colored card inside. If it's a gold card, they'll receive $500, if it's silver $100, if it's bronze $25 — to spend "according to their heart's desire." They're not likely to forget that title.

As every retailer knows, one of the most difficult parts of selling anything is getting a passerby to stop and take a look. To accomplish this the trade has long been depending on what it disrespectfully calls "dumps" — those large cardboard cartons converted into displays and placed in the middle of an aisle or on the top of a counter. Now the dumps are being embellished as never before.

• To crown its dumpfulls of *The Pride of the Peacock*, Fawcett has a large "riser card" showing a bird spreading its plumage. To house its forthcoming book about U.F.O.'s, *Close Encounters of the Third Kind*, Dell has designed a star-shaped dump aglitter with silver foil. To promote *Ragtime* last year, Bantam had dumps shaped like oldtime pianos; to promote *Sinatra* this year, NAL has displays resembling jukeboxes.

• To induce browsers to prolong their stay, NAL has come up with some novel tricks. In many stores the floor displays for *First, You Cry* will invite them to press a button to hear the recorded voice of Betty Rollin tell them why they should buy her book. And, thanks to an offer the publisher is extending to all booksellers — 50 bottles of "the essence of Alyx" for every 150 copies they order of the novel *Alyx* — many stores besides Mr. Louvis's will be smelling very flowery next month.

The paperback houses are also using many new as well as time-honored gimmicks to prompt the millions of Americans who rarely visit a bookstore to drop into one.

Under their auspices, more than 100 wholesalers across the country are carrying advertisements for the programs of local radio stations on the side panels of their trucks in return for free air time to play cassettes touting new softcover releases.

• Among the prizes many television stations award contestants on their daytime game shows are bundles of paperbacks given them by the publishers in return for a mention of their titles by the show's host.

• This fall Dell will be having airplanes with trailers advertising *The Seventh Game* fly over big-league ball parks during important games. Come October, New York's Times Square will see a 40-by-25-foot ad in lights for the same publisher's *Blood and Money.*

• This week Electra Records is releasing a romantic vocal-and-instrumental number, *This Loving Torment* — which just happens to be the name of Warner Books' current best seller.

"We've got a lot more 'firsts' coming up," one of the most active of the paperbounders assures us, "but we don't want them publicized now — or people will steal them. Yep, it's down to that."

The TV Spot

May 22, 1977

It flashes on the little screen, an interruption in a morning quiz show or an afternoon soap opera. A pretty little blonde girl, the picture of innocence, is having tea with her doll to the accompaniment of soft music and the dulcet patter of an announcer. Suddenly the camera's vision shifts to reveal that the doll's arm has been twisted off. The child's face is distorted now and she's screaming hateful epithets at the toy. Finally there's a large view of a glistening paperback cover featuring a doll with a severed arm while the announcer sonorously declares that "innocence dies so easily, evil lives again . . . and again . . .and again." It's all over in just half a minute and the tube is back to its routine of quiz shows and soap opera.

This TV commercial will be aired next month on stations in New York, Chicago and Los Angeles to promote *Suffer the Children* (Dell), the first published work of John Saul, a 32-year-old former actor, at present a staff member of an Oshkosh, Wisconsin, drug rehabilitation center. If it arouses the curiosity of enough viewers to make them pick the book out of the racks on their next visit to the supermarket or suburban-mall bookstore, the campaign will be extended to half a dozen or more large cities.

Such campaigns have become standard practice in promoting mass-market paperbacks during the past five years. Because TV ad rates are relatively high—up to $500 for 30 seconds of non-prime time in New York—publishers plan their campaigns and monitor them assiduously. As daytime audiences are largely feminine, the book must have a special appeal to housewives. During the past year novels in which the security of the home and the children is menaced, by either natural or supernatural forces, have proved most successful: Avon's *The Auctioneer*, in which the community is threatened by an evil newcomer (1,268,500 copies), Dell's *Where Are the Children?* a tale of tots vanishing when Mom isn't looking (2,150,000); Warner's *Audrey Rose*, a reincarnated child on Manhattan's Central Park West (3,289,000).

The lure of *Suffer the Children* is writ plain on its cover: "In Port Arbello the children are disappearing, one by one. An evil history is repeating itself." Dell, convinced that it has another *Where Are the Children?* on its hands, has ordered a first printing of 500,000 copies—large for a previously unpublished first novel—and is ready to go back to press and step up its campaign if they move fast.

September 25, 1977

Did the TV ad for *Suffer the Children* live up to its publisher's hopes? Very much so, according to Lee Simmons of Franklin Spier Inc., the advertising agency in charge of the book's promotion. During July the spot was shown in eight large cities, in August on two nationally televised game shows. When the returns were tallied afterwards, it was found that *Suffer the*

Children had sold 1,225,000 copies, most of them within a few days of the ad's airing. It is a remarkable record for a first novel that got no reviews, was supported by neither an author tour nor other promotional tie-ins.

Mr. Simmons hastens to add that he doesn't believe TV spots alone can always sell a book. The national mood, he says, is right just now for "bad seed" stories.

Author's Tours

June 14, 1981

No matter where you are in the United States this month, if you turn on your television or radio set, read a newspaper or a magazine, you're apt to come across Gay Talese discussing his book *Thy Neighbor's Wife*, Martha Weinman Lear her memoir *Heart Sounds*, Erica Jong her novel *Fanny*, Adrien Arpel her *How to Look Ten Years Younger* and Craig Claiborne his *Craig Claiborne's Gourmet Diet*. They and a score of other writers of recently released paperbacks are on coast-to-coast tours, carrying on the tradition established a generation ago by Jacqueline Susann and Mickey Spillane—a tradition founded on the notion that an author's job isn't over once he's written a book, but that it behooves him to get out there and help sell it when it's published.

Most authors' tours nowadays last three or four weeks, including stops in 10 to 15 cities, with scarcely a moment to rest. They may call for a half-dozen engagements a day—a breakfast meeting with the truck drivers who deliver paperbacks to mass-market racks and can see that they get a proper display there, a mid-morning appearance on a television show, a lunchtime interview with a newspaperman, an autograph session at a large bookstore, perhaps a dinner meeting with a group concerned with the book's subject, evening encounters with the jockeys of radio talk shows. Through it all, the author must remain smiling, quick-witted and gussied up, undaunted by the travails of travel, sometimes helped in and out of airplanes and limousines by an accompanying publisher's publicist, more often by the publisher's local sales rep. Grueling though the experience is, many writers thrive on it.

Thirty cities are currently favorite stops for authors, because they are good markets for books and are what the trade calls "good media towns." The big three: New York City, originating point of such nationally televised programs as Today, Good Morning America, Tomorrow and The Dick Cavett Show; Chicago, home of The Phil Donahue Show; and Los Angeles, home of The Merv Griffin Show. Washington, D.C., long hospitable to books with a political slant, is becoming even more important thanks to the new, syndicated Charlie Rose Show. Like Mr. Donahue, Mr. Rose devotes a full hour to a single author, rather than the six minutes that most nationally televised programs allow.

Other good book towns? San Francisco, Houston, Boston, Atlanta, Philadelphia and Detroit. Towns on the rise? San Diego, Seattle, Portland, Oregon, and Norfolk, Virginia.

With the cost of travel skyrocketing, many publishers have begun to wonder whether the author's tour is worth all the cost and bother. Bantam Books' Stuart Applebaum has an answer to that: "Recently we talked Mickey Spillane into coming to New York for a three-night stand in behalf of his first book for young people, *The Sea Rolled Back*. We got a tremendous amount of press and media attention. It would have cost us many times the $1,100 the tour cost us to buy a few seconds of television advertising time."

September 29, 1981

This week, for the sixth time, a book listing some 600 widely prescribed drugs that remain on the market although they have been shown to be ineffective in government-ordered studies claims a place on the trade paperback best seller list. *Pills That Don't Work* by Sidney M. Wolfe, M.D. and Christopher Coley has an unlikely publisher—Farrar Straus & Giroux, a house noted for its works of literary distinction.

Even more curious is how this all came about. The book is the product of the Washington-based Public Citizen Health Research Group, founded ten years ago by Ralph Nader. Dr. Wolfe is the organization's director. The Group distributed *Pills* to its own loyal following by mail last year, but was anxious to take it to the general public through the bookstores. Dr. Wolfe called it to the attention of Roger W. Straus Jr., an old friend and FS&G's president. Mr. Straus quickly signed up the book and, last September, hopefully sent out 50,000 copies to the stores.

What Mr. Straus hadn't taken fully into account was that Dr. Wolfe, an accomplished hand at personal appearances in behalf of his cause, had entree to the nationally syndicated Phil Donahue television talk show, a great favorite with concerned American housewives. As soon as Dr. Wolfe's hour-long conversation with Mr. Donahue about pills that don't work went on the air, orders for the book began pouring into FS&G's offices. To date, the book has sold 280,000 copies.

Word-of-Mouth

April 12, 1981

Along Publishers Row, a neighborhood whose residents seldom all agree about anything, there's one matter about which opinion is unanimous—nothing sells a book like "word-of-mouth." Favorable reviews, advertisements in the press, on television and radio, book-club adoptions, attractive cover designs and elaborate displays in bookstores help launch a book, but to become a true popular success, it must possess a magic quality that impels readers to recommend it to others.

To see how word-of-mouth operates, we've just studied the case of *A Woman of Substance* by Barbara Taylor Bradford (Avon), which last week completed a 43-week run on the mass-market paperback best-seller list—an all-time record exceeded only by *The Complete Scarsdale Medical Diet.* (Sales of the latter have undoubtedly been helped by the fact that the author was the victim in a sensational murder case.) Among mass-market books, a 12-week appearance on the list is considered an excellent record, even for a "blockbuster." Since publishing *A Woman* last June, Avon has gone back to press 12 times; it now has 2,750,000 copies in print.

In the course of our inquiry, we talked with the folks at Avon, with the mass-market buyer at the Ingram Book Company, the nation's largest wholesaler, and with the owners of a dozen representative independent bookstores from Florida to the state of Washington. Almost everyone said that when *A Woman* was first shown to them, they expected it to be a good but not phenomenal seller. It was a first novel, and first novels aren't easy to sell. It did have several things going for it: the Literary Guild had made it an alternate selection. It received generally "good" reviews. Doubleday's $12.95 edition sold

45,000 copies, giving it a brief stay on the hardcover best-seller list. Avon paid $315,000 for reprint rights.

It was only after *A Woman* had been in the store racks for a few weeks that it began to show it had that word-of-mouth magic in rare degree. Book industry economists estimate that 60 percent of the nation's book readers are women. Mrs. Bradford's novel is the sort that women enjoy—a long (360,000-word) story about the rise of a strong feminine woman from humble origins to command of an international business enterprise, a story duly laced with family conflicts.

The booksellers told us what happened in their stores: "Women came in from the beauty parlor down the block demanding a copy of the book they'd heard all about while they were having their hair done." . . . "I've seen women standing in front of the racks trying to decide what to buy and other customers run up to them and point at it and say, 'You'll *love* that!' " . . . "It's one book that I can honestly recommend—like *The Thorn Birds*." . . . "There's a reading club in our town and all the members came in to buy it."

Did the television time that Avon bought to advertise *A Woman* inspire any sales? "I didn't know there were any TV ads," all the booksellers said.

A final, promising word for everyone who's loved *A Woman of Substance*. Mrs. Bradford, a 48-year-old native of Leeds, England, now a resident of Manhattan and a longtime conductor of a syndicated column on home decorating, is presently finishing her second novel. It's about not one, but two strong women.

Sales Reps at Work

March 6, 1977

"Over the years," writes one of our readers who works for a major paperback house, "you've sung the achievements of authors, editors, cover designers, publicity and promotion people—but never said a word about those who sell the books. Won't you give us sales reps a break?"

The man has a point. So the other day we called on Alex Holtz, a New American Library sales vice president, to find out just what a sales rep is and does. Herewith some notes:

- There are more than a thousand of them—men and an increasing number of women—employed by U.S. paperback firms, national distributors, regional wholesalers and jobbers, whose task it is to see that the 400 mass-market titles published each month get into the store racks.
- The typical sales rep is a traveler, constantly on the road calling on his several hundred accounts. In populous areas he visits each one every two to eight weeks, in the wide open spaces of the West several times a year. He does his traveling by car—except in New York, where parking is a problem. One rep gets around Manhattan by motor scooter.
- Although historically paperback distribution evolved out of the magazine business, the newest breed of sales rep cut his eyeteeth in a bookstore, usually as a manager, where he learned the necessity of matching what he had to sell with the taste of his clientele. When he calls on buyers for bookstores, he finds himself dealing with kindred spirits. When he calls at variety stores and supermarkets, he finds his advice accepted eagerly, for their buyers' knowledge of the world of books is slight. His advice had better be good: paperbacks are fully returnable and unsold copies will come back to darken his record.
- Some sales reps are chairbound creatures, stationed at telephones in the publishers' headquarters to answer the "800-line" toll-free calls that come in from stores between the travelers' visits. Most of these are women, who deftly mix a little friendly talk about the weather with the serious business of taking reorders.
- A successful traveling sales rep keeps his ears and eyes open in stores and out to learn of sudden shifts in taste and the appearance of new trends. He passes what he learns on to his firms' sales managers and editors back in that often out-of-touch place called Manhattan.
- When the author of a book the sales rep is handling visits his territory in the course of a promotional tour, he's expected to provide advice and help in arranging appearances on the most influential local TV and radio shows and at the most strategically located bookstores. Sometimes he drives the visiting celebrity around from one date to another.

All this doesn't tell the whole story of the sales rep by any means, but it should suggest why authors and editors and top executives acknowledge they couldn't last very long without him.

Selling Through Bookstores

February 1, 1981

Twenty years ago, whenever New York publishers visited Chicago, they made a point of dropping by one of Kroch's & Brentano's stores to see something extraordinary. This very respectable bookseller accorded valuable display space to a kind of merchandise than known only to newsstands, drug-stores and airport shops—papercovered books. They were, of course, segregated in the basement.

How things have changed! A survey of 500 independent booksellers in all sections of the country recently conducted by the trade journal *Publishers Weekly* gleaned the following statistics and impressions:

• Mass-market paperbacks constitute 41 percent of their current unit sales, trade paperbacks 28 percent.

• Mass-market books occupy 39 percent of their display space, trade paperbacks 27 percent.

• Nearly 70 percent of the stores now integrate their display of hardcover and softcover books. The 500-store B. Dalton chain, a recent convert to integration, reports that it made the change because customers seemed to prefer it that way.

• Booksellers predict that by 1990 paperback sales will account for 70 percent of their dollar sales.

• A familiar refrain from the customers: "The price of hardcover fiction is now too high for a one-time read. I'll wait until those novels come out in paperback."

February 3, 1980

For most Americans, the name of the Tennessee capital evokes visions of the Grand Ole Opry and sounds of country music. For 7,000 booksellers across the country, Nashville is the place from which they can order urgently needed books, delivered expeditiously with the aid of sophisticated computers.

When one of these booksellers finds that his stock of a new book is running low or receives a request from a customer for some backlist titles, he is often reluctant to order them directly from the publisher or even a nearby wholesaler; from experience he knows it may take weeks for them to arrive. He'd rather go to a computer terminal in the back of his store, insert one of the microfiche films listing 23,000 titles currently stocked by the Ingram Book Company, and if the books he wants are on it, telephone his order to Nashville.

At 39 computer stations in a sprawling building on the outskirts of Nashville, women are waiting to take calls like his. A phone conversation is held, orders taken and discussed. One day recently, within a span of ten minutes, we watched Ingram order takers chatting with booksellers in Alaska, Nevada and Virginia.

If the order is from a bookstore in the American heartland, a printed copy is rushed to the vast adjoining warehouse. There a corps of young men and women are moving about, filling up shopping carts from long rows of well-arranged stacks. Within a few hours the order is packaged and on its way to the bookstore by truck. If the order is from a bookstore in a more distant part of the country, it is telephoned to an Ingram warehouse in Jessup, Maryland, City of Industry, California, or Bellevue, Washington, to be filled in a similar fashion from there.

Ingram is a major contributor to the revolution that has been taking place in American bookselling during the past ten years. While large chains like B. Dalton and Waldenbooks were opening branches in shopping malls from coast to coast, many locally-owned bookstores at first found themselves hard put to compete. For many, Ingram, with its fast delivery service, has proved a godsend.

Ingram is a venture of a family deeply involved in such earthy industries as petroleum refining and marine transportation. One of the family's companies constructed one-third of the Alaska pipeline. Nine years ago, the Ingrams bought a small Tennessee textbook supply house and from it have developed the Ingram Book Company, a wholesaler whose sales last year exceeded $100 million.

Much of Ingram's success has been attributed to its executives' combination of computer and bookselling expertise. It was quick to respond to the challenges of the 1970's. Six years ago, at a time when bookstores were just starting to be hospitable to mass-market paperbacks as well as trade paperback books, Ingram began handling complete lines of both. Until that time the distribution of mass-market paperbacks had been dominated by some 550 regionally-oriented independent distributors—"ID's." The ID's specialty was magazines; paperbacks were no more than a sideline.

The people who run Ingram make much of the fact that they are "real book people," with a knowledge of and instinct for what will appeal to bookstore patrons. They are eager to supply any backlist title a customer seeks. Their paperback buyers insist that for all the data about current and developing trends made available to them by their computers, they still act on the hunches of any true bookman. In the promotional pieces they send out to their customers, they don't always push the sensational "blockbusters" that the mass-market houses are featuring, but concentrate on the titles they feel bookstore customers prefer.

Ingram's relationship with paperbacks has been a happy one financially. They accounted for one-half of the company's sales last year—a situation shared by most bookstores.

Selling Through ID's

May 10, 1981

In troubled times, remember your old friends. That adage is being heeded these days by the 550 independent distributors—who see that one-half of the paperbacks sold get into the nation's mass-market racks.

The friendship between the largely family-owned ID's and the paperback publishers dates back to the years right after World War II, when the distributors agreed to take on the new softcover books to supplement their magazine lines. Thanks to the ID's efforts, drugstores, stationery stores and other retail outlets began displaying books in neighborhoods where books had never been sold before. Best-selling authors like Jacqueline Susann made a point of making personal appearances before groups of ID deliverymen to ask that they give their latest books a prominent place in the racks. Gradually, paperbacks came to represent one-third of the ID's business.

The friendship cooled during the 1970's. The ID's became annoyed when the number of copies of books they sold stopped growing, while the costs of handling unsold copies kept rising. Meanwhile, their sales of magazines—titles like *Playboy* and

Penthouse for men, *Family Circle* and *Woman's Day* for women, hundreds of titles for special-interest readerships—rocketed.

There were other irritations. Thousands of new bookstores opened across the country. All bookstores began selling paperbacks, which, in many cases, they purchased directly from the publishers or from jobbers who specialized in books. By the end of the decade, paperbacks accounted for less than one-fifth of the ID business, and some of them were heard to say they wondered if books were worth all the trouble they entailed.

But this year, when ID's get together at their regional conventions, they're talking of their old paperback friends in another tone of voice. Magazine sales have stopped growing and in some cases have dropped a bit. Perhaps, the ID's say, they should start paying more attention to paperbacks.

The new marketing possibilities they're thinking about include "Family Reading Centers," books and magazines displayed in such a manner that they become a bookstore within a large variety store or supermarket. There are now 1,000 such centers across the country.

At the convention of the American Booksellers Association late this month, the Council of Periodical Distributors of America, the ID's trade organization, will have an exhibit urging booksellers to open magazine sections in their stores. The paperback-magazine connection, it appears, is about to grow stronger.

December 2, 1979

As the owner of three bookstores in San Jose, California, the Milligan News Company, an enterprising magazine wholesaler, plays an important role in the cultural life of its community, but it is by no means unique. Today some 200 ID's in every section of the country operate more than 650 retail bookstores. Their interest in books dates back to the introduction of mass-market paperbacks during World War II. When national chains such as B. Dalton and Waldenbooks began opening stores in their regions half a dozen years ago, they countered with chains of their own. All carry both hardcover and softcover books. Among the leaders are the Portland News Company in Maine, the Scott Kraus News Agency in Columbus, Ohio, the Delmar News Company in Delaware and the Charles Levy Company near Chicago.

Typical of this new breed of bookman is Roy Newborn, circulation manager of the late *New York Herald Tribune*, who describes himself as "a zealot for the printed word." On moving to central Pennsylvania to set up the Altoona News Agency, he found himself amid a blue-collar population that was eager to read, but without a single bookstore to serve it. In the past half dozen years he has established a flourishing chain of five stores. The bookish spirit runs in the Newborn family: his daughter Barbara is in charge of Altoona News' sales to schools and libraries.

Mr. Newborn has a conviction that is shared by many others in the business. If more wholesalers would become involved in book retailing, they'd learn how to match various types of books with their reading public's tastes and could therefore greatly reduce the high percentage of paperbacks returned unsold—a percentage that is threatening the industry's health.

Some Remarkable Markets

Special States: Hawaii and Alaska

July 26, 1981

Although Alaska and Hawaii are celebrating their 22nd birthdays as full-fledged members of the United States this year, both remain lands apart. This is partly because they are far from any of their sisters—Alaska's principal city is some 1,250 miles from the nearest point in the "lower 48 states"; Hawaii's capital is 2,000 miles from the California coast. Each state is unique in its compound of diverse cultural and ethnic heritages and its geographical and economic conditions.

How do these differences affect the roles they play in the American book world? We asked that question of wholesalers who distribute paperbacks to retailers in the two states. Herewith a precis of their replies:

• For the three million tourists from the American mainland and the Orient who annually visit the isolated cluster of 124 tropical islands that is the 50th state, Hawaii is a bit of paradise. But Gene Sturtevant of Honolulu, head of Hawaiian

Magazine Distributors, supplier of paperbacks to 450 outlets in the state, finds that paradise has its problems.

Although in land area Hawaii is a small state—only slightly larger than Connecticut—many of Mr. Sturtevant's troubles result from distances. It usually takes eight weeks for copies of new books to make the land-and-sea journey from a Midwestern printing plant to the HMD warehouse in Waikiki. Shipments from there to stores in the outer islands are by barge, another slow and, sometimes in winter, stormy passage. This delay creates embarrassments for retailers when tourists arriving from the mainland complain that the titles on display as "new releases" were on sale in their home towns long ago.

There is, according to Mr. Sturtevant, hardly one first-rate bookstore in Hawaii. Most books are sold in stores specializing in the tourist trade, alongside souvenirs, T-shirts and suntan lotion. For such visitors, James A. Michener's 1959 *Hawaii* has a perennial appeal (2,250 copies sold each month). There is a constant interest in fiction about the Orient, especially Japan. James Clavell's 1975 *Shogun* is a brisk seller, as are two current novels, Eric Van Lustbader's *The Ninja* and Robert Shea's *Shike.*

Recently tourism, the lifeblood of Hawaii's economy, has been having a wobbly time. Do the one million people who live there help keep the book trade alive? "The local people aren't good readers," says Mr. Sturtevant. "They buy comic books, picture magazines and Harlequin-type romances."

Mr. Sturtevant sighs when he looks over the releases that paperback publishers are sending him these days. "Always more of the same. Rarely anything excitingly new. Perhaps it's time to give the good books on the backlists a new life."

• For Russ Riemann of Anchorage, who is both president of the Alaska News Agency, which supplies 273 retail outlets throughout the state, and owner of the Book Cache, a chain of 15 retail stores, the 49th state is a land of boundless opportunities. Its distances are magnificent—its land area is one-fifth of the size of the whole United States. Its population is sparse—400,000, about the size of Harrisburg, Pennsylvania. Its oil and mineral resources are abundant—with the result that in recent years it has attracted thousands of well-paid, well-educated, highly literate young settlers, most of them male.

As in Hawaii, remoteness from the rest of the nation creates problems for Alaska bookmen. It takes a consignment of books three to four weeks to arrive by sea or air freight from the printer. From Anchorage, orders are flown to stores in cities as far away as Nome and Kotzebue.

Alaskans' reading tastes, according to Mr. Riemann, are in general similar to those of other Americans. The most popular book currently is *Coming Into the Country,* John McPhee's account of his experiences in Alaska's wide open spaces. Mysteries and Westerns—particularly the stories of Louis L'Amour—have strong followings. There is relatively little demand for romances in the Harlequin style.

Mr. Riemann refuses to join bookmen in other parts of the nation who take a gloom-and-doom view of their trade. Sales are steady throughout the year—the long winter nights are conducive to reading, but there are many book-buying visitors during the summer. Nor is there any resistance to the high price that many paperbacks now bear. "A price of $3.95 may seem a lot of money for a book in Omaha," he says, "but compared to what a sandwich costs in Anchorage, it's a bargain."

Washington, D.C.

March 28, 1982

How's business? Ask that question of booksellers in most parts of the country nowadays and you're apt to see long faces and hear laments about inflation and high unemployment and the soaring cost of books.

Ask the question of a dealer in the metropolitan area of Washington, D.C.—an area whose book sales now rate fourth or fifth in the nation—and you'll get quite different responses:

• "Our business is inflation-proof," says Doug Talley of the District News Company, supplier of mass-market paperbacks to newsstands, supermarkets and variety stores. "And, of course, sales will go up as spring brings the tourists."

• "Business is good, and we expect it to stay that way," says Jim Tenney, buyer for the Book Annex, whose three stores are richly stocked with special-interest and backlist titles.

• "Business was soft in January, because of the terrible weather, but it's back to normal now," says Bill Kramer of Sidney Kramer Books, one of whose four stores has a cafe as an added attraction. "Some government agencies have had their book budgets cut, but we've adapted to that."

- "Business is very good," says Robert M. Haft, president of Crown Books, a discount chain that has just opened its 29th store in the area.

The reason for these high spirits is, of course, the fact that Washington's chief raison d'etre is politics and government, a way of life that has lured thousands of well-educated professionals—lawyers, journalists, bureaucrats, lobbyists, foreign diplomats—to the city. They and their families are especially devoted to books, a love they can indulge because their per capita income is the highest in the nation.

The typical Washingtonian, like most of his countrymen, buys many more paperbacks than hardbacks—the ratio is more than three to one—but the titles he chooses aren't average American. He's particularly fond of nonfiction books about politics, national and international, past and present. Current favorites in capital bookstores include Henry Kissinger's *Years of Upheaval,* Joseph Alsop's *FDR: A Centenary Remembrance,* Anthony Samson's *The Money Lenders,* Robert Lacey's *The Kingdom* and David Holden and Richard Johns' *The House of Saud.* Such accounts of the Japanese way of life as *The Art of Japanese Management, Theory Z* and *A Book of Five Rings* sell very well. Ballantine's new Espionage/Intelligence Library has many fans.

The Washingtonian's fascination with espionage and intrigue extends to the fiction he buys. Booksellers have had great trouble getting enough copies of Robert Ludlum's new thriller, *The Parsifal Mosaic,* to satisfy the extraordinary demand.

In general, the Washingtonian's taste in fiction closely resembles that of his fellow Americans. Romances, family sagas and whodunits are extremely popular. "After all," as one bookseller puts it, "no matter what your line of work, after a hard session at the office, when you read nights and weekends you're likely to seek entertainment and escape."

Silicon Valley

December 2, 1979

One sunny Saturday several weeks ago, 3,000 people packed a civic auditorium to hear eight authors of current best sellers discuss their literary philosophies, then lined up to have the visiting celebrities autograph copies of their books. Later, several of the guests, veterans of many a book-promotion tour, were heard to say that this was the most exciting encounter with readers they'd ever experienced. That pleased, but hardly surprised their hosts. This was the fourth annual author-reader encounter they'd held, and writers attending the preceding ones had said the same thing. It took place in the heart of the eighth largest book market in the United States, a market that is, per capita, one of the richest.

Washington? San Francisco? Dallas? No, San Jose.

San Jose is the seat of California's Santa Clara County, chief city of what quipsters call Silicon Valley, the home of hundreds of companies that manufacture sophisticated electronic devices and employ thousands of highly educated young men and women who spend a lot of their high salaries on reading matter. On the peninsula that is Santa Clara County are half a dozen institutions of higher learning, including Stanford University, which helped start the computer revolution. Local partisans contend that more books are bought in San Jose's metropolitan area than in San Francisco, 60 miles to the north.

Partisans include *The San Jose Mercury-News*, the daily that sponsors the encounters, and the Milligan News Company, a magazine wholesaler that operates three bookstores in the city and services most bookstores in the 45 shopping centers that dot the valley.

Airports

March 30, 1980

"Paperbacks? Sure. I often pick up one at the airport. Helps kill the time of the plane ride." Over the years that comment has been made so frequently that many people assume that sales at airport stores constitute a considerable portion of the nation's paperback business. But do they?

None of the marketing specialists we queried recently were willing to hazard a guess as to what percentage of the paperbacks sold these days are from racks in airports. But all agreed that the number has declined steadily in recent years, because rising rents have obliged the stores' operators to allot more space to merchandise like souvenirs and jewelry on which the profit margin is greater.

One man who's unhappy with the trend is Ed Elson, whose companies service the airports of Atlanta, Chicago, Boston, Houston and Pittsburgh. "We don't have room for titles over which a buyer's got to browse. He must know about them in advance from the best seller lists or from the authors' reputations. Most people who use airports are men traveling on business. They're put off by the length of many of the current books—1,000 pages is too long for an airborne read." But Mr. Elson is happy about the current spate of suspensers—books by the likes of Robert Ludlum and Len Deighton. They're the sort of thing businessmen on the move love to read.

Special Sales

May 21, 1978

On the backs of the title pages of several publishers' paperbacks appears a cryptic legend: "Our books are available at discounts in bulk for sales-promotional use." Just what does that mean?

Quite a number of houses—most don't advertise the fact so openly—conduct a lively trade in what is known variously as "premiums, special sales and co-publishing ventures." Thus a house with a "cheese cookbook" on its list—or willing to have one—creates a special edition for a cheese maker to offer its customers as a premium; meanwhile it sells its own edition through bookstores. A book about sports may be similarly useful to a sports-equipment manufacturer and sporting-goods stores.

An important figure in this unsung side of the book business is Roy Benjamin, who got started back in 1953, when he brought Pocket Books and Johnson & Johnson, the baby powder manufacturer, together as co-distributors of Dr. Benjamin Spock's *Baby and Child Care.* Today the Benjamin Company has a staff of 20, who are busy devising variations and elaborations of the original idea. They'll even go so far as to track down subjects for which a need has recently developed, locate an interested commercial sponsor and a publisher, find a suitable author and assist in the editorial and production work.

At present, Mr. Benjamin reports, Americans seem most concerned about home security, consumerism and money management — and his organization is working with manufacturers and services willing to sponsor books on such topics. Come June, for example, one of his ideas, *Protect Yourself: The Complete Guide to Safeguarding Your Life and Home* by N. H. and S. K. Mager, will be on sale in hardware stores, courtesy of the Master Lock Company, and in bookstores as a Dell paperback. In its pages the products of the Master Lock Company are duly mentioned, but so are many devices and services in which it has no interest.

Mr. Benjamin feels that his kind of publishing serves the common good. Millions of Americans, he says, seldom venture into a bookstore. Start them reading books on topics close to where they live, and they may develop into bibliophiles.

The Fate of Unsold Copies

November 22, 1981

What is the design below — the like of which you see every day on cans of coffee, boxes of soda crackers and bottles of ketchup — doing in a book about paperback publishing? It's here because it's one of the devices by which mass-marketeers hope to reduce the number of copies returned to them unsold, which is now in the neighborhood of 45 percent.

The design is the Universal Product Code symbol — a series of bars and numbers that can be scanned and tabulated by machines at checkout counters of chain supermarkets and bookstores, stores that sell millions of paperbacks every month. Almost every book published, hardcover and soft, is given a number by the International Standard Book Agency. An ISBN number identifying the book by title and other numbers

identifying its publisher, distributor and price are incorporated in the design. When exposed to scanning devices at checkout counters, these mazes make it possible for a clerk to add up a customer's bill automatically and quickly—and provide the store manager with information he needs to replenish his stock.

Blockbuster books like *The Key to Rebecca* sell equally well in all kinds of stores and in all kinds of neighborhoods. On the other hand, there's little demand for Westerns in supermarkets in sections of town that are crowded with fashionable boutiques or for teen-age romances in open-all-night convenience stores along interurban highways. The wholesalers who keep the nation's supermarkets and variety stores supplied with paperbacks hope that the day will come when the universal use of the UPC will enable them to construct a profile of the reading tastes of each store's customers and so put into its racks only books that are certain to find a welcome there.

Paperback publishers have been relatively slow in joining the UPC parade. Especially vociferous in opposition have been their art directors. ("Spoil a beautifully designed cover with a blotch like that? Oh, no!") But when Pocket Books and New American Library begin using the code on their books early next year, all the major mass-market houses will be playing the game and the prospects for reducing the rate of returns will be considerably brighter.

October 23, 1977

Shredder. Just the sound of the word is enough to make the blood of otherwise undauntable writers turn cold. A machine that can turn thousands of printed copies of their wit and industry into unreadable shavings within a matter of minutes! For as every well-read author knows, it is the practice of all publishers and distributors of mass-market paperbacks to destroy the copies of books they have not been able to sell within a few months of publication and for which there seems to be no likely demand in the future.

Just what does a shredder look like in operation? There are nearly 2,000 varieties on the market, no one of which is particularly favored by the more than 750 wholesalers and jobbers who use them in their daily operations. To satisfy our curiosity, we decided to go see the one in use at the Hudson News

Company, a 50-year-old New Jersey wholesaler now in the midst of a vigorous effort to increase its book business in a highly competitive area, metropolitan New York. It occupies a sizable warehouse among the expressways and small houses of North Bergen, 45 minutes from Broadway.

Every morning Hudson's 88 trucks fan out across New Jersey, Manhattan, the Bronx and Yonkers, leaving boxes filled with what the trade calls "new issues" at supermarkets, newsstands and stationery stores, each night returning with bundles of "old issues" that had not been selling briskly enough to warrant their keeping a pocket in the paperback racks. From most, the front covers are stripped off to be returned to their publishers for full credit; their innards are then tossed onto a conveyor belt.

Bob Tipton, Hudson's vice president and sales manager, suggested that we follow the conveyor belt. High above us, in a vast storage room, the coverless paperbacks glided toward and then into a great square green-covered metal enclosure. "Jaws," he said, "is inside that. Let's go take a look."

We opened the door of the enclosure and peered inside. There was not much to see. A cluster of large pipes and several pulleys spinning belts. "There are a lot of metal fingers and sharp knives in there," Mr. Tipton said, pointing at the piping.

We emerged, feeling a little depressed, and walked to the other side of the enclosure. Here was another conveyor belt, onto which was popping a line of small metal-tied bales containing shreds of printed matter. "We sell that to people who'll recycle it," he exclaimed, with what sounded like a cheery note.

At the latest count, 45 percent of all mass-market paperbacks printed in the United States end up in a bale headed for the recycler. With manufacturing and distribution costs rising fast these days, the whole trade is working hard to reduce that figure. "We've got our returns down to 35 percent," Mr. Tipton said proudly. "We're trying not to order more copies of a book than we think we can sell, and we're watching each dealer's record to see that he gets only the sort of titles and the quantity he's likely to sell."

The Crisis of the '80's

The Revolution Winds Down

The Paperback Revolution was three decades old when the *New York Times Book Review* published a cautionary editorial:

February 16, 1969

Is the Paperback Revolution dead?

The Revolution's ministry of propaganda keeps on cranking out press releases full of glowing statistics. Last year the American public bought more than 350 million paperbacks for an estimated $66 million, accounting for approximately 15 percent of the publishing industry's income. There were some 12,000 new titles, upping the list in this month's issue of *Paperbound Books in Print* to 63,000.

But the press releases are deceiving. Thirty years after the first appearance of the low-priced paperback on the newsstands, 16 years after the debut of the higher-priced, high-intellectual-content paperback in the bookstores, there are signs that the Revolution is standing still—and may even have slipped into reverse gear.

The total number of paperbacks sold annually has remained substantially the same for ten years. Almost as many paperbacks were sold in 1959 as in 1968. Meanwhile, the population has increased 15 percent.

While the dollar volume has gone up, it has gone up because cover prices have gone up.

Ten years ago, less than five percent of paperback sales were to the school and college market. Last year the figure was 25 percent. Thus it appears that the *general public* is actually buying fewer paperbacks today than in 1959.

Why?

Have the more expensive cover prices created sales resistance? Many salesmen claim that if the public wants a book it will pay whatever the industry charges, but there have been no controlled tests to determine the facts.

Does the industry need more outlets? The number of sales outlets—100,000 newsstands, cigar stores, etc., handling mass-market paperback titles and 1,700 bookstores dealing in paperbacks of all types—hasn't increased in a decade. The individual with a modest amount of capital and a knowledge and love of books finds it difficult to enter a business taken over by big retailers. And the big retailers look on paperbacks as just one consumer product among many. (To assist these busy, non-bookish men in stocking titles, some publishers are experimenting with computers.)

What about libraries and schools? There is a bureaucratic and traditional resistance on the part of many institutions to the use of paperbacks. At a time when librarians complain that 70 percent of the population has "dropped out" of the circulating system, only 36 percent of public libraries give paperbacks shelf space. And while three-quarters of the nation's schools use paperbacks, at least 17 states forbid the spending of public funds for them. The industry has to educate the educators.

Have the Paperback Revolutionaries gotten tired? The industry today wears a middle-aged look. The men in power entered the field a dozen years ago, during its great period of expansion. More editors and salesmen in close touch with members of the younger generation might result in titles with a greater attraction for under-35 readers.

Is Marshall McLuhan right? Has the Now Generation dropped out of print culture? If so, not only paperbacks, but the whole publishing industry is in trouble, not to mention the intellectual life of the nation.

As it turned out, the alarm of the *Book Review's* editorialist was quite premature. During the next decade, the paperback industry resumed its growth, then settled onto a plateau that caused a number of leading publishers to express fears and apprehensions:

November 20, 1977

What's been happening to the Paperback Revolution? Oscar Dystel, president of Bantam Books, spoke like a Dutch uncle at a recent wholesalers' convention:

• It's stopped growing. The number of paperbacks sold soared steadily from the late 1960's to 1973, when the total was 520 million copies. The number has been static ever since. Last year it was off three percent, and this year there'll probably be little change.

• Its growth has been stopped by great increases in cover prices—since 1971 almost twice as fast as the Consumers Price Index. Price tags are still climbing. Five years ago "a person could put down a $5 bill and walk out with four or five paperbacks. Today he'll buy only one—and pocket the change."

How can the industry escape its developing crisis at a time when competition "is more intense than I can ever remember"? According to Mr. Dystel, a 23-year veteran of the business:

• Publishers should show more restraint in the number of titles they publish. Five years ago 350 titles came out each month, now it's 400.

• Publishers should offer a more varied product. They now concentrate on: books for which they've paid $1 million or more for reprint rights; books that they can back up with expensive coast-to-coast television campaigns, in the hope of hyping them into best sellers; books tied to movies and television series, a formula that sometimes works, sometimes does not. Instead of concentrating on imitative titles, publishers should be more inventive in their editorial product: "We mustn't forget writers like Henry James and William Faulkner, important new books on social, political and economic themes. Some of us know that money can be made that way and can prove it."

September 11, 1977

The way things are going in book publishing, it's only a matter of time until the business is dominated by seven giant companies—with a little room on the side for a few wildcatters. That's the prediction Richard E. Snyder, head of Simon & Schuster, made several months ago to a *Publishers Weekly* interviewer.

Start a mass-market paperback house from scratch? In today's bitterly competitive market, it would require at least $10 million capital. That was the estimate given us the other day by the president of a major mass-market house.

November 27, 1977

"Once upon a time," some people whose job it is to watch what goes on in American business are saying, "book publishing was a cottage industry, a wide spatter of mom-and-pop enterprises. But during the past 20 years there have been more than 200 book publishing mergers. That's only a beginning. Before long, for example, the 20 mass-market paperbacks will be reduced to six or seven. All book publishing will become part of the world's fastest-growing, most high-powered industries, the media business.

Soaring Costs

April 2, 1979

Two years ago this week the average price of the paperbacks on the mass-market best seller list was $2.10. A year ago it was $2.36. This week it is $2.56. Almost all the "big books" announced for this summer will bear price tags of $2.95. Small wonder that we've received a number of letters from readers asking whether the publishers aren't "getting greedy."

Ask that question of anyone on the mass-market side of Publishers Row and you'll hear a moan and an appeal for sympathy and understanding. "The situation is getting scary," some will concede. "Nineteen seventy-nine is the crunchiest year in two decades."

Publishing is an industry in which the latest official statistics are usually at least a year old, but everyone we've talked to agrees on a number of things:

• All costs are soaring—paper, printing, shipping, promotion and advertising, authors' royalties and advances. The publishers haven't passed all the increases on to the book-buyer because the reader who used to carry two or three titles to the checkout counter is now taking one. The result is a decrease in the total number of copies being sold. To offset this, some houses are embarking on costly television advertising campaigns and bookstore displays. The overall effectivenes of these countermeasures has yet to be proved.

• One publisher willing to cite some specific figures and cases is Robert Diforio, vice president of New American Library. He's particularly concerned about the galloping increases in authors' advances and royalties. Ten years ago, he points out, the reprint rights for Mario Puzo's *The Godfather* cost $400,000. The paperback publisher charged $1.50 a copy. Last year NAL paid $2.2 million at an auction for the rights to Mr. Puzo's *Fools Die*. Mr. Diforio calculates that to break even next year, NAL will have to sell 3.5 million copies at $2.95 — perhaps even $3.50.

December 17, 1978

One million nine. Two million five fifty. The figures sound like bids for the services of a star pitcher. But no, they're the sums being paid nowadays for paperback reprint rights to "hot literary properties" at auctions so frenzied that they make headlines and feature stories in publications that usually pay little attention to the world of books.

In 1975, Bantam paid $1,850,000 for E. L. Doctorow's *Ragtime*. In 1976, Avon acquired *The Thorn Birds* for $1,900,000. Last spring, New American Library bought Mario Puzo's *Fools Die*, along with reprint rights to *The Godfather*, for $2,550,000. A few weeks ago, Fawcett paid $2,250,000 for an astrology book, *Linda Goodman's Love Signs*, the largest sum ever paid for a nonfiction work.

These are just the highest peaks in an alpine range that everyone in the trade has come to take for granted. "High six figure prices" are now commonplace. Not much attention was paid when NAL recently paid $1,020,000 for *Born to Win*, a handbook on Transactional Analysis. The paperback business has come a long way since 1953, when $28,000 seemed a fantastic sum for John Steinbeck's *East of Eden*.

Along Publishers Row, some concern is being shown over this drift of things. A little of it is outspoken, as were the remarks of Nat Wartels, Crown's veteran head, to a *Publishers Weekly* interviewer: "Years ago some of us used to go down to Atlantic City on vacation. On the boardwalk were any number of auctioneers with various trinkets on their stands. Around each one would be a small crowd of people bidding. But when the bidding was over, we inevitably had paid more than the item was worth. In any auction you are likely to get too involved and go beyond the limits of sound judgment."

Some paperbounders object that this overstates the case against auctions. After all, most publishers are getting returns on their gambles. Bantam has recouped its investment in *Ragtime* with the sale of 2,787,000 copies. With 7,000,000 copies in print, Avon is now in the black with *The Thorn Birds.* But it will be another year before NAL can start selling *Fools Die,* two years until Fawcett can get *Linda Goodman's Love Signs* into the racks.

Most publishers with whom we've talked acknowledged that the fact that they have large portions of their capital tied up in such purchases is contributing to continuing hefty increases in prices of mass-market paperback books. This time last year the average price of a book on the best seller list was $2.34; this week it's $2.58. (Other elements contributing to the price increase: spiralling costs of paper and printing.)

There's still another unhappy consequence of the current emphasis on "blockbusting leaders," our confidants acknowledge. As the publishers stage all-out campaigns to put over the books in which they have so much invested, many worthy books of less than mass appeal are being left unpublished or inadequately promoted.

Is Publishers Row likely to mend its ways? Well, it's aware of the problem, so there's hope.

September 30, 1979

Like most people, paperback publishers sometimes find it hard to practice what they preach. For several years now, spokesmen at many houses have been decrying those multimillion-dollar auctions of reprint rights that periodically make newspaper headlines. Yet on two days this month, the key people at nearly all the major houses participated in auctions that reached stratospheric heights. Ballantine Books paid $1,910,000 for reprint rights to Marilyn French's new novel *The Bleeding Heart* (her first was *The Women's Room).* Bantam Books paid an all-time-high amount—$3,200,000—for Judith Krantz's new novel, *Princess Daisy* (her previous novel was *Scruples).* The reasons given? "It'll show we're still very much in business," said Ballantine, referring to the fact that Ballantine's owner, Random House, is for sale. The word from Bantam: "It's necessary to show we're still the industry leader."

August 10, 1980

A year ago, we reported that Bantam Books had bought at auction, for an all-time high of $3,200,000, the paperback reprint rights to Judith Krantz's *Princess Daisy*.

What's happened since? That sale hasn't been topped, nor does it seem likely to for some time to come. Lou Wolfe, new head man at Bantam, attributes his house's relatively poor profit performance during 1979 in part to the large sums spent for advances and says that a ceiling will be held on future purchases. Other publishers, sobered by the current state of the economy, indicate they'll be playing the reprint-rights game more cautiously.

The biggest purchaser of late seems to be Fawcett, which paid $1,633,000 at auction for Phil Donahue's *Donahue* and $1,045,000 for Jeffrey Archer's *Kane & Abel*. Other books bought "on option" include Erma Bombeck's *Aunt Erma's Cope Book* ("near $2,000,000") and Alistair MacBain's yet-to-be-published *Athabasca* ("in the seven figures").

Three other houses cracked the million-dollar barrier recently. Erich Segal's *Man, Woman, and Child* went to Ballantine for "over $1 million," Mary Higgins Clark's *The Cradle Will Fall* to Dell for "over $1,250,000," and Avery Corman's forthcoming *The Old Neighborhood* to Bantam for $1,450,000.

Gloom and Doom

June 1, 1980

"Some of our biggest accounts are in arrears," said the director of accounting and finance in a large paperback house. . . . "Dollar sales are up a little over a year ago, but unit sales are way, way down," said the vice president in charge of sales. . . . "It used to be that wholesalers waited ten days before returning new titles that didn't move. Now it's five days," said the assistant sales manager. . . . "So far as I can tell, only the Sun Belt is immune from the recession," said the marketing director. . . . "There's an old saying that, in a recession, books are relatively secure. That doesn't seem to be the case now," said the publicity person. . . . "We're having all we can do just to survive," said the head of the children's book department. . . . "There's a real danger that all this gloom-and-doom talk will be self-perpetuating," said the president-publisher.

"Complete Publishing": Is It the Solution?

April 4, 1976

The word these days in many businesses is "synergism." It's borrowed from biologists, who use it to describe the action of two or more organisms to achieve an effect that neither one is capable of individually.

We came across it recently in an announcement from Michigan General Corporation, a Dallas-based conglomerate deep into such things as motor homes and concrete pipe. Until recently Michigan General's only publishing property was Pinnacle Books, a paperback house remarkable mostly for its numerous series of men's-action stories. Michigan General says it intends to develop Pinnacle into a major mass-market house and will shortly "acquire a major hardcover house." It expects the two firms to "synergize" each other.

Certainly this is not a unique idea in publishing. Ballantine is owned by Random House, Berkley by Putnam's, Pocket by Simon & Schuster, Pyramid by Harcourt Brace Jovanovich, Tempo by Grosset & Dunlap. Penguin recently bought Viking. Popular and Holt are both owned by CBS. Dell, owner of Delacorte, is about to be acquired by Doubleday.

Will the yen for synergism strike other firms? Avon, Bantam and Fawcett, which have no hardcover affiliates, say they have no plans to purchase one, are watching the developments with interest, think there are still plenty of good books and authors to go round.

October 14, 1979

The following announcements came within a few days of one another, three variations on a single theme:

• Next spring, New American Library, one of the largest and oldest mass-market paperback houses, will begin issuing new books, both fiction and nonfiction, that "combine literary merit with commercial strength" in hardcover. NAL will bring out many of these titles in softcover later themselves; some they will sell to other firms for reprinting.

• Early next year, Warner Books, one of the fastest-growing mass-market houses, will start a hardcover program, teeing off with *The War Called Peace*, Richard M. Nixon's ideas about American foreign policy during the 1980's. Some of these books will be reprinted in softcover by other houses; others, like the Nixon book, will become Warner paperbacks.

• Two separately owned companies, Bantam Books, largest of the mass-market houses, and William Morrow, a leading trade publisher, have established a new imprint, Perigord Press. Books published under this arrangement will be issued first in hardcover as Morrow/Perigord Press Books, later in paperback as Bantam/Perigord Press Books. This cooperative effort will not affect their other operations as independent companies. Perigord has just made its first acquisition—an as-yet-to-be-written novel by Gerald Green, author of *The Last Angry Man* and *Holocaust.*

What prompts firms that came into being largely as reprint houses, whose sales outlets were largely newsstands and variety stores, to venture into a more traditional form of book publishing? In recent years, paperback publishing has been changing fast. More and more softcover books are being sold in bookstores. The competition for big-name authors and "good literary properties" keeps growing more intense. The three houses feel that their new arrangements will enable them to operate more flexibly, to develop authors and properties of their own and at the same time continue to compete in the open market for reprint rights to works originated by others.

This vision isn't exactly new. Back in 1964, Dell Books, another house that got into the paperback business through the newsstand route, established its own hardcover division, Delacorte Press. Today Delacorte has some 60 best-selling authors under contract, including Irwin Shaw, Kurt Vonnegut, William Goldman, Richard Bach, Belva Plain, Nancy Friday and Rona Jaffe. Dell reprints their books in paperback.

Most of the other large mass-market houses benefit in various ways from the fact that they are owned by conglomerates, members of families that include trade publishers. Pocket Books is a sibling of Simon & Schuster's many divisions, Ballantine of Random House, Berkley/Jove of the Putnam group.

There are two exceptions: Fawcett is owned by CBS Inc., which also owns Holt, Rinehart & Winston. Avon is owned by the Hearst Corporation, which recently acquired Arbor House. Both insist that they'll continue to operate "completely independently" of their siblings—or, perhaps more accurately, "cousins."

The Times Grow More Anxious

March 8, 1981

What's the mood along Publishers Row as the nation makes what President Reagan calls "a new beginning"? We asked that question at the major paperback houses, which together sell over 30 million books each month through racks placed in 100,000 bookstores, supermarkets and variety stores across the country. When we asked it in years past, we were told almost everywhere, "We're having lots of fun." This time we heard the phrase only once.

The general sobriety rises from the fact that for the past half dozen years the number of copies of mass-market paperbacks sold has remained "flat," while production and distribution costs have rocketed, resulting in the slimmest of profit margins.

To meet this predicament, few of the houses any longer think of themselves as "reprinters" of books originated by hardcover firms—as they all were when they were founded 30 or 40 years ago. Most of them have assumed the role of "complete publishers"—which means that in many cases they acquire all rights to a promising manuscript and in some cases publish it as a trade paperback before putting it into the rack-size format. Dell, New American Library, Warner and Pocket Books also give some of their "properties" a debut in hardcover. "We try to be as flexible as possible, selling rights or buying them from other publishers as seems most advantageous in each case," we were told by several heads of houses. As a consequence, editorial offices are no longer monopolized by men and women with an acquisitive eye—"we have to have editors who can really edit."

At almost every house we heard lamentations about the huge amounts being paid at auctions for "hot properties." The titles of books for which their competitors paid multi-million dollar sums in the past were usually recited along with the comment, "I don't think they'll ever get all their money back. But this is a situation for which we're all to blame—it's hard to resist the urge to gamble." The recent purchase of a first novel for more than $800,000 was a particular object of scorn.

Some of the publishers' current anger rises from the fact that they are all owned by conglomerates and subject to the whims and fluctuations of fortune of their Big Daddies. Recently, the Hearst Corporation, which already owns Avon, Arbor House and Hearst Books, bought the middle-size general trade house William Morrow. Warner Communications, which owns a record company, a motion picture firm, television and cable companies, as well as Warner Books, bought a sizable block of the stock of Harcourt Brace Jovanovich, which, besides publishing books, owns an insurance company and Sea World, a theme park. CBS Inc., whose subsidiaries operate a radio-television network, manufacture toys and musical instruments and publish books under the Holt, Rinehart & Winston and Fawcett Book imprints, has "officially denied" reports that it is considering divesting itself of Fawcett. Rumors about other conglomerates and their subsidiaries are circulating along Publishers Row these days.

What do the power plays of the conglomerates portend for the future of book publishing? Probably not even the powers-that-be at the conglomerates know. But it all gives Mr. Reagan's new beginning an uncertain, yet most interesting start.

October 11, 1981

"Nervousness" seems the only word to describe the air pervading the executive suites and editorial sanctums of many paperback houses these autumn days. For example:

• At Bantam, a publisher that used to boast that it had had four different owners in the past 25 years, all of whom had left it "completely free to do its own thing in its own way," a representative of its latest owner, the West German publisher Bertelsmann, now occupies an office on its executive floor.

• At Fawcett, whose management once expressed pleasure that it felt no pressures from its owner, CBS Inc., there's talk of an imminent shake-up.

• At Dell, which in the past few months has lost several key people to other houses, new directions are awaited from its owner, Doubleday & Company, the family-owned publishing empire that has been having some financial reverses of its own, among them losses incurred through its ownership of the New York Mets baseball team.

1982: A Year of Mourning

April 11, 1982

Ten days ago, in the Belasco Room of Sardi's Restaurant, just off Times Square, some 60 persons attended a wake for Fawcett Books, dead at the age of 32. The sixth largest of the 13 major mass-market paperback houses had been at death's door for three months, ever since CBS, Inc., the conglomerate that had owned it for five years, arranged to sell its rich backlist to Ballantine Books, the eighth largest house. Ballantine is owned by the Newhouses, the newspaper, magazine and book-publishing family whose properties include Random House, Knopf and Pantheon. In the past, Ballantine has acknowledged that its backlist is weak; the acquisition of Fawcett's titles may lift it to the No. 2 or No. 3 spot in the industry.

The wake was a particularly sad occasion because approximately 170 Fawcett employees are joining the ranks of the unemployed at a time when the troubled book business has many old hands looking for work.

It was a sad occasion, too, because it marked the death of a house that made important contributions to the development of the modern mass-market paperback. Like several others, Fawcett Books was an offshoot of the old-time mass-market magazine business.

The Fawcett publishing empire started in a most unlikely place—a footlocker filled with barrack-room jokes that an Army captain brought home from World War I. In 1920, while working on the night desk of *The Minneapolis Tribune*, William H. Fawcett sorted out his cache, then persuaded a printer to produce some of it as a pamphlet called *Captain Billy's Whiz-Bang*. (A whiz-bang was one of the small-caliber shells that disturbed the peace of front-line soldiers during the war to make the world safe for democracy. The jokes, considered quite "risque" at the time, wouldn't cause anyone's maiden aunt to blush nowadays.)

With the aid of two teen-age sons, Captain Billy trundled his pamphlets around Minneapolis on a coaster wagon, dropping them off at drug stores for sale on consignment. They moved so fast that he soon had more selections printed. Because there were no national distributors of magazines at the time, he got hold of lists of drug stores across the country and started sending them copies, again on consignment. Thus was a great publications empire founded.

In 1937, when it was issuing more than half a dozen successful pulp movie fan magazines, not to mention *True Confessions* and *Woman's Day*, and operating its own nationwide distribution organization, Fawcett Publications moved to New York.

Fawcett's entry into paperback publishing was as happenstance as its founding. In 1945 Victor Weybright, a onetime magazine editor just returned from war service, and Kurt Enoch, who had once worked for Tauchnitz, the German paperback house, came to it seeking distribution facilities—and some credit—for a new line of softcover books to compete with such pioneers as Pocket and Avon. Thus was New American Library born.

Once they saw how eagerly the public grabbed up NAL's reprints of hardcover books, Captain Billy's sons, running his empire now, decided to enter the paperback sweepstakes for themselves. In 1950, they started Gold Medal Books, the first line of original paperback books in modern mass-market publishing. "Through Gold Medal, Fawcett was able to give many not-well-known authors a chance at book publication early in their careers—among them John D. MacDonald and Kurt Vonnegut," we were reminded the other day by Knox Burger, the literary agent who was one of the line's first editors. "It also gave established writers like William Goldman and MacKinlay Kantor a chance to flex their creative muscles under pseudonyms."

"From our entrance into the paperback business," recalls Ralph Daigh, who retired ten years ago as Fawcett's editorial director, "we paid authors at a more generous rate than had been the custom. And in 1955, when we started the Crest line to reprint hardcover books, we extended this practice to what we offered for softcover rights. It caused quite a sensation in the trade when we paid $100,000 for Vladimir Nabokov's *Lolita*, $101,005 for James Gould Cozzens' *By Love Possessed*, later $400,000 for William L. Shirer's *The Rise and Fall of the Third Reich* and $700,000 for James A. Michener's *The Source*. Giving the author a bigger share of the pie paid off handsomely. Those were the days when Fawcett was definitely No. 2 in the paperback world. However, I gather that the practice has been overdone in recent years and has led to some of the book industry's current troubles."

In the mid-'70's, as a large corporation owned wholly by three brothers and a sister, Fawcett found itself facing an uncertain future. None of Captain Billy's grandchildren had entered the business. And there were those inevitable inheritance taxes . . .

Meanwhile, over at Black Rock, the Sixth Avenue headquarters of a half-century-old television and radio broadcasting empire, the top brass was debating whether, in keeping with its continuing program of diversification, CBS should plunge deeper into publishing.

The question was moot. In 1967 CBS had acquired Holt Rinehart & Winston, one of the oldline hardcover publishers. In 1971 it had tiptoed into the paperback field by purchasing Popular Library, a relatively small house. Both ventures proved profitable enough to lead it to buy Fawcett Publications from Captain Billy's offspring in 1977. But in less than five years, Black Rock came to realize that paperbacking was not its kind of game, with that recent wake at Sardi's the sorry end.

July 18, 1982

The news had been expected for months, yet it created a shock when it reached Publishers Row on the eve of the Fourth of July weekend. MCA Inc., the Hollywood-based conglomerate that owns the Putnam Publishing Group (G. P. Putnam's Sons, Coward McCann & Geoghegan, Perigee and Philomel Books) and the Berkley/Jove paperback publishing group, had completed its purchase of two more book publishing houses:

• Grosset & Dunlap, one of the great houses early in this century, when its hardcover reprints of popular fiction and series of children's books (Tom Swift, the Bobbsey Twins, Nancy Drew, etc.) found a place in virtually every American book-reading household. For some years, G&D has owned Ace Books, a softcover imprint that has been counted one of the best in science fiction for three decades.

• PEI Books, Inc., the book-publishing arm of Hugh Hefner's Playboy empire. Of late, PEI's Playboy Paperbacks has been issuing not only books related to themes of the men's magazine but works by Shirley Hazzard, Anne Tyler, Francine du Plessix Gray and Alberto Moravia, among others.

Why did MCA buy these houses? Victor Temkin, head of

Berkley/Jove, points out that the cost of book publishing, particularly mass-market publishing, has rocketed in recent years, while sales have not. Prices of paper, printing and shipping are way up. As a result of the increase in gasoline prices and hotel rates, it now costs $50,000 a year to keep a sales rep on the road. The cost of maintaining editors and promotion people in Manhattan offices has risen comparably.

"To meet the overhead," Mr. Temkin says, "a mass-market publisher must be able not only to offer an attractive list of new titles every month, but to maintain a large, rich backlist. Ace's science fiction titles and Playboy's fine novels, for example, should help us enormously. Both imprints will be continued under the Berkley/Jove banner." (Much the same reasoning motivated MCA earlier this year to purchase Quick Fox, a line of books about popular music that is becoming part of the Perigee imprint. The same thinking lies behind the Newhouse publishing group's recent purchase of Fawcett Books to augment its Ballantine softcover line.)

As a result of Berkley/Jove's absorption of Ace and Playboy, it is quite possible that Berkley's place in the mass-market industry will rise from ninth to sixth place, following Bantam, Pocket, Ballantine, Harlequin and New American Library.

What happened to the 100 editorial, promotion and sales people who worked at the acquired houses? Most of them have been "let go," to join Publisher Row's now sizable corps of unemployed. The acquirers say that's the only way they can keep operating costs under control. They say they will hire them back when and if they are needed.

Yes, these are parlous times on Publishers Row—as they are in the automobile business, the airline business, the teaching profession, journalism and many other sectors of American life.

The Hopes of the Trade

The Trade Paperback

March 14, 1982

Back in 1971, one million copies of trade paperback books were sold in this country; by 1980, the number had risen to 44 million. This year, the "trades" will account for approximately

20 percent of the whole book market; by 1985, probably between 30 and 40 percent: by 1990, as much as 60 percent.

Facts, figures and just plain guesses like these set the mood for a meeting of the Association of American Publishers held recently in Washington, D.C. Among the 450 participants at two days of discussions of the topic "The Trade Paperback Phenomenon" were editors, production and marketing managers, wholesalers, booksellers and librarians.

Herewith some impressions gained from what was said during panel discussions in crowded conference rooms and over cocktails in lobbies in between:

• Bookpeople are a tribe of individualists, and it's almost impossible to get them all to agree on any question. As Peter Minichiello of Pocket Books put it, trade paperbacks are seen "simultaneously as a revelation and a kind of curse."

• Booksellers and book distributors are most enthusiastic about the future of the trades. Melanie Fleischman of Words Worth, a Cambridge, Massachusetts, bookstore, declared that they are the staff of life to the under-35 generation that constitutes her clientele. Alan Kellock of Waldenbooks showed slides to illustrate the imaginative ways his nationwide chain has developed to display trades in its 732 stores, most of which are in shopping malls. Two wholesalers, David Youngstrom of Denver and David Turitz of Portland, Maine, told of their success in getting supermarkets to sell books, especially trade paperbacks.

• Libraries, as their funds are cut and the costs of hardcover books soar, are buying more and more trade paperbacks. James O'Neill of the District of Columbia Public Library system said that it is increasingly common to order two copies of a book in hardcover, seven or eight in paperback.

• The publishing executives were markedly cooler. Some subjects are "naturals" for trade paperbacks, they conceded, but nonfiction books on "hot topics" and fiction by "big-name" authors, they insisted, should first be published in hardcover. Publishing a novel simultaneously in hardcover and trade paperback—as is currently being done in the cases of Jerzy Kosinski's *Pinball* and Thomas McGuane's *Nobody's Angel*—aroused little enthusiasm among those on the panels. Magazines and newspapers remain reluctant to review original paperbacks, which places a new author of serious fiction at a disadvantage.

• Curiously, not until late in the discussions was any attempt made to define the trade paperback. The distinction between mass-market and trade paperbacks is not based on their price, size, shape, quality of paper and printing or subject matter, as many outside the book world suppose. It's a matter of distribution practices. The covers of unsold copies of mass-market paperbacks may be stripped off by the dealer and returned for full credit, as is the practice with magazines. Unsold copies of trade paperbacks must be returned in their entirety, as is the practice with hardcover books. Slight though this difference may seem, it profoundly affects the way the books are promoted and sold, the size of first printings, the royalties allowed authors.

• Only over cocktails did anyone mention that the cost of manufacturing a hardcover book averages only 50 to 75 cents more than that of manufacturing a trade paperback—a difference that is greatly magnified in the price tags of the two editions. Clearly, useful as it was, the conference did not offer the last word on the trade paperback and its future.

August 8, 1982

Take heart, you who are troubled about the state of the book world: help is on the way. A special issue of the book-trade journal *Publishers Weekly* that is scheduled for release next Friday says succor will come from the trade paperback. The *P.W.* supplement chronicles the evolution of this type of book from the mid-1950's, when serious literature bound in soft covers appeared in the bookstores for the first time, to the present, when volumes about cats, cubes, preppies and other trendy subjects are selling millions of copies. Fourteen articles report the feelings that bookpeople have for the still developing form. Here are some of their views:

• During the past several years, while sales of hardcover books have sharply declined and those of mass-market paperbacks have decreased or at best remained flat, sales of trade paperbacks have risen prodigiously. An official of the B. Dalton chain estimates that within five years "the trades" will constitute one-third of the chain's sales.

• A generation of executives who read their way through college with the help of softcover books is now taking command at many publishing houses. They believe that income from trade paperbacks can help make up for lost sales of reprint rights to the mass-market houses. Old-line firms like Farrar, Straus & Giroux, Little, Brown, Scribner's, Dutton, Putnam's and Morrow are issuing softcover editions of worthy out-of-print titles from their own backlists and the backlists of other houses. Many are distinguished works of literature that they expect to keep in print for years.

• Both the old-time houses and the mass-market publishers are issuing more new works, particularly those intended for a youthful readership, in trade softcover format. Literary agent Ron Bernstein explains: "It costs only five bucks to go to the movies. If it cost the moviegoer $15 to sample a movie by a new director, there wouldn't be much of an audience. If a first novel is available only in hardcover for $15, few people are going to take a chance on it." Thomas McGuane, whose novel *Nobody's Angel* was released simultaneously in hardcover and trade editions, says: "I wouldn't want my book out first on the revolving rack at the Trailways Bus Terminal, but the Random House $6.95 paperback is a fairly handsome book. With an offbeat writer like me, my readers would find a $14.95 price tag a tough lick."

• However, authors and their agents do have some misgivings. The agent Georges Borchardt points out that because the royalty rate allowed on trade paperbacks is normally lower than that for hardcover books, an original trade paperback must sell several times as many copies for the author to make the same amount of money.

• Promotion people also have reservations. Roger W. Straus, president of Farrar, Straus & Giroux, says, "One reason trade paperbacks can be priced between $5.95 and $8.95 is that the advertising budgets they're allotted are far less than for cloth editions."

• There's a wide difference of opinion about the attention original trade paperbacks receive from the media. Editors of newspaper and magazine book sections insist that it's not the format of a book but its content that dictates the coverage they give it. One publisher's editor retorts, "Whatever they say, the review apparatus is still attuned to the idea that if a book is important, it's published in hardcover."

• Libraries, which consititute an important market for publishers, are increasingly buying paperbacks because of decreased budgets. "Who needs a book that will live forever?" One librarian asks. "What we need are multiple copies now."

• Booksellers generally welcome trade paperbacks. Yet they present problems. "There must be 9,000 different sizes," says the paperback buyer of the Ingram Book Company, the giant wholesaler. "Our bookseller customers have had their ingenuity sorely tried to come up with ways to handle the odd shapes and sizes in store fixtures designed for either hardcover books or rack-sized paperbacks."

• The trade paperback may in time dominate the publishing field, but the hardcover book won't disappear. One bookman puts it this way: "Because of the troubled economy, more people want smaller, more efficient cars. So Detroit is making them. But some people still want Cadillacs. So Detroit continues to make them too. Similarly, publishers are planning to shift over to more books at a cheaper price. But just as the Cadillacs continue to roll off the assembly line, so will hardcover books."

Small Presses, Great Hopes

November 9, 1980

"A troubled time for book publishing. Lists cut, staffs reduced as buyers balk." So run the headings of recent articles surveying the situation of the large New York hardcover houses whose blockbuster titles, designed for spots on the best-seller lists, attract the widest attention these days.

But what about the hundreds of small, independent enterprises that during the past half-dozen years have sprung up outside of Manhattan, in such unlikely places as Deephaven, Minnesota, Charlotte, Vermont, Santa Fe, New Mexico, Emmaus, Pennsylvania, Sag Harbor, New York, and Summertown, Tennessee, with an especially thick cluster of them in Berkeley, California? A study just released by the Library of Congress suggests that their rapid growth is offsetting the drift toward concentration and stagnation so much talked about in New York City.

We asked the heads of two dozen houses whose books have been reported on here—since the new breed of publisher tends to favor the trade paperback format—how they are doing. With hardly an exception their answer was "Great!" Several said their business is 40 percent higher than last year. One said it is double. Several said they are so busy expanding their lists that they don't want to make comparisons. One publisher, whose business is off, attributed it to special circumstances not likely to be repeated.

Why are they doing so well? Partly, they said, because their overhead is relatively low. They operate out of low-rent quarters, often with staffs of a dozen or less, many of them part-time workers.

The chief reason for their success, as they see it, is that they know exactly for whom they are publishing books and what those people want. As one put it, "Most New York houses, because they're so large and bureaucratic, publish hundreds of unwanted or badly conceived titles each year and hope that what they lose on them will be offset by the profits they make on a few big hits. Because our resources are limited, we have to specialize, to make our imprint stand for things that concern people these days—career-changing, parenting, health, solar housing and the like. Few of our books are returned unsold by bookstores, most become steady backlist sellers. We've had to let very few of our books go out of print."

But these are how-to books. What about literary works? Several houses are bringing back into print worthy novels and biographies that their original publishers dropped because they weren't selling briskly enough. Several are making modest ventures into the publishing of fiction and several others are talking about doing so in the near future.

If these small houses are doing so well, won't they sooner or later be gobbled up by the big-city corporations? "I've already been propositioned by several," the owner of one of the most successful told us. "But I've heard about the poor fellows who sold out to the conglomerates in the past 20 years. I'd rather enjoy life being a struggling publisher than bored stiff as an unemployed millionaire."

March 14, 1976

Who introduced the trade paperback—the softcover book notable for its scholarly or literary content, often referred to as a "quality paperback"—to American publishing? Knowledgeable folk in the business are apt to say Anchor Books, back in 1953. What were the first large-format paperbacks, those albums of photographs and paintings currently so popular? The usual answer is the Sierra Club and the Ballantine series that bowed in the late 1960's.

Actually, first-rate examples of both types of books were published several years earlier by Dover Publications, one of the least-publicized paperback houses in the country—and one of the most innovative. Today, in its 31st year, Dover has more than 2,000 active paperbound titles, all of them printed on excellent paper with sewn, durable bindings. They cover subjects from fine arts to science, with three dozen other fields, including crafts, humor, children's books and cookbooks in between.

Dover, the domain of fiftyish Hayward Cirker, is housed on two floors of a seedy warehouse building on Varick Street. Except for Grove Press, it is the only New York trade publisher south of 14th Street. As far as Manhattan's tight little publishing world is concerned, it might as well be in Santa Fe, New Mexico or Wayzata, Minnesota. You won't find any of its six editors swapping trade talk at Elaine's or lunching with agents at Le Mistral. Most of them are lifelong New Yorkers, bookworms deep into a host of hobbies they constantly mine for book ideas. Some of their best ideas come from the firm's large circle of loyal mail-order customers. All very clubby.

Mr. Cirker is proud of his "substantial" sales abroad. In Dover's lobby, beside the creaking elevator, he has posted a clipping from the *Frankfurter Allgemeine,* in which a reporter who visited his exhibit at last year's International Book Fair expresses surprise that such fine examples of publishing should come out of the U.S.A.

November 27, 1977

From his Santa Fe, New Mexico, home that also serves as his office, Ken Luboff, president and general handyman of John Muir Publications, has just sent out the one-millionth copy of *How to Keep Your Volkswagen Alive: A Manual of Step by Step Procedures for the Compleat Idiot.* This spiral-bound paperback, with a format resembling *The Whole Earth Catalog,* is a creation of Mr. Luboff's partner, John Muir, nephew of the famous naturalist.

Ten years ago Mr. Muir, then a middle-aged dropout from mechanical engineering, found himself spending more time than he liked repairing friends' VW's. He wrote the book in self-defense. Unable to find a publisher, he published it himself. Bookpeople, a Berkeley, California, book distributor, took it on and it became a best seller up and down the West Coast. Today it's in its 19th printing, and another volume, designed for owners of the new VW Rabbit, is in the works.

John Muir Publications isn't a one-book, one-author firm by any means. Its current catalogue lists 16 other titles by other writers, including a guide to Mexico (100,000 copies sold), two novels (2,500 copies each), a volume of verse, books on gardening, solar greenhouses, self-defense—and a book by Mr. Muir on how to remake society that has sold 30,000 copies.

"It's sort of a family affair," Mr. Luboff told us. "John and I and both of our wives get involved in every book. We want to keep it that way. I hope that whatever you write won't get us so much publicity that our fun will be spoiled."

November 16, 1980

Whatever became of those young people of the '60's and early '70's who talked a lot about the New Consciousness and counter-culture, who experimented with psychedelic drugs and pursued alternate life styles in communes? Some are making their mark in the world of books. A case in point:

In 1971, 270 flower children from San Francisco, headed by a young guru named Stephen Gaskin, pooled their assets and headed for south-central Tennessee, where land was cheap. There, in a village named Summertown, they set up a commune called, quite simply, The Farm. During the past decade, it has become the largest commune in the country, with a membership of more than 1,000, nearly half of them children, on its 450 acres. Its enterprises, too, have proliferated. Besides farming, the activities it now engages in include building construction, videotape production, printing and a book publishing company called, quite simply, The Book Publishing Co.

At present, BPC has a dozen active titles, whose sales are almost all in the 150,000–200,000 copy range. All reflect the concerns of the commune—the telepathic philosophy of Mr. Gaskin *(Mind at Play)*, planned parenthood *(A Cooperative Method of Natural Birth Control)*, natural childbirth *(Spiritual Midwifery)* and vegetarianism *(The Farm Vegetarian Cookbook)*. Curiously, the biggest seller (800,000 copies) has been *The Big Dummy's Guide to C.B. Radio*.

Like many other small publishers, BPC's people take a cheery view of their prospects. Their books are being commented on approvingly by many "establishment publications," more bookstores are stocking them, and British and European houses are buying reprint rights.

June 14, 1981

America, particularly the West Coast, is dotted with thriving small book publishers, each with its own beguiling success story. For example, there's Klutz Enterprises, whose home is a stucco house in Palo Alto, California, two blocks from the Stanford University campus. Among the house's residents half a dozen years ago was John B. Cassidy, a Stanford graduate and part-time teacher who suffered from an embarrassing problem. Because his voice lacked the necessary timbre, he was unable to hold his own when his friends started singing on river outings. Undaunted, he trained himself in another art that would amuse and impress his peers—the art of juggling with bean-bags. He was so successful at it that he decided to share his secrets with others. In 1977 he wrote, and with the help of housemates, published a paperback called *Juggling for the Complete Klutz* (Klutz Enterprises, Stanford, California).

At first, sales of the book, in California bookstores and novelty shops, were quite slow. But when national book distributors—Ingram Book Company and the B. Dalton and Waldenbook chains—added it to their stock, copies began moving fast. Today its sales total 200,000.

Klutz Enterprises still operates out of the Palo Alto house where it began, but its affairs keep a trio of partners busy—not to mention 15 youngish "little old ladies" from the neighborhood, who periodically gather together to handsew the three beanbags that come with each copy.

April 20, 1980

With the book industry increasingly dominated by conglomerates, it's becoming increasingly difficult for creative writers—poets, essayists, fiction writers—to find publishers for their work, and the quality of literature is suffering as a result.

That's a cliche for which Bill Henderson, president of the Pushcart Press of Yonkers, New York, has little use. Seven years ago he quit his job with a leading Manhattan house to devote himself to a desperate cause—the nurture of promising talent that the publishing "mainstream" was neglecting. Today, he says, he's "exhilarated" by the quality of the writing being published by the hundreds of small literary presses that are blossoming across America.

To this exhilarating state Mr. Henderson has contributed more than one man's share. His *The Publish-It-Yourself Handbook* has become an indispensable how-to book for small presses. Each spring he publishes in hardcover *The Pushcart Prize*, a selection of short pieces originally published in the literary press. Nine months later the anthology is made available in an attractive trade paperback format by Avon Books, whose publisher, Walter Meade, takes a particular interest in the enterprise. Usually the hardcover edition sells some 3,300 copies, the paperback over ten times as many.

The just-released paperback edition of *The Pushcart Prize IV* includes 61 pieces from over 4,000 nominations by publications ranging from *Partisan Review* to *Jam Today*. Helping Mr. Henderson and a volunteer committee make the selections were John Gardner, Jerzy Kosinski, Malcolm Cowley and John Irving. *The New York Times Book Review's* critic found it "an extraordinary amount of writing of genuine distinction."

January 20, 1980

"Many a good book fails after publication from neglect or poor distribution or inadequate promotion or an act of God." With those words an item in the "Book Ends" column of *The New York Times Book Review* a little over a year ago invited authors who thought their works deserved another hearing to submit them for republication by the Second Chance Press of Sag Harbor, New York.

Unlike many noble endeavors, the word is that the Second Chance Press is coming along most promisingly. The "Book Ends" item brought 400 responses from out-of-print authors and their agents. Six of these, novels and memoirs that Second Chance's editors particularly liked, were published last fall, simultaneously in hardcover and paperback editions. Printings ran between 3,000 and 4,000 copies. One title, Charles O'Neal's *Three Wishes for Jamie*, a romantic adventure tale originally published in 1949, already has gone back to press. A new, larger list will be issued during 1980.

And just what is Second Chance Press? It's a mom-and-pop

operation, run by two New Yorkers who became all-year-round summer people in Long Island's Hamptons half a dozen years ago. They've found libraries and some chains most receptive. The Shepards aren't making much money yet, but they're having a lot of fun.

April 13, 1980

In a warehouse within eyeshot of Chicago's Tribune Tower, sharing quarters with Midwest Newsclip Inc., Anita and Jordan Miller operate Academy Chicago Ltd., a young publishing house that is winning esteem from literary folk across the country. The clipping service is a most welcome neighbor, for its profits provide Mr. and Mrs. Miller with the working capital they need to publish books dear to their hearts—attractively made, mostly paperbound feminist books and new editions of hard-to-come-by literary treasures of the past.

Anita and Jordan Miller first discovered they had a lot in common back in the '50's, when they were classmates in literature courses at Chicago's Roosevelt University. It wasn't until 1975, when Mrs. Miller was teaching at Northwestern and looking around for someone to publish her dissertation—an annotated bibliography of the works of Arnold Bennett—that they seriously considered getting into the business themselves. They found an established house willing to take on the bibliography, but in the course of their investigations of the ways of book publishing they turned up a number of promising manuscripts. Their first venture, *A Guide to Non-Sexist Children's Books*, published in January 1976, is now in its third printing.

Most of the 70 titles on Academy Chicago's list are by writers the Millers greatly admire: Arnold Bennett's *The Old Wives' Tale*, Robert Graves' *Wife to Mr. Milton*, Sarah Gertrude Millin's *Mary Glenn*, *The Last Poems of Elinor Wylie*.

The Millers are sanguine about the prospects for mom-and-pop ventures like theirs. They hear that the accountants of leading New York publishers are insisting that many fine back-list titles be let go out of print because they don't sell briskly enough to cover warehousing costs. Small out-of-Manhattan houses like Academy Chicago and Second Chance Press, whose overhead is considerably lower, will be able to give such works another life.

February 14, 1982

Two paperbacks published this week—W. M. Spackman's *An Armful of Warm Girl* and George Stade's *Confessions of a Lady-Killer*—have a number of interesting things in common. Both are novels by well-known teachers of literature. Mr. Spackman taught classics at New York University and the University of Colorado. Mr. Stade teaches English at Columbia University.

Both books were published in hardcover to high critical acclaim a few years ago but failed to interest the mass-market reprint houses, which felt they lacked that magic ingredient that makes a paperback "jump out of the racks" within ten days of its release.

Both attracted the attention of entrepreneurs anxious—as one of them puts it—"to keep literary works available in these days when many large publishing houses are controlled by bottom-line accountants."

• David Van Vactor and his wife, Pat Goodheart, have been involved in the publication of *Canto*, a literary quarterly, for the past half-dozen years. Now they've set up Van Vactor & Goodheart in Cambridge, Massachusetts, to issue books of comparable quality: *An Armful of Warm Girl* will be followed by such titles as *The Power of the Dog*, a 1967 novel by Thomas Savage, and *The Problem of Style*, a book by the poet J. V. Cunningham.

• Norman Loftis, who has taught film at Lehman College and worked as an editor at W. W. Norton, is running Alpha/Omega Books out of his Morningside Heights home with the aid of a small staff of freelancers. *Confessions of a Lady-Killer* will be followed later this year by four other books, including *Squeeze Play*, by Paul Benjamin, a new whodunit featuring a Jewish detective.

Both houses are troubled by the problem that nags all small independent publishers—getting their books into stores in all parts of the country. They are heartened by the examples recently set by such firms as David R. Godine of Boston; North Point Press of San Francisco; Academy Chicago of Chicago; Second Chance of Sag Harbor, New York; and Persea Books of New York City.

September 19, 1982

For the executives of many of the giant paperback houses, grimly devising ways to cut their losses, these seem the worst of times. For the head of one small, young house, these seem the best of times. He's Walter Zacharius, chairman of the board of Zebra Books, which this year is selling one-third more copies of its publications than it did last year. His company's total sales will approach $10 million, giving it a place in the industry just below the Big 10.

Zebra is owned almost entirely by Mr. Zacharius, who founded it seven years ago with an investment of $50,000 of his own money and a wealth of knowledge gained from 25 years' experience in publishing paperbacks at Ace and Pinnacle and owning a string of popular newsstand magazines. We say "owned almost entirely" because he recently assigned some of its stock to Roberta Grossman, who has worked closely with him since Zebra's birth and now has the title of president-publisher. The firm has a staff of 22 in its Manhattan offices; it issues 160 titles a year and, *mirabile dictu*, has no outstanding debts.

Why is Zebra doing so well at a time when its giant competitors have so many woes? To hear Mr. Zacharius tell it, it's because Zebra is a small, privately owned corporation in the old tradition of book publishing: "The people who run it are free to operate as they see fit and can react quickly to changing conditions. The conglomerates that own all the other houses require their M.B.A.-type executives to spend most of their time preparing projections and plans for years to come. When they got deeply into book publishing a decade or so ago, they hired too many editors and told them to spend too much money for literary properties that couldn't possibly pay off."

"Lately this has given us a great advantage," according to Mrs. Grossman. "We buy the books that aren't 'big' enough to meet the conglomerates' grand notions, the middle-list fiction that didn't sell when it was put up at auction. We play a very tight game. We pay between $2,500 and $50,000 for a title, design an attractive cover that plays up the author's name, put an edition of perhaps 75,000 copies into the racks, and let readers' word-of-mouth carry on from there. A recent example of the way this works is a family saga called *The Lion's Way*, by Lewis Orde, released last March. We've had to go back to press several times for a total of 408,000 copies to date."

Most of Zebra's books are fiction—family sagas, romances, horror, occult, science fiction-fantasy, mysteries. Recently it's been doing especially well with historical romances, nurse-

and-doctor stories, men's action tales and, a new twist, the "women's adult Western." "We're not impressed," says Mr. Zacharius, "with what's selling on Fifth Avenue or Rodeo Drive. Our readers patronize suburban shopping malls."

Zebra plays its own game another way. Of the eight men on its sales staff, four are veterans of large publishing houses who were forced to retire by company policy. "For a real salesman," says Mr. Zacharius, "living is being able to visit distributors and dealers. The retirees would like to work full time, but we don't want them to overdo it and limit them to two or three days a week." Their ages? Sixty-three to 81.

The Book In Our Times

An Age of Exuberance, 1939–1982

March 1983

Last year, over a long weekend in May, 17,000 booksellers, publishers, authors and agents from every section of the United States and many foreign lands congregated in a vast hall in Anaheim, California, where the American Booksellers Association was holding its annual convention. In many ways the affair bespoke the prevailing spirit of the world of books. Anaheim, the home of Disneyland and only an hour's drive from Hollywood, seemed an appropriate place for the meeting. California accounted for 20 percent of the nation's book sales, as much as the whole Northeast. Many of the social affairs that filled both daytime and evening hours were graced by stars of show business and politics. Naturally television and newspapers reported what transpired. The most dazzling of the exhibits that bedecked the hall were those of large publishing houses owned by large conglomerates listed on the stock exchanges. Before the year was out, it was said, 40,000 new book titles would be issued. Naturally the business press reported what transpired.

But in guarded tones, insiders traded sober talk. Many houses were planning to cut their lists. Mergers of a number of houses were imminent. Many talented old hands would soon be unemployed. A business that traditionally considered itself "recession-proof" was facing the worst crisis in its 200-year history.

How the American book world fell into this predicament can best be understood by contrasting the affair at Anaheim with the A.B.A.'s 1939 convention, held at New York's Hotel Pennsylvania. On that occasion, although some of the 500 attendees came from "as far away as Kansas City," the vast majority were from the Northeast, where 40 percent of all American books were then sold. At that time, 10,000 books were scheduled for publication within the year.

The changes that transformed the book world during the intervening third of a century mirrored the changes that were taking place in the nation's economic and social life. In that period, the book became for the first time truly a medium for the masses. Previously, most middle-class and blue-collar Americans had relied on their local public library systems, models for the Western world, for whatever books they read. Some patronized privately-owned lending libraries or bought popular magazines. Thanks to what has come to be known as the Paperback Revolution, they now had become accustomed to buying books of their own.

Paperbacks in the modern sense of the word first appeared in 1939, when Pocket Books introduced softcover reprints of hardcover books. Their 25-cent price made the lending libraries' five-cent-a-day charge seem costly. Then, after World War II, two dozen companies, most of them magazine publishers, with the assistance of a nationwide network of periodical distributors, put paperbacks on sale in towns and neighborhoods where books had never been sold. Several firms began to issue original books in paperback, giving writers like Kurt Vonnegut and John D. MacDonald their first chance to have their work published in book form. Ordinary Americans welcomed the paperbacks as substitutes for popular magazines that, thanks to the competition of television for advertisers' dollars, were dying a slow death.

Paperbacks became conveyors of high culture during the 1950's, especially among college students, their ranks swelled by millions of veterans whose tuition was paid by the Government under the G.I. Bill. Wouldn't they prefer to buy copies of the fine books their professors assigned as supplementary reading rather than wait in line at the library? The first publisher to perceive this opportunity was Doubleday, which started Anchor Books, a line of "trade" paperback editions of works like Edmund Wilson's *Literary Chronicles* and Sigmund Freud's *Origins of Psychoanalysis*. Soon most houses, including university presses and mass-market firms, hastened into this exploding market. Until that time most booksellers had been reluctant to handle soft-covered volumes because they found it difficult to think of them as *real* books, but the eminently respectable trade paperback made them change their attitude.

By 1960, 360 million paperbacks a year were being sold in 90,000 outlets—newsstands, drugstores, stationery stores and an increasing number of bookstores. They accounted for nearly half of the books sold in the United States and one-fifth of the book industry's total income.

The Paperback Revolution had barely peaked when a radical change began in the way books were marketed. Twenty years ago there were approximately 1,200 stores in the United States that maintained stocks of any consequence, not many more than there had been at the time of the Civil War. Many were not profitable operations. In the words of one veteran publisher, they were "the hobbies of retired librarians and widows with a little money who wanted to devote their lives to books."

Half the outlets upon which the hardcover publishers depended to sell their books were department stores in three dozen major cities. There was a score of chains, most of them small and regional; only Brentano's and Doubleday, each with fewer than two dozen stores, could be described as national in scope. A few booksellers prided themselves on carrying on the tradition of the 19th-century personal bookshop and made a point of knowing the particular tastes of their regular customers and alerting them to books that might interest them. Stuart Brent of Chicago once declared at a literary luncheon: "I can't tell you what a burden it is being a guardian of the human spirit in this city."

But the potential market quickly outgrew the personal bookseller as massive numbers of people moved to the suburbs and thousands of shopping centers were built amongst the new urban sprawls. Two large retailing corporations, sensing that the rising educational level, increasing leisure time and affluence of Americans had created a new public for books, began opening chain stores in suburban centers. In 1966, the Minneapolis department store firm Dayton Hudson opened its first B. Dalton Bookseller store and two years later absorbed Pickwick, a highly respected Southern California chain of bookstores. In 1969, Carter-Hawley-Hale of Los Angeles, another retailing conglomerate, bought and began expanding Waldenbooks, a chain that had evolved out of franchised lending libraries and bookstores in department stores.

Lured into the new chain stores by splashy displays, people who had never set foot in a bookstore browsed and bought books. To take advantage of this interest, publishers gradually developed "the impulse book," one bought for its appealing subject or cover. Top sellers in this genre were how-to, self-improvement and humor books. And, as sales increased, the chains grew: by 1979, Dalton had 380 stores and Waldenbooks had 560. The two chains accounted for nearly one-fifth of the books sold in stores in the United States.

Meanwhile, the publishing industry also changed profoundly. At the end of World War II, publishing remained pretty much what it was in the 19th century, a profession for gentlemen. Most leading houses were relatively small, privately held businesses. Since the 1920's, the industry had been invigorated by the entrance of sons of men who had done well in other businesses — Bennett Cerf, Alfred A. Knopf, Harold Guinzburg, Richard L. Simon, Roger W. Straus Jr., among them. Like the old-timers, they realized they had to turn a profit, but a more important motive was the opportunity to work and socialize with writers. To underwrite their chancy enterprises, some houses had allied operations that produced a reliable income — textbook publishing (Harper and Harcourt Brace, for example), printing plants (Doubleday, Houghton Mifflin), book clubs (Doubleday) and remainder books (Crown, Simon & Schuster).

That snug situation was eroded by a series of social and political developments. The growing exactions of federal inheritance taxes caused many family-owned houses to "go public" during the 1950's so that families might preserve their assets for their heirs. The industry began enjoying unprecedented prosperity. The baby boom that started in the late '40's increased the market for schoolbooks. The G.I. Bill increased the college market. In 1958 the National Defense Act, passed after the Soviet Union launched the first space satellite, Sputnik, made large sums available for books. In 1963 and 1965, at the behest of Lyndon B. Johnson, a onetime teacher, Congress appropriated billions of dollars for the use of schools, colleges and libraries. As one consequence, the head of a children's book department of a middle-sized publishing house recalls, "at every staff meeting I was able to announce: 'Our department has just had another million-dollar month!'"

It was a time, too, when the structure and spirit of many hardcover firms was dramatically changed by the Paperback Revolution. In 1949, Norman Mailer's publisher was pleased to share in the $35,000 a mass-market firm paid to reprint *The Naked and the Dead;* in 1975, E. L. Doctorow's *Ragtime* brought $2 million to the author and the originating publisher. In many houses the person in charge of selling reprint rights became more powerful than the editor-in-chief.

As a result of these explosions, a number of publishing houses registered annual profits of between 15 and 18 percent. And, as word of that seeped through Wall Street, entrepreneurs and conglomerates eyed Publishers Row covetously. A frenzy of takeovers began in 1965:

• Communications corporations felt that book publishing would complement their activities: CBS Inc. bought Holt, Rinehart & Winston from its small band of shareholders and Fawcett Publications from the Fawcett family. RCA Inc. bought Random House and Knopf from their founders. (Later, the Samuel I. Newhouse family, owners of a large newspaper chain and an array of magazines, took over the Random House consortium and Fawcett Books.) Time Inc. acquired Little, Brown. The Times Mirror Company acquired New American Library and Harry N. Abrams. The Hearst Corporation bought William Morrow and Arbor House.

• Entertainment corporations were moved by the same spirit: Filmways took over Grosset & Dunlap. MCA Inc. bought G. P. Putnam's Sons, a family-owned corporation, and later bought Grosset & Dunlap from Filmways.

• Conglomerates seeking to diversify their holdings jumped into the publishing game: Gulf & Western bought Simon & Schuster from its founding families. ITT Inc. bought Bobbs-Merrill. Crowell-Collier, controlled by Wall Street entrepreneurs, bought Macmillan, long dominated by the Brett family, and later changed the conglomerate's name to Macmillan Inc.

• Foreign investors perceived profits to be had on America's Publishers Row: The British conglomerate S. Pearson & Sons, owners of Penguin Books, bought Viking Press from the Guinzburg family. The Dutch publisher Elsevier bought E. P. Dutton from the Macrae family. Italian and German interests bought Bantam Books.

• Privately-held houses, to prevent takeovers by outsiders, diversified their activities. Doubleday became a communications corporation that bought chains of radio and television stations and the New York Mets. Harcourt Brace Jovanovich acquired properties ranging from amusement parks to insurance companies.

Many of the new owners replaced old executives with people trained in business administration, and the newcomers made no secret of their contempt for what they saw as the antiquated ways of book publishing. They referred to each book title as a "product" and a "profit center." Their constant concerns were the bottom line and projections of future profit-and-loss. Aggressive editors were hired to undertake costly ventures with great commercial prospects—in some cases, tie-ins to movies and other activities of the parent conglomerate. Marketing specialists were engaged to apply the marketing techniques used to sell household and consumer products. E. L. Doctorow, who served as an editor at one of the taken-over houses, told an interviewer why he quit within a year: "Publishing is a business of personal enthusiasms, hunches, instincts. The new owners brought in their business consultants and personnel people who had no sympathy for this kind of work. The soul went out of the place."

One effect of the deluge of riches in publishing was a marked change in the old-fashioned personal relationships among writers, editors and publishers. The new world of big money attracted very different personalities. The changes in the role played by agents were most dramatic. When that profession came into being early in this century, almost all were former editors who could provide writers with creative help and moral support, find a sympathetic editor at an appropriate house and arrange such business details as advances and royalty rates. With the book world's increased emphasis on business and showmanship came another style of agent, of whom the most colorful are Irving Paul Lazar of Hollywood and Morton Janklow, a veteran of New York corporate law.

Some of them were less interested in having their clients maintain a long relationship with a publishing house than in finding one that would pay large sums in advance.

Some great deals were made on little evidence. No longer was it necessary for an author or agent to submit a complete manuscript; a sample chapter and a brief outline would do, and the same proposal might be sent to several publishers at the same time. Often a $25,000 to $30,000 advance was requested by a writer with a middling reputation. In the case of "blockbuster" books, rights were sold at auctions, dramatically staged affairs that provided fodder for gossip columnists.

New species of editors appeared, most notably acquisitions editors whose duty was to maintain close relations with important agents. Some of these editors made a point of regularly occupying a prominent table at one of the Manhattan restaurants favored by the publishing community. "Once editors were known by the authors they worked with," Robert Giroux of Farrar Straus & Giroux observed. "Now they are known by the restaurant table they occupy."

Since the social rules observed in fashionable restaurants differ from those that used to govern literary relationships, less charismatic editors often felt that the only way they could get a higher salary was to take a job at another house. So many did so so often that authors began to complain about "floating editors." An author might work for years to complete a manuscript only to find that the editor who had contracted for it had departed for greener pastures, leaving him in the hands of a stranger who might not care for his style of work. Inevitably authors too began to float from house to house. Many who had been nurtured by one publisher until they built a popular following were lured by big bucks and the better distribution promised by another house.

Finally, writing well was no longer enough. To be a successful author, one had to be a public personality. The book world discovered that television viewers are potential book buyers in 1960, when appearances of the Tonight Show made best sellers of books by four personable writers—Alexander King, Harry Golden, Cliff Alexander and Jack Paar, who was then the host of the show. As the years passed, exposure on television came to be considered essential in making a bid for bestsellerdom, particularly of nonfiction books. Many publishers, considering a manuscript for publication, now make it a practice to ask the agent if his client will "travel." The author must be willing to make long, grueling tours of major cities, autographing books at bookstores, submitting to interviews with journalists and, most important, talking engagingly on television and radio shows.

Inevitably, having discovered vast new markets and having become a part of really big business, the book industry was now acutely vulnerable to economic and political strains. Budget cuts had forced schools and libraries to reduce their book purchases. The baby boom was over, college enrollments had levelled off. Inflation had affected the cost of everything in the industry—paper, printing, binding, warehousing and transporting books, sending salespeople on the road and authors on tour, and maintaining large staffs. Even before a great business recession set in late in the 1970's, publishers acknowledged that they were lucky if they made an annual profit of five percent.

Ironically, it was the paperback that was affected most acutely by the recession. The price of a book that had once cost a quarter now ran as high as $3.95, in some cases even more. Blockbuster titles that once sold three to four million copies now sold half as many. Annual sales of paperbacks, which had reached a plateau of 835 million copies a year, would have been considerably lower if it hadn't been for the popularity of impulse books and a rage for "women's romances," formula love stories that accounted for one-fifth of the total. As a result of the crunch, four large mass-market houses were merged in 1982, leaving only ten in the field. The distinction between paperback and hardcover publishing had become blurred as many paperback houses now published original books in both hard and soft covers.

Hardcover publishing had its problems too. Booksellers who reported to the New York Times best seller list said that the number of copies of the 30 top fiction and nonfiction titles sold in the first quarter of 1983 was down by more than 30 percent from the first quarter of 1982. Particularly hard hit was the "mid-list book," one written by a little-known author or one that deals with a subject for which there is no well-defined market. As a result, authors who had once been able to count on incomes of $40,000 to $100,000 a year were advised by their agents to take full-time jobs and do their writing at night or on weekends.

After several decades of tremendous and sometimes boundless prosperity, people in the book world found it necessary to ponder ways to survive and prosper in the new and quite different age that was dawning.

The Shape of Things to Come

June 1985

"Sanguine" was the word to describe the prevailing mood at the American Booksellers Association convention in San Francisco last month. Over the Memorial Day weekend 17,550 bookpeople from all over the world—the greatest number in history—crowded the aisles of Moscone Center, unveiling their plans for the future, catching up on each other's activities and, most significant of all, doing business.

Gone was the glitzy, showbiz air of many conventions past. Gone was the doleful feeling that first appeared four years ago, when the industry was sliding into the most harrowing recession it had ever experienced. The high spirits and relaxed optimism on the edge of San Francisco Bay made it clear that the people who live by the book are now convinced their world has a great future ahead of it—even if that world will, in many respects, greatly differ from that of the past.

What will that future be like? Herewith a digest of what some knowledgeable bookpeople see in their crystal balls, as expressed at trade meetings and during private discussions:

• The book world will expand greatly, even as it becomes exceedingly diverse. Yet its inhabitants, no matter what roles they play in it, will continue to share a collegial spirit.

• The public for books will continue to grow in the immediate future. By the end of the decade, the "reading population" will have increased by 15 to 20 percent. There are, however, reasons for concern. The number of illiterate Americans is currently estimated as high as 60 million, one-fourth of the U.S. population. The percentage of readers younger than 21 years is said to be declining.

• The number of books published will increase. In 1980, only five years ago, some 40,000 titles were published. This year the number will exceed 90,000 and the growth is likely to continue.

• More books will be published that are designed to appeal to special interests and tastes. According to the professional prognosticator John Naisbitt, author of the best seller *Megatrends*, this will be in response to the growing heterogeneity of the population. The national best seller list will become relatively less significant.

• The number of publishing houses will multiply. Two dozen or so very large firms will live on, but the number of small houses will proliferate. In the operations of all, much of the dedicated spirit and some of the highly personalized procedures of the cottage industry that characterized publishing early in this century will prevail.

• Most of the houses, particularly the large ones, will pay more attention to the ways they market books, an area in which the industry has traditionally been inept.

• Although the Paperback Revolution that began during World War II is now over, its legacy will live on. The readers it attracted to the book as a medium of entertainment and information, the authors and subjects it introduced and the marketing methods it pioneered enriched and enlarged American cultural life. Almost every publisher now issues and will continue to issue books in both hardcover and soft. Paper covers will remain the prevailing format.

• The number and variety of bookstores will increase, their operations made more effective through the use of computers.

• Indeed, the computer and the technological revolution it represents will transform the lives of authors, publishers, booksellers, librarians and readers. It may give the word "book" many new meanings.

The buoyancy that characterized last month's affair at Moscone Center is all the more remarkable because the spate of takeovers and mergers that struck Publishers Row early in

1982 and sent its denizens into a depression at the time has not yet ended. Since then, the conglomerate Macmillan Inc. has bought Charles Scribner's Sons, Atheneum and Rawson-Wade from their founding families, Bobbs-Merrill and other imprints from the conglomerate ITT Inc. The conglomerate Gulf & Western has acquired the textbook and business book publishers Prentice-Hall and Esquire Inc. The management of the New American Library has acquired control of their firm from the Times Mirror Company and ownership of E. P. Dutton from the Dyson family, which not long before had bought the latter from the Dutch publishers Elsevier.

What's behind all this buying and selling and realigning? Certainly federal taxes continue to make families quite happy to consider attractive purchase offers. Moreover, takeovers of all kinds are the prevailing rage on Wall Street. Most significantly as far as book publishing is concerned, in many boardrooms the concept of highly diversified conglomerates has lost much of its charm. ITT, one of the first to proclaim that the profits of any business could be increased largely through the application of strict accounting and "modern management methods," has abandoned the notion and is now concentrating on industries with which its management feels most comfortable. In this same spirit, Macmillan is selling off such disparate units as a specialty store chain and a musical instrument manufactory to concentrate on "publishing and information services." Gulf & Western, which formerly coupled Simon & Schuster with Paramount Pictures in a division devoted to "entertainment and communications," is now integrating it with what remains of Prentice-Hall and Esquire Inc. in a new unit devoted to "publishing and information services."

The continuing rage of realignments make many bookpeople believe that the Publishers Row of the future will have some two dozen large houses, almost all of them based in New York, whose forte will be commercial fiction and nonfiction tailored to make the best seller lists. Most of them wil be "complete" or "full-line" publishers, issuing hardcovers, trade paperbacks and mass-market paperbacks. As such they will be able to buy all rights to promising manuscripts, thereby avoiding some of the perils of the auction mania of the late 1970's.

Their location in New York creates a number of problems that the large houses must overcome. They're having to reorganize their operations in many ways to minimize the high cost of doing business in Manhattan. Many are moving downtown to the lower-rent area that was Publishers Row when that expression originated early in this century. They're having to take more steps than ever to keep in touch with trends and talents across the country by maintaining close contact with booksellers and agents in every region and by sending their editors on frequent scouting trips. They're making liberal use of the free-lance publicists able to promote books and authors in their regions.

The large houses are facing up to a problem that has long dogged publishers, that of getting their creations into the hands of every possible buyer. They've borrowed methods developed by other industries and have put into regular use tricks learned during the Paperback Revolution. "Back in the 1970's, when mass-market publishers were offering huge sums for reprint rights," one oldtimer at a leading trade house has observed, "it was often said that the person in charge of selling subsidiary rights had more clout here than the editor-in-chief. Now it's the marketeers who have the clout."

The emphasis that New York publishers are placing on the technical and marketing aspects of their business was highlighted in a recent poll of employment agents recently published in the trade newsletter *BP Reports*. According to the agents, young people wishing to enter the book world can now choose between a job as an editorial assistant paying $11,500 a year and one as a production or marketing assistant paying $13,000. The former, it should be noted, requires longer hours of work, sometimes at home during evenings and on weekends. In marketing, in addition to salary, a beginner may also receive a bonus and fringe benefits, ranging from cars to vacation time.

Even so, an assistant marketing manager in a publishing house is likely to receive $16,000 a year, little more than half the $30,000 he would expect in any other industry. Such is the magic of the book that, in this age of Yuppies, "young upwardly mobile achievers bent on getting into the fast lane to success," at a time when many talented oldtimers who were declared redundant back in 1982 are still looking for jobs in publishing, many recent college graduates are striving to find a place in the industry.

The big houses aren't forgetting that books are products of the imagination. To counteract some of the stifling effect that a large, "impersonal" organization can have on the creative process, a number of them now identify certain editors by placing a "personal imprint" on their books. These editors maintain close relationships with a small stable of authors. Many have won reputations for their special skills. (As one owner of an imprint observed, "You're sure to do the best job of which you're capable if your name appears on the title page between the author's and the publisher's.") The tradition was begun 30 years ago by Harcourt Brace Jovanovich's Helen and Kurt Wolff and is being continued by the likes of Dutton's William Abrahams and Seymour Lawrence, Ballantine's Judy-Lynn del Rey, St. Martin's Richard Marek, Atheneum's Margaret K. McElderry, Viking's Elisabeth Sifton and Harper's Cornelia and Simon Michael Bessie.

To lessen their overhead costs, publishers are making increasing use of the services of "book packagers" — or, as some of them prefer to be called, "book producers" — individuals or small groups that conceive an idea for a book, find talented people to write and illustrate it, and sell it to a publisher-distributor in any stage from a finished manuscript to a finished book. Paul Fargis, who is one of them, says that packagers can "concentrate on the creative aspects of the project, which editors no longer have time for." Bill Adler, another successful packager, predicts that within the next several years more than one-quarter of all nonfiction books will be products of his fraternity. Currently there are more than 130 packagers, among whom the most visible are John Boswell, Bernard Geis, Richard Gallen, Philip Lief, James Monaco, Lyle Kenyon Engel's Book Creations Inc., Jeffrey and Daniel Weiss's Cloverdale Press, the Chanticleer Press, the Hudson Group and the Rolling Stone Press.

But Publishers Row is no longer merely a concentration of houses in Manhattan. Over the past several decades thousands of small presses have sprung up in every section of the country, with thick clusters on the West Coast and in New England. There are so many — estimates run at more than 17,000 — that the R. R. Bowker Company, publishers of the trade journal *Publishers Weekly*, has started a magazine called *Small Press*. Sometimes they're run by one person or a mom-and-pop couple out of their home, more often by a dozen people out of a small suite of offices. They're in publishing more out of love for it than for the money they may make.

Among the best-known small presses are 49-year-old New Directions of New York, 15-year-old David R. Godine of Boston and 5-year-old North Point Press of Berkeley, California.

The most successful of the newcomers specialize in particular areas of interest. Lord John Press of Northridge, California, for example, is notable for random works by such literary figures as John Updike, John Barth and Joyce Carol Oates. Northland Press of Flagstaff, Arizona offers books about the history and culture of the Southwest, John Muir Publications of Santa Fe, New Mexico, about auto repair and travel, Peanut Butter Publishing of Seattle, Washington, cookbooks and restaurant guides. The concerns of women are the metier of the Feminist Press of Old Westbury, New York, the lives of pop-music and film stars that of Delilah Books of New York. Among the houses that have done well in reissuing novels and other literary works that have gone out of print are Academy Chicago of Chicago and Second Chance Press of Sag Harbor, New York.

In their efforts to bring their creations to everyone who might be interested in them, the small presses are reinforcing the collegial spirit that has traditionally characterized the book world. Many presses now share staffs of sales reps as well as the warehousing and distribution facilities of other firms, sometimes the very largest firms.

The curious bifurcation between bigness and smallness, between mass taste and special taste that has taken over the book world in our time is reflected in the growing number and diversity of U.S. bookstores. One measure of this is the membership of the American Booksellers Association: in 1970, 2,575; today, 4,400.

The most spectacular growth has been that of chains with a supermarket air, frequently located in shopping malls. In the past decade, the largest, Waldenbooks, has increased its outlets from 400 to 920; the close runner-up, B. Dalton Bookseller, from 168 to 732. Crown Books, a chain whose specialty is discounting best sellers, has grown from a young man's idea to 158 stores during the same period.

Discounting has become such an important practice in

retailing in recent years that it seems likely to increase its role in bookselling. Dalton is opening 50 to 60 such stores under the name of Pickwick and Waldenbooks has plans to open 25 to 30 under the name of Reader's Market. The recent purchase of Waldenbooks by the K Mart Corporation, a huge retailer whose specialty is mass-marketing discount merchandise has raised much speculation as to its future effect on the second largest bookstore chain.

The proliferation of the large chains has greatly alarmed independent booksellers. By combining the orders of their various branches the titans are able to obtain books from publishers under far more favorable terms than are single bookstores or small chains.

What many independent booksellers regard as a godsend has appeared in the form of the Ingram Book Company of Nashville, Tennessee. This large, conglomerate-owned firm now provides counselling service and order fulfillment to some 15,000 bookstores and libraries throughout the country. From its three strategically located warehouses it can deliver copies of 60,000 new titles and older titles still in demand anywhere in the U.S. within several days—considerably faster than the two weeks or longer usually taken by publishers and regional wholesalers.

Meanwhile, there has been some increase in the number of stores that provide personalized service to their customers and feature books appealing to the particular tastes of the community in which they're located. There has been a proliferation of stores specializing in particular genres—children's books, mysteries, science fiction, travel books and the like.

This growth, fragmentation and specialization in publishing and bookselling has been tremendously facilitated by the coming of the computer during the past decade. The computer is affecting much more than management; it is revolutionizing the ways in which books are written, produced, circulated, and read.

It is estimated that two-fifths of all published authors now use home computers or "word processors" instead of typewriters. Jimmy Carter wrote *Keeping Faith: The Memoirs of a President* on one. The best-selling novelists Andrew M. Greeley and Stephen King, the poet-novelist Erica Jong, biographers like Jane Howard and Andrew Cave Brown use them. Douglas R.

Hofstadter set type for his Pulitzer Prize-winning *Gödel, Escher, Bach* on his computer. It seems only a matter of time until this becomes the normal practice in book production.

In one form or another, computers are providing booksellers and publishers' sales departments with instant access to the information they need for controlling and filling orders. One of the reasons for the swift growth of the Dalton chain was its network of computers, which made it possible for a person at the Minneapolis headquarters to tell at any moment the sales record of any book in any of its stores. This lesson wasn't lost on its competitors or on the houses along Publishers Row.

Computers are changing the ways in which reference, scientific, technical and educational works are published. It is now possible for business and professional people to project on screens in their offices the complete texts of encyclopedias, legal decisions, periodicals and similar works hitherto available only in a few libraries. Textbooks and manuals are similarly available for use in schools and colleges. As most readers still prefer to pore over words and illustrations on paper rather than on a screen, machines have been developed that can print out the text of electronically recorded material at the rate of 60 pages or more a minute.

The computer promises to solve a number of problems currently troubling librarians and to make it possible for them to expand their services to the public. As the number of books and magazines published escalates, they are running out of storage space. The shoddy paper and binding now used in most books are reduced to shreds in as little as 25 years. The Library of Congress has launched an experiment that will put the texts of its books and periodicals on small disks. These are virtually indestructible, take up a minuscule amount of space and can be used by many people at the same time.

Some crystal-ball gazers suspect that within a few years all books and magazines will be computerized as soon as they are issued. They see a day when, thanks to a global network of libraries, a reader sitting at a computer in a branch library will be able to call upon the screen in front of him books and articles stored in computers all over the world.

But will the computer ever share the place or even take the place of the book in the affections of the average American? That question was anxiously discussed throughout the recession-troubled book world as the sales of microcomputers designed for use in the home soared to 2,200,000 in 1982. When plied with appropriate pieces of "software," their manufacturers declared, these home computers would provide families with sophisticated entertainment and information about such subjects as dieting, recipes, sewing and continually updated research material. For those seeking intellectual stimulation, there would be software requiring interplay between the reader and the computer. For young people, adventure tales that were both educational and entertaining would be "published."

This seemed to open up a great opportunity for book-people. Manufacturers of computer hardware, nuts-and-bolts people by nature, frankly admitted that they lacked the experience necessary to produce software and welcomed their cooperation. Many larger publishing houses that had successfully issued books about computers and their use hastened to set up separate divisions for the purpose, among them Addison-Wesley, Bantam, Harper & Row, Houghton Mifflin, McGraw-Hill, Prentice-Hall, Random House, Scholastic, Simon & Schuster, Van Nostrand, Warner and John Wiley. A host of software producers, with names like Mindscape, Paperback Software, Spinnaker, Softie Inc. and Sublogic, mushroomed across the land, in many cases arranging with book publishers to distribute their creations to the trade. Early in 1983 *Publishers Weekly* inaugurated a monthly "software publishing and selling" section.* The Association of American Publishers authorized the admission of "software houses" into full membership and instituted a program to protect their wares, both software and allied books, against copyright and infringement.

Booksellers were equally eager. "It's a chilling yet exciting opportunity for us," Andy Ross of Cody's Bookstore in Berkeley, California, told his fellow members at the American Booksellers Association's 1983 convention. With a challenging reference to the 2,000 computer stores that were then selling software, he added, "Computer users need support and information whey they buy books and software. If we booksellers make the effort, we can become the best equipped persons to provide

---

*Publishers Weekly has dropped the monthly software feature and will substitute a much smaller weekly round-up.—R.W. 7/85.

them with it." Donald Laing, owner of the Boulder Bookstore in Boulder, Colorado, warned, "We mustn't make the mistake we made with paperbacks. We refused to sell them because they weren't books as we were raised to think of books, and as a result we lost out in the Paperback Revolution for nearly 30 years."

A number of bookstores lost no time staking their claims in the new electronic world. They set up sizable "computer sections" and, frequently with the help of high school and college students who had grown up in the electronic age, organized them to make computer users feel at home. The Ingram Book Company made available to the bookstores it services 2,000 "key software titles" to round out its large inventory of books about computers and computer operation.

All the while, the talk of the trade was that every purchaser of a home computer would buy three to five of the 3,000 paperback titles then in print bearing such titles as *The Commodore 64 Programmer's Guide, Bits, Bytes and Buzzwords* and *The Word Processing Book: A Short Course in Computer Literacy.* A Dalton executive predicted that in 1983 such books would account for ten percent of the chain's sales, exceeding that of fiction. Doubleday gave Stuart Brand, author of *The Whole Earth Catalog* $1,300,000 to create a *Whole Earth Software Catalog.*

But the next year, even as the book industry was beginning to recover from its recession, many a soul began to wonder whether his vision of computers as a great bonanza hadn't been just a pipe dream. Although more than 4,800,000 home computers were sold in 1984, manufacturers and retailers complained that, because of bitter competition and price-cutting, they weren't making a profit. Some of the gloomier souls began saying that, except for entertainment and word processing, there wasn't much that a home computer could be used for, certainly not enough to warrant their high price tags.

The gloom quickly spread to book publishers and booksellers. Copies of the 4,000 books about computers and software programs then in print found relatively few takers in the bookstores; obviously the market was glutted with "me-too" titles. Doubleday's 100,000 copies of Stuart Brand's *Whole Earth Software Catalog* didn't exactly race to the checkout counters.

By the spring of 1985, the entire computer industry was in a deep recession; the result, it was generally said, of too rapid expansion. Many manufacturers have drastically cut back on their production of all types of computers; a number have gone out of business. This turn of events has had its effect on the book world. Harper and several other publishers have dropped their software divisions, a number have cut back their lists and staffs.

Even during the days when the book world was most ebullient about the prospects for home computers and software, little was said about their providing anything for persons who wish to read literary works for pleasure. Their most enthusiastic advocates at the 1983 American Booksellers Association meetings acknowledged their limitations in this respect: "Yes, it is uncomfortable to read fiction and poetry on a screen." "Poetry must be read many times to be appreciated." "Computers are hard to read in bed or carry to the beach." "Nothing can replace the satisfaction to be derived from the look and feel of good printing on good paper."

The late Christopher Evans, a British computer scientist, had an arresting answer to such skeptics. In his 1979 book *The Micro Millenium*, he envisioned a "computer book" that is the size, shape and weight of a paperback and, since it is elegantly bound in leather, a pleasure to hold. When a tiny silicon chip is inserted into it, the entire text of a literary work may be read and reread on a screen of any color its owner chooses at whatever pace he wishes.

Visions like these distress some bookpeople while delighting others. Certainly they will remain only daydreams until the computer industry has completed its current shakeout and institutes more orderly product development and business practices.

In any event, as Gail See, owner of The Bookcase of Wayzata, Minnesota, and president of the A.B.A., pointed out during a meeting at last month's convention, "It is not technology which threatens the book, but illiteracy." At another session, Bette Fenton, of B. Dalton Bookseller, cited figures indicating that more than one-quarter of all Americans cannot read and the number of illiterate Americans is rising at the rate of ten percent a year.

Fittingly, the theme of this year's convention was "Towards a Reading Society." That problem was addressed in many ways and at many sessions. A hopeful note was evident at the many exhibitors' booths and a number of meetings where publishers showed a new determination to hook young people onto the habit of reading by vigorously promoting their books for children. A cautionary note was struck by Jonathan Kozol, author of the widely acclaimed book *Illiterate America,* who appealed to all bookpeople to participate in private programs to reduce illiteracy at all age levels and to resist the Reagan administration's reduction of public funding for such purposes. Not only the future of the book depends on it; as Mr. Kozol pointed out, "the future of democracy may depend on it."

Index